AT THE SHARP END

UNCOVERING THE WORK OF FIVE CONTEMPORARY DRAMATISTS

Peter Billingham

Reader in Drama and Performance
School of Creative Arts Films and Media
University of Portsmouth

'I do not ask the wounded person how he feels,
I myself become the wounded person.'
Walt Whitman, 'Song of Myself'

Methuen Drama

At the Sharp End

is dedicated to Millie and Joshua

First published 2007
A & C Black Publishers Limited
38 Soho Square
London W1D 3HB
www.acblack.com

Copyright © 2007 Peter Billingham

Peter Billingham has asserted his right under the Copyright, Designs and Patents Act, 1988, to be identified as the author of this work.

ISBN: 978-0-713-68507-7

A CIP catalogue record for this book is available from the British Library.

Typeset in Dante MT by SX Composing DTP, Rayleigh, Essex
Printed and bound in Great Britain by Caligraving Ltd.

This book is produced using paper that is made from wood grown in managed, sustainable forests. It is natural, renewable and recyclable. The logging and manufacturing processes conform to the environmental regulations of the country of origin.

CONTENTS

ACKNOWLEDGEMENTS

I would like to thank the following people for their help and support in the research and writing of this book.

First, I would like to thank the five writers whose work is at the very heart and centre of this book for their generosity of time and spirit in agreeing to be included in the book. The subsequent interviews and various other demands upon their time at different stages in the process were engaged in with goodwill and patience. It has been a genuine pleasure to meet with David Edgar, David Greig, Mark Ravenhill, Tim Etchells and Tanika Gupta, and a privilege to talk with them about their work.

Second, I would like to thank my editor at Methuen Drama, Mark Dudgeon, for his willingness to support the original concept and proposal for this book and the process of its subsequent evolution. I also wish to express my sincere personal thanks to Sally Njampa for her advice and copy-editing at significant stages.

Third, I would like to thank friends and colleagues at the University of Portsmouth who have shown such an encouraging and continuing interest in my researching and writing of this book: (alphabetically) Dr Dave Allen (Head of the School of Creative Arts Film and Media), George Burrows, John Caro, Stuart Olesker, Karen Savage, Gareth Somers, John Stanton and Dr Dominic Symonds (Course Leader for Drama). I also wish to express my thanks to Lawrie Tippins who provided significant technical advice and assistance at a crucial stage in the transcribing process. Also I'd like to thank Rachel Crowther, a Drama student at the University of Portsmouth whose comments upon the work-in-progress gave an invaluable undergraduate's perspective on the material.

Fourth, I would like to acknowledge the ongoing friendship and support of a small but significant number of people whose interest and provocative stimulation over a long number of years has sustained my lecturing, playwriting and theatre-making work. To Edward Bond, a valued friend and mentor and his wife Elisabeth, Professor John Bull (University of Reading), Dr Cesar Villa, Richard Hurford, Velda Harris, Dr Bill McDonnell (University of Sheffield), Dougie Hankin, Nick Drew (Bath Spa University), Dr Roger Grainger and, last but not least, Linda Taylor (University of Huddersfield).

Finally, but uppermost in my mind, I want to express my deep, affectionate appreciation to my family for their continuing interest in and support of my writing. To Marilyn, whose faith in this project and my wider creative and professional achievements and endeavours is priceless and profoundly appreciated. Also my pride and joy in the lives of Eve, Chris and Millie, Tom, Sally, Leo and Joshua and William and Ruth. May we all dare to be 'at the sharp end' of social justice and progressive change in whatever ways we can, now and in the years to come.

Peter Billingham
June 2007

1 POINTING AT SHARP ENDS – AN INTRODUCTION

Sharp ends hurt. Handle with care! Sharp ends aren't polite. The sharp end is the shouting end. Not the 'Sorry I'll go away and come back' end. Being at the sharp end is being where the action is. Getting involved. Making a point. Something serious is going on. You've got to make yourself heard. No looking on or shouting from the sidelines. At the sharp end is out there centre stage making a difference. 'Come on over here if you think you're sharp enough!' That's the shouted challenge from the mix, the scrum, the scuffle: the sharp end.

Talking about sharp ends, what's the *point* of contemporary British theatre? Does it have one apart from bums on seats, happy investors and the odd soundbite for the politician at election time? Think Cool Britannia, think froth. Think froth, think empty, think here and then gone. Is that all British theatre has become? What drives it, what are its principal concerns? What kinds of purpose does it have? Who's bothered enough to go and see it apart from the coachloads from Dudley, Tunbridge Wells and beyond, buying their overpriced ticket to consume interval ice creams watching roller skaters in cat costumes? Or perhaps Abba's back catalogue hung on a storyline so thin it must break? What value does theatre have in our current world in the first decade of the twenty-first century? Questions like these have fuelled the five conversations at the heart of this book. They've been equally provoked through the conversations themselves. 'To be or not to be?' It's a well-worn question that even Hamlet couldn't answer, yet it's one we might ask of British theatre today outside the West

End-dominated commercial mainstream. You need a compass on a journey entering new territory. In mapping the work of the five writers in this book I've needed to make my own compass in order to engage fully with and analyse their work. Some of the writing across the five writers has been new territory to me. Sometimes on my journey into new plays and their ideas I've needed to put down way markers like 'political', 'social relevance' and 'innovation'.

It really has been a great journey. No one had mentioned carbon footprints when I started. There are also the footmarks one's own discoveries make as one leaves the beaten tracks of what one knew before. Exciting! It's been an exhausting and exhaustive trip. It's a journey that's carried a sense of genuine privilege to meet with the five very diverse modern writers: David Edgar, David Greig, Mark Ravenhill, Tanika Gupta and Tim Etchells of Forced Entertainment. Their generosity of time and spirit was tangible in agreeing to be the subjects of *At the Sharp End*. Each of them contributed with enthusiasm, honesty, insight and sometimes humour, making our conversations stimulating, thought-provoking and enjoyable.

Sharpening Up: Reading and Using *At the Sharp End*

This book is structured to be as user-friendly as possible to you, the reader. It's based around the extended interviews or conversations that I had with each of the five writers. They are, in order of appearance in the following pages, David Edgar, David Greig, Mark Ravenhill, Tim Etchells (of Forced Entertainment) and Tanika Gupta. Each interview has been edited with valuable input and advice wherever possible from the writers themselves. In terms of the presentational format of the interviews, I've endeavoured to remain consistent across all five of them. Clearly, as they are not academic essays but the accurate, edited transcripts of actual conversations, there is a tempo and flow that

I've tried to retain. There are also sequences where the writer concerned was speaking in full flow. Rather than package those sentences into formal sentence structures I have made extensive use of dashes and sometimes parentheses to help catch and communicate the immediacy of the sudden insight or revealing aside. The dashes should therefore be read as conversational breaks and pauses, while the parenthesis signals the reflective aside or afterthought.

The transcript interview is followed by a critical essay about each of the dramatists. These essays can't, of course, discuss the entire output of these five writers. I've therefore focused upon individual plays that offer a chronological journey through their work to chart the development of the writer's dramatic voice. My other criteria in selecting the plays under discussion were that:

- they were plays that were discussed or significantly referred to in the interviews;
- they were plays whose themes are centrally important to each writer's work and also to issues facing contemporary British society and the wider world.

With the single exception of David Edgar, whose output reflects a career that spans over three decades, there is a principal focus upon the most recent work of the writers, though not exclusively so. In this sense I was very fortunate that each of the writers had new work (or new revivals of work) produced during my research and writing period, which I was able to see in live performance. Therefore my discussion, for example, of Mark Ravenhill's *The Cut*, *Product* and *Citizenship* is among the first, if not *the* first, 'academic' appreciation and analysis of those plays.

Famous Five
Each of the five dramatists discussed in this book is chosen according to the following criteria:

- *Timescale* It's important that the works of more contemporary writers such as Mark Ravenhill, David Greig, Tanika Gupta and Tim Etchells are placed in the longer-term developments of modern British theatre. David Edgar represents those writers of a previous generation who were committed to a theatre that served a function of social and political enquiry and commentary. *At the Sharp End* explores and discusses plays from 1976 – David Edgar's *Destiny* – through to 2006: Tanika Gupta's *Sugar Mummies*, Mark Ravenhill's *The Cut*, *Product* and *Pool (No Water)*, and revivals of David Greig's *The American Pilot*, Tim Etchells and Forced Entertainment's *Bloody Mess* and *Dirty Work*, Mark Ravenhill's *Citizenship* and David Edgar's *Nicholas Nickleby*).
- *Issues* All of the five writers and their work relate directly to key issues facing contemporary British theatre and society. As an important dimension of *At the Sharp End* is to map out the territory of modern British theatre, the themes and concerns in the plays are as important as the undoubted creative skills and talents of the five dramatists. I've no wish to package up the writers in this consideration but the following summary should prove helpful to the reader:
- *Alternative sexuality and gender* – Mark Ravenhill and Tanika Gupta.
- *Racial and multicultural perspectives* – David Edgar and Tanika Gupta.
- *Left and postmodern, post-Marxist political perspectives* – David Edgar, Mark Ravenhill, David Greig and Tim Etchells.
- *The emergence of new national identities* – David Greig and David Edgar.
- *New aesthetics and genre* – Tim Etchells and Forced Entertainment.

Short Cuts

These are short, helpful summaries of each writer's main themes and major stage plays. Please note that they don't include all plays by each writer but are representative indicative lists of significant plays. It's my expectation that readers will pursue their own further examinations and explorations of other plays by the five authors. These summaries precede each of the interviews. They also incorporate:

Downloads
A Download section is provided for each writer at the end of the chapter. The Download is an easy way of making contacts with other writers, plays, companies or even films, which connects as an influence or comparison with that writer. These are only indicative and my hope is that readers will follow these connections through and begin to make their own discoveries of relevant related material.

Time Zones
Time Zones identify some of the key plays and social and political events from the 1950s through to the present first decade of the new millennium. Key years are highlighted in the historical period covering the work of the five writers and the plays discussed in *At the Sharp End*. They will help you to identify all the writers and their work in the context of other important events.

There is also a list of Recommended Further Reading and Websites at the end of the book.

1956: Look Back in Nostalgia?

All journeys happen in a context and a significant context of my journey of research and writing was that 2006, the year this book began, was the fiftieth anniversary of the founding of the English Stage Company at the Royal Court Theatre, Sloane Square, London. This was under the inspired and visionary artistic leadership of the Royal Court's founding Artistic Director, George Devine. Of course, in reality, single productions and single dates of opening nights don't literally define time or history. There's more than just journalistic convenience nevertheless in the date of 8 May 1956 as the defining moment of a new wave in British playwriting, a modern renaissance driven in its first and second phases principally, though not exclusively, by new writers.

The date of 8 May 1956 was the opening night of John Osborne's iconic, ground-breaking play *Look Back in Anger*, first produced at the Royal Court and directed by Tony Richardson. The debate surrounding this play, its meanings and significance has been well and often rehearsed in the ensuing fifty years. It met with mixed critical reaction initially. Its anti-hero Jimmy Porter was a prototype of the post-war anti-hero. He was the confrontational, provocative embodiment of the 'anger' of the play's title. He looked back with problematic nostalgia at a lost past of just causes to fight for and human values that made life worth living. He looked back in order to look around him at a Britain moving like a sleepwalker though the decade of the 1950s. 'Wake up!' Porter shouted at his wife, his best friend and a world of sterile, empty moral hypocrisy and political indifference. He looked back to help him look forward to see if and how British society could be revolutionised, though not in terms of conventional politics.

Jimmy's anger embodied the bitter disappointment, frustration and alienation felt by a new, emerging hybrid of left-wing working-class and liberal-bourgeois men and women in their twenties and early thirties. Britain might have won the war but the intervening decade had been characterised by the economic austerity of a 'Ration Book Culture'. These 'Angry Young Men' reacted collectively against the parochial Britain of the 1950s.

You may wonder where the young women were. Ironing perhaps, like Jimmy's wife, Alison? If they were, it wasn't out of choice, but facing powerful societal and government pressures to return them to domesticated roles after their temporary economic and social liberation of the war years. Following the unexpected landslide victory of the Labour Party in the General Election of 1945 there were major advances in progressive social engineering.

These included the establishing of the Welfare State, the National Health Service and increased educational opportunities for the working class (1944 Education Act). The stage looked set for a new kind of Britain. The short-lived Labour government and the re-election of a Conservative government in 1951 led instead to a social and cultural inertia with dominant moral values that owed more to Victoria than Elizabeth, who became queen in 1953. This was, after all, a society in which divorce laws were restrictive and biased against women, and where homosexuality was a criminal offence, punishable by prison.

Why am I, like Jimmy Porter, looking back, in a book that's about contemporary British playwriting and asking by implication whether contemporary theatre is at the sharp end or sedated and irrelevant? While avoiding the temptation of 'Looking Back in Nostalgia' like Jimmy, it's none the less important to recognise the achievements of that first generation of new British playwrights such as Osborne, Edward Bond, Arnold Wesker, Shelagh Delaney, John Arden and others. British theatre needed a revolution and, in an important sense, got one from those writers. Might it be that British theatre today needs a radical change but doesn't realise it? Would it again be playwrights who led the charge? I might be in danger of making my own misguided stumble down Memory Lane through an idealised, selective view of a privileged period in the reawakening of British theatre and society. Living now at the sharp end of increasingly dangerous and worrying times, it's essential to ask some hard, challenging questions about where contemporary British theatre and playwriting is. What, if anything, does it have to say to contemporary society?

Aleks Sierz coined the memorable phrase 'In-Yer-Face Theatre' in his seminal book of the same name (Faber, 2001) to define and describe some of the young, emerging playwrights of the 1990s. One of them, Mark Ravenhill, was one of the leading young dramatists of that decade. So was the late lamented Sarah Kane, who would undoubtedly have been close to the heart of this book had suicide not terminated her potential genius. While David Edgar's playwriting career spans nearly forty years and was thus exempted from Sierz's discussion of new writers, it's interesting that Tim Etchells, Tanika Gupta and David Greig were not included in his analysis of innovative, ground-breaking writers. Greig is mentioned, albeit only on five occasions and then as one of a number of 'footnotes' to that decade.

What is clear without prejudice is that the work done by the English Stage Company in the decades following on from Osborne's first night, and also by Joan Littlewood and Theatre Workshop at the Theatre Royal Stratford East, meant that there were opportunities for new writers to have their work staged in a way that's never been surpassed since. Their innovative plays were often produced by a generation of younger emerging directors such as Bill Gaskill, John Dexter, Tony Richardson and Lindsay Anderson.

Furthermore there was an audience hungry for new plays reflecting the radically changing world of the period. It wasn't only that there was this floodtide of new writers and directors crashing like Atlantic breakers against the old barriers of British theatre and society. It was that people like Devine and Littlewood were prepared to privilege the challenging, radical dramatist's vision over financial and commercial considerations alone. It is unimaginable, for example, that either John Arden with plays such as *Serjeant Musgrave's Dance* (1958), Edward Bond with *Saved* (1965) or Shelagh Delaney with *A Taste of Honey* (1958) would have been produced without the vision and commitment of Devine and Littlewood towards theatre's power and right to be innovative, provocative and controversial. Do we have the equivalents of those tough visionaries in our theatres today? Can the radical voice be allowed to speak above the clamour of self-interested focus groups, funding priorities and the search for the next theatrical fashion?

2006: Looking Forward – in Expectation?

Two articles from the *Guardian*, the first in 2004 and the second in 2006, offer cause for concern and debate about the state of contemporary British theatre. What are the opportunities for major, innovative and challenging new writing, and also what is the relationship between the New Labour government and its attitude towards and funding of the arts?

In an article entitled 'Where have all the playwrights gone?' (*Guardian*, 7 October 2004), the journalist Maddy Costa articulated a question in her title that other established critics and commentators such as Michael Billington had been asking in the preceding years. Her article opened with:

> At a press conference in the spring, Nicholas Hytner, artistic director of the National Theatre, threw up a challenge. As journalists clamoured for more details of David Hare's *Stuff Happens*, he said: 'The question you should be asking is where is the new generation of playwrights to write this play?'

Even considering whether Hare's play represented 'new writing' in the strict sense of the term or whether its conventional format should be presented as an inspiration to a new generation of playwrights, the deeper question nevertheless remained. The article went on to discuss the commitment by the two major state-subsidised theatres not only to recruit new writers but also writers who could write for their main stages. Costa continued:

> We are, it seems, witnessing a shift in the theatre culture, an explosion of energy not witnessed since the emergence of Joe Penhall, Mark Ravenhill, Sarah Kane, Conor McPherson et al through the Royal Court a decade ago. That energy has, however, long since dissipated. As Penhall says, 'It's not in the air now, as it was eight years ago, that new writers are bankable and exciting.' Instead, the pervading feeling is that theatres have been suffering from the virtual ghettoisation of new writing into smaller spaces.

Remembering that George Devine supported *Serjeant Musgrave's Dance* in the context of audiences at a suicidal average of between seventeen and twenty-eight per cent capacity, Penhall's observation about new writing being perceived as 'bankable' illustrates one of the major problems facing British theatre. That is the dominance of concerns of commercial profit and viability resulting too often in an embracing of mainstream writing. Clearly business is business and building-based theatres in particular have staff needing to be paid. Nevertheless, the continued appearance of revivals of commercial favourites or of established, 'bankable' writers is counter-productive and depressing. It seriously undermines any real, sustained chance of either artistic innovation or a scheduling policy taking risks outside a guaranteed, homogenous, Home Counties audience. Terence Rattigan's fictional Aunt Edna seems, like a zombie in a twin set and pearls, to have risen from the grave and to be occupying at least the front stalls. Can you imagine the accountants at the time of Bond's *Saved* calculating the financial cost of losing a large part of the audience walking out in the infamous Scene Six when a baby is stoned to death in a park? Calculators clutched in their hands, would they have gambled on the lucrative sponsorship deal from pram makers and quarry owners to offset those box-office losses?

In the second article entitled 'The gulf between the arts and New Labour is growing wider' by Martin Kettle (*Guardian*, 20 May 2006), he opened by identifying that overall spending on the arts from government in the Blair decade (1997–2007) had actually risen around eighty per cent. He then went on to discuss and consider what he perceived as a widening gap between the government and the arts, and especially theatre:

> The fissure between the arts and politics is increasingly obvious and may be growing deeper. Few people in the arts speak about the government with anything resembling goodwill any longer . . . Surprisingly few people in the government are prepared to value the arts publicly, in the way they value football, even though far

more people attend arts events . . . It is as though the arts and politics now inhabit increasingly different worlds – two cultures you might say.

Kettle goes on to argue that there has been a significant change in the attitude of the political Left and certainly the New Labour centre-right, to the value and function of the arts. He recalls an earlier post-war period when 'arts for all' as a slogan had its roots in something more than a political soundbite. While writers such as Osborne were never in any formal sense politically of the Left, it's true that many of the major writers from 1956 to the beginning of the Thatcher period in 1979 were, in one sense or another, political.

What do I mean by political? Well, for most of those thirty-odd years (1956–79) and indeed into the early-to-mid years of the Thatcher government (1979–90) it was fair to assert that 'political' carried with it a sense of the oppositional and interventionist. Theatre should be in a position where it could critically question and constructively oppose the social, cultural and political mainstream. Much, though of course not all, theatre of the period existed to ask difficult and challenging questions. It was at the sharp end. Plays like Wesker's *Roots*, Delaney's *A Taste of Honey* and Bond's early play *The Pope's Wedding*, though very different stylistically, were by writers focused upon a historically marginalised working class. Those plays were about the possibilities of radical political and social change, though never in some naïve or Utopian sense. They grappled with previously taboo issues of teenage pregnancy, mixed-race relationships, homosexuality and violence as a symptom of economic and social deprivation.

Later, diverse plays such as Bond's *Lear*, Martin Sherman's *Bent*, David Edgar's *Destiny*, Howard Brenton's *Weapons of Happiness*, Trevor Griffiths's *Comedians* through to Caryl Churchill's *Cloud Nine* and *Top Girls* had continued that tradition of sharp-edged writing and theatre.

Tony Marchant's powerful play *Welcome Home* (1983), about

traumatised British soldiers returning home from the Falklands war to bury a comrade and consequently revealing their own traumatised psychological wounds, potently captured the mood of that period. It was a war that was fought in part to help keep Margaret Thatcher's government in power when economic failure and increasing unemployment might have suggested otherwise. Its twenty-fifth anniversary was being commemorated at the time of writing (June 2007).

Edward Bond's savagely provocative musical-political satire *Restoration* (1981) critiqued the seemingly endemic deference within the British working class that could be exploited by Rupert Murdoch's *Sun* to secure the Conservatives' victory: the equivalent of turkeys voting unanimously for Christmas. Interestingly, *Restoration* was 'restored' in the autumn of 2006 and, on a short regional tour into London, played to large houses and widespread critical acclaim. These writers and their plays were therefore engaged to one extent or another in the conviction that theatre could and should intervene in and respond to the various problems and issues within society. Kettle continued:

> Through most of my lifetime the arts have always been overwhelmingly well disposed towards Labour. Partly this was Margaret Thatcher's doing, but it ran deeper, drawing on a shared vision of the role of the arts in a good society. But the Blair years have marked a divide, perhaps a parting of the ways. Ministers say this is mainly due to Iraq, and undoubtedly there's truth there. If there is a growing disillusionment in the country with Labour, it's no surprise to see it reflected in the arts.

One of the ways in which contemporary theatre has sought to rediscover its role as an oppositional and interventionist voice is through what has become known as 'verbatim' theatre. This has been most completely identified with and produced by Nick Kent and his Tricycle Theatre in Kilburn, north London. Verbatim theatre might also be called 'transcript' theatre. It works on the basis of the written transcribing of spoken testimony and accounts of real-life people. Inevitably and invariably those people have been involved as perpetrators, victims or onlooker-participants in events and decisions relating to issues of injustice or the repression of justice and truth. It has emerged in circumstances where the mainstream media reporting of such issues has either been censored or incomplete. Tanika Gupta's recent *Gladiator Games* (2006) is one good example of such a play, although it is not formally verbatim theatre. It does, though, incorporate a very large proportion of real-life testimony and eyewitness account relating to the murder in custody of a young British Asian man, Zaheed Mubarek. He was savagely beaten to death by his psychotic white racist cell-mate while both were imprisoned in the same cell at HMI Feltham. This is a notoriously overcrowded young offenders' prison in south London. Plays like *Gladiator Games* (a co-production between Sheffield Crucible Theatre and the Theatre Royal Stratford East) along with earlier landmark verbatim plays such as Richard Norton's *The Colour of Justice* and *Guantanamo* (both Tricycle Theatre productions) are essentially drama documentaries. Their existence was necessitated by the failure of the political authorities and law enforcement agencies in cases of clear institutional injustice and failures within the judiciary. *The Colour of Justice* dealt with the circumstances surrounding the racist murder of Stephen Lawrence, a black teenager. *Guantanamo*, as its title indicates, was concerned with the prisoners held at the detention camp of the same name by the US authorities.

Powerful and necessary as these dramatic reconstructions are, they're essentially documentary rather than dramatic in form. Is the emergence of verbatim theatre not only a comment upon serious structural inadequacies in the administration of British justice? Might it also reflect an absence or failure of British theatre to provide opportunities for single-authored plays on such issues to be produced? David Greig's *The American Pilot* is quite clearly a political play in that broader tradition of oppositional and interventionist theatre. Mark Ravenhill's *The Cut* explores issues of state-authorised political violence and its moral implications. His one-man show *Product* deals with the volatile territory of how our perception of both Islam and Islamic terrorists helps perpetuate prejudice, injustice and mutual misunderstanding. Ravenhill's *Citizenship* is political in that it deals with the politics of sexual identity and the help or otherwise that the liberal rhetoric of political correctness brings to that territory. Tim Etchells of Forced Entertainment famously asserted, 'We're not interested in rousing plays for the barricades.' However, their phenomenal output over twenty years *is* concerned with raiding the 'dressing-up box' of consumer capitalism's mass-mediated propaganda project. Etchells and the company try to re-dress some of the devastating impact of mass globalisation upon our contemporary world. It's as if this writer and these performers are cutting up those old ideological costumes to refashion them anew, provoking our own renewed, radicalised perspectives.

Does it matter? What, you might ask, is my point in all of this? Do art and theatre have to be political? Should they be? Am I guilty of a glassy-eyed, dated optimism in revisiting and reviewing (through rose-tinted spectacles?) a lost period when theatre dared to matter and get engaged? Returning to Maddy Costa's article about the scarcity of new playwrights, she quotes Dominic Cooke (then newly appointed Artistic Director of the Royal Shakespeare Company) in relation to this debate about political theatre:

> Cooke says people are deeply suspicious of politics. 'In the 1970s and 80s when people were writing big public plays, their role model was Brecht. But when the iron curtain came down the ideology that supported the Brechtian model was brought into crisis. Playwrights now have a much harder job because the critique of government and capitalism is a more complex task than the 1970s theatre forms reflect.'

Since that interview took place, Dominic Cooke has gone on to become the new Artistic Director of the Royal Court. While Cooke's central points are fair and correct, there are some underlying assumptions within his analysis that are open to question.

Is it completely accurate to view one of the great plays of the post-war period such as Bond's *Lear* (1971) or an important 1970s play such as Brenton's *Weapons of Happiness* (1976) as anything less than 'complex'? David Edgar's *Maydays* (1983) also offered a most searching and complex analysis of post-war revolutionary Left politics and their demise. These three plays and a significant number of others from the period were profoundly self-questioning. Without resorting to narrow polemic or a simplistic, reductive, outdated Marxism, they engaged with the nature of political authority, state-sanctioned and 'terrorist' violence, and the crisis facing the historical trajectory of the Left political project. The fall of the Berlin Wall in 1989 and the subsequent dis-integration of the former Soviet Union were, of course, major global events with equally major consequences. Disaffection and disillusionment with the Soviet Union as a global political alternative to capitalism had already begun back in 1956 with the Soviet invasion of Hungary followed by their mirror-effect invasion of Czechoslovakia in 1968.

It's inescapable and probably inevitable that interest in not only politics but the wider field of social and moral debate has changed over the last twenty years. This is a period in which Margaret Thatcher proclaimed, 'There is no such thing as society,' followed by John Major who assured us that class had also ceased to exist. Finally Tony Blair as Prime Minister made it clear that ideology and class conflict had joined the other corpses in the cemetery of redundant concepts. Without any need for society, the disap-pearance of class and the absence of ideology, it's a wonder that contemporary British society doesn't feel more completely like a neo-liberal, democratic, twenty-first-century Eden. If there is no society, no class and effectively no debate, what could there be left to write plays about, except possibly 'reality TV' shows, home and garden 'make-over' programmes and Oprah-style confessional 'sofa TV'?

As plays like Mark Ravenhill's *Shopping and Fucking* and *Some Explicit Polaroids*, David Greig's *The Architect* and *Europe*, David Edgar's *Maydays*, *Pentecost* and *Playing with Fire*, Tanika Gupta's *Fragile Land* and *Gladiator Games* and Forced Entertainment's *Bloody Mess* illustrate, we are living in a Britain and a wider world where the 'big issues' that have informed theatre are now subject to critical revisiting and questioning. As you engage with these five writers in *At the Sharp End* you'll see a new landscape slowly emerging.

It's characterised by a new postmodern politics of sexuality and the environment as well as the new and problematic nationalisms of a post-Soviet Eastern Europe and a gradually devolving Britain. It's a world in which the ideology of Islamic fundamentalism and United States neo-conservatism has taken over the territory previously held by the old Cold War politics of capitalism versus Soviet Communism. How can we have cross-cultural dialogue in a mass-mediated world post-9/11 and -7/7? What are the challenges and opportunities presented by living within contemporary multicultural Britain? This is where the sharp end of our times is. This is where the five writers are fighting to engage. Are they on the losing side of a battle too big to be won?

Playwrights, after all, can't stop the tanks or prevent the bricks thrown through a Pakistani corner shop window in Oldham or Whitechapel. They *can* and should ask questions about who sold the armaments to which regimes, who cast the first stone and why human beings seem terminally addicted to violence and discrimination.

The answers will be complex, if they can be found at all. Better to make that journey than to stay in the supposed safe harbour of lack of interest or ignorance.

Revisiting My Route

That the venues for my London-based conversations were both the Royal Court and also their offices generously provided by

Paines Plough felt both symbolic and auspicious. Alongside the journeys around England and Scotland, I also visited a diverse range of theatre venues. This entailed travelling from the main house of the Chichester Festival Theatre with its predominantly older, white, neo-conservative, upper-middle-class audience through to the main stage of the Theatre Royal Stratford East. There, remarkably, I gave heartfelt thanks for being one of a relatively small number of middle-aged white faces in a high-energy-field audience of young black British and British Asian theatregoers. My travels also took me to the Soho Theatre, like Paines Plough, a leading light in new writing, and also to the privileged metropolitan audience of a Press Night at the Donmar Warehouse. I'd also travelled literally with Forced Entertainment on a piece (*Nights in This City*, 1995) performed on a coach tour through Sheffield, walking at the end through a derelict bus depot that they had magically re-created as a sacred space for atheists and agnostics.

This résumé of my geographical journey of interview locations and venues reflects, I hope, the diverse and eclectic nature of the five writers and their work. It would take an encyclopaedia of a book even to begin to try to map 'where British theatre and playwriting is now'. It would also require a misguided arrogance of purpose and critical judgement. Not guilty.

'Now' like 'contemporary' is a shifting space and concept. It is prey to the vagaries of fashion and the socio-cultural ephemera of what is viewed variously as 'relevant', 'accessible', 'hip', 'exotic' and 'cool'. Beyond such transient and superficial markers on my map lies the exciting potential for innovation and the redefining of what does or should concern or celebrate us in this new millennium. Each of the five writers under discussion can lay legitimate and serious claim to be a significant reference point at the sharp end of this challenge.

Theatre can play an essential role in helping to sustain and build a more human-centred, human-valued society in which what it means to be human can be provisionally articulated. Theatre can never afford to be simply the decorative icing on the cake, however sweet tasting and delicious. Writers, directors, performers and designers, and everyone involved in making theatre, need instead to be right down in the rough centre of the mix – at the sharp end.

Time Zones

The following *Time Zones* are intended to help locate the five writers and the plays discussed in the critical essays into a chronological context. The zones represent each of the six decades from and including 1956 to the present. The zones also list some but not all of the principal plays of that decade, along with a selection of the key indicative political/social events. This will help to give you a historical overview of the post-war period from the 1950s onwards.

Plays by the five writers are indicated in bold beneath the year in which they premièred. The *Time Zones* cannot of course be comprehensive but will, it is hoped, help you to map your own journeys of the five writers and their work against a wider social, cultural and political background within the post-war period.

1950s

- The first space satellite sent into outer space by the Soviet Union.
- The Suez Crisis.
- The Soviet invasion of Hungary.
- The formation of the Campaign for Nuclear Disarmament (CND).
- The Royal Court and the Theatre Royal Stratford East open.
- John Osborne's *Look Back in Anger* and *The Entertainer*.
- Harold Pinter's *The Birthday Party*.
- John Arden's *Serjeant Musgrave's Dance*.
- Arnold Wesker's *Chicken Soup with Barley*.
- Shelagh Delaney's *A Taste of Honey*.

1960s

- Labour government 1964–70: Capital punishment and theatre censorship abolished, homosexuality partially decriminalised, abortion legalised.
- Left-wing political riots in Paris (1968) especially, but also in

London and throughout Western Europe and the USA, against the Vietnam war.

- The Soviet Union enters Czechoslovakia with armed force to crush non-violent uprising for a democratic socialism.
- Edward Bond's *Saved*.
- Joan Littlewood's Theatre Workshop *Oh What a Lovely War!*
- Arnold Wesker's *Chips with Everything*.

1970s

- Conservative government under Edward Heath 1970–74: Mounting unemployment, mass miners' strikes, rising crime figures.
- Labour government under Wilson and Callaghan 1974–79: Initial partial political stability ends with 'Winter of Discontent' of mass industrial action. This leads in 1979 to the election of Britain's first ever woman Prime Minister, Margaret Thatcher.
- Increasing violence in Britain's conflict in Northern Ireland with IRA bombs in England and 'Bloody Sunday' in Derry when paratroopers killed thirteen non-violent Irish Catholic demonstrators.
- Edward Bond's *Lear*.
- Trevor Griffiths's *Comedians*.

1976

- David Edgar's **Destiny**.
- The opening of the National Theatre on the South Bank.
- Gay Sweatshop, the first gay theatre company in Britain, is formed.
- The Manchester Royal Exchange Theatre opened.

1980s

- Margaret Thatcher's Conservative government – unleashed free market, privatisation, cuts in public spending – defines the decade.

- The Falklands war.
- David Edgar's *Nicholas Nickleby* (1980).
- David Edgar's *Maydays* (1983).
- Caryl Churchill's *Top Girls* and *Serious Money*.
- Sarah Daniels's *Masterpieces*.
- Howard Brenton's *The Romans in Britain*, produced by the National Theatre and directed by Michael Bogdanov. The director faced legal proceedings 'for procuring an act of gross indecency' in a scene of attempted anal rape. The legal action, brought by the right-wing moral campaigner Mary Whitehouse, was unsuccessful.

1990s

- Margaret Thatcher deposed as Conservative leader and Prime Minister in 1990 and replaced by John Major, who wins a surprise election victory in 1992. Tony Blair's New Labour elected in 1997 with landslide victory as the first Labour government to be in power for eighteen years.
- The first Gulf war.
- The Good Friday Peace Agreement in Northern Ireland.
- *'In-Yer-Face Theatre'*: Aleks Sierz employs this term to describe a new wave of young British dramatists including Mark Ravenhill, Sarah Kane, Joe Penhall and Jez Butterworth. These writers largely appear through Stephen Daldry's tenure as director at the Royal Court and Max Stafford-Clark's Out of Joint theatre company.
- Sarah Kane's *Blasted*.
- Ayub Khan-Din's *East is East*.
- Richard Norton-Taylor and the Tricycle Theatre: *The Colour of Justice*.

1994

David Edgar's *Pentecost*.

Tim Etchells and Forced Entertainment *Hidden J*.

1995

Tim Etchells and Forced Entertainment *Nights in This City*.

David Greig's *Europe*.
1996
Mark Ravenhill's *Shopping and Fucking*.
David Greig's *The Architect*.
1998
Mark Ravenhill's *Some Explicit Polaroids*.
Tim Etchells and Forced Entertainment *Dirty Work*.
1999
David Greig's *The Cosmonaut's Last Message to the Woman He Once Loved in the Former Soviet Union*.
Tim Etchells and Forced Entertainment *Disco Relax*.

2000s
- Islamic fundamentalists hijack aeroplanes resulting in '9/11': (11 September 2001) the aerial destruction of the World Trade Center in Manhattan, New York, with up to 3,000 civilian deaths.
- The second Gulf war in which the USA and Britain invade Saddam Hussein's Iraq.
- (7 July 2005): Tragedy on the London Transport system when underground trains and a London bus are bombed by British Islamic suicide-bombers leading to over fifty civilian deaths and many more seriously injured.
- (21 July 2005) Jean de Menezes, a Brazilian migrant worker, is shot and murdered by British police on a London Underground train on the mistaken assumption that he is a suicide-bomber.
- (June 2007) Tony Blair resigns as New Labour leader and Prime Minister and Gordon Brown succeeds him.
- Civil partnerships are introduced for same-sex couples in Britain.
- Dominic Cooke moves from the RSC to become the new Artistic Director of the Royal Court.
- Roy Williams's *Sing Yer Hearts Out for the Lads*.
- Kwame Kwei-Armah's *Elmina's Kitchen*.

2000

David Greig's *Victoria*.

Tanika Gupta's *The Waiting Room*.

2002

Tanika Gupta's *Inside Out*.

Mark Ravenhill's *Mother Clap's Molly House*.

2003

Tanika Gupta's *Fragile Land*.

2004

Tim Etchells and Forced Entertainment *Bloody Mess*.

2005

Mark Ravenhill's *Citizenship* and David Edgar's *Playing with Fire*.

2006

Mark Ravenhill's *The Cut* and *Product*. **Citizenship** revived at the National Theatre. *Pool (No Water)* his first collaboration with physical theatre company, Frantic Assembly.

Tanika Gupta's *Gladiator Games* and *Sugar Mummies*.

2 DAVID EDGAR

SHORT CUT
- Major dramatist originating from the 1970s generation of left-wing political writers such as Howard Brenton, Trevor Griffiths and David Hare.
- Political analyst, socio-political commentator and map maker of post-war British and European political and cultural change.
- Important anti-racist writer and activist.
- Active in contemporary multicultural initiatives.
- Devised and was Course Director for Britain's first ever MA in Playwriting of which Sarah Kane was a particularly infamous graduate.

PLAYS
(Bold titles are plays discussed in the critical essay)
The National Interest 1971
Dick Deterred 1974
Destiny 1976
Nicholas Nickleby 1980
Maydays 1983
Entertaining Strangers 1985
That Summer 1987
The Shape of the Table 1990
Pentecost 1994
The Prisoner's Dilemma 2001
Playing with Fire 2005

Interview with David Edgar

The following is an edited account of two conversations recorded at the Royal Court Theatre in May 2006 and in Chichester in July of the same year.

PB David, I wonder whether you could talk about your early writing for the stage and any particular influences upon both that and your subsequent involvement in theatre?

DE I think I'm odd amongst some of my playwriting contemporaries in that I come from a theatre family – both my parents met on the Stage Door steps of the Birmingham Repertory Theatre – where my father was Stage Manager and my mother was joining the company as a student actor. My aunt ran the company in the post-war period up until the early 1960s. So the first plays I wrote were plays that I wrote myself to act in for a model theatre that my father built for me. I then decided at school (I went to public school at Oundle) that I wanted to direct and spent some time doing that and then went to university at Manchester, but as my second year was 1968 I pretty much lost interest in theatre (because what was happening outside was so much more exciting). Although I was President of the Student Socialist Society for a short period, I think my most influential position was as editor of the Manchester University student newspaper and out of that arose the belief that I would like to earn my living 'by the pen', but also much more importantly a commitment to a political movement. When I left university, I think I'd come back round – partly because I hadn't succeeded in directing at university.

There'd been a particularly catastrophic production of Oscar Wilde's *Salome* at the Manchester University Drama Studio back in 1967. I had written a play whilst at university, which was entered but failed to get into the final of the National Student Drama Festival. However, the reason that I got back into writing was writing for a student theatre group in Bradford, where I was working as a journalist. The University of Bradford didn't have a drama department (which was probably a saving grace) but it did have a Fellow in Theatre, Chris Parr, who later became a television producer. He commissioned writers to write plays for students, so there weren't endless productions of [Edward Albee's] *Zoo Story* or [Harold] Pinter 'three-handers'. What there *were*, were plays by Richard Crane, John Grillo, Howard Brenton and myself – which was very thrilling. I wrote a large number of plays and I think settled really into an agitprop mode of writing.

Out of this university group came a group called 'The General Will', which was one of the principal agitprop political companies of the early 1970s, for whom I wrote half a dozen 'political cartoon' plays over the next four years. I was also writing more conventional plays for studio theatres at the same time. Gradually the foreground and the background changed, and I became more interested in writing for the theatre and less interested in writing for the small-scale touring circuit. I ended up writing political dramas which (although they continue to be accused of being agitprop) were self-consciously and formally breaking with that tradition.

I go through the whole of that story because the influences were dormant, because they go back to when I was very, very small. I had seen Shakespeare about the age of nine, and also I went to see lots of bad plays – Agatha Christie and the like. I think my parents took a decision to let me go and take me to pretty much all the theatre that I wanted to see. In the summer of 1969 I went to see the Living Theatre at the Roundhouse, and I was bowled over by the energy and possibility and revolutionary explosiveness of that. That obviously was an influence on the work that I did, even though I've probably exaggerated that a bit in its terms of influence, just as I probably exaggerated the influence of productions like Peter Brook's production of the *Marat/Sade*. I remember once thinking, because I'd read it very often, that I'd seen [Hochhuth's] *The Representative*, which I actually didn't but that was very influential too in terms of large-scale political drama – so

I think there was a breadth rather than a depth of influence in my early career in which I wrote in a lot of different styles.

PB That leads us rather nicely into our first 'sub-theme' of theatre and politics. Where did your political sensibilities grow from originally, David?

DE I really came into politics and political thought at public school where I joined the Campaign for Nuclear Disarmament, but more seriously at university where I was inspired by two things. One was the events in Paris of 1968 and the other was the way in which the Vietcong, with vastly smaller resources, had managed to get virtually into the compound of the American embassy during the Tet offensive in February 1968. I was really much struck and much taken with that. I came to Left politics through a pretty traditional route: that is, a kind of 'romance' about the heroism of the oppressed, which is a rather dangerous route because of when that perception is broken down, as it inevitably will be (because nobody stays a 'revolutionary hero' for ever). That's a very well-worn course to Conservatism and, as you know, my play *Maydays* is very much about how I might – and my generation of people might – have moved to the Right. Certainly a large part of that is how those of us who came into revolutionary politics by being impressed with the heroism of the poor and the oppressed might come to feel the oppressed and the poor had stopped behaving 'suitably heroically', or felt the poor stopped behaving appropriately to their 'victim status'. Those are the two disillusionments which are at the core of and characterise almost everybody who has defected from the far Left to the far Right. So I was conscious really from quite early on of that historical movement from the Left to the Right of so many people in their middle age – and I wanted to try and avoid that.

PB Did you ever feel constrained by any particular ideology on the Left or any political party on the Left when you were writing those early agitprop plays for the General Will? Did you view yourself as working autonomously as a writer or did you have a greater sense of wider obligation and commitment?

DE   Well, it was very interesting that none of us was in a political party. I was, as I used to joke, 'always going to join the Socialist Workers Party tomorrow' – for several years! In some senses I am very glad that I didn't. Certainly I was never even attracted to the Workers Revolutionary Party, which a lot of the people in the theatre were at that time. On the other hand, I think we felt in a strange kind of way even more committed to the fact that we needed to be different sorts of people from those that we were. Then, perfectly properly, one member of the group who was gay decided that he was the only person who was genuinely aligned because of his sexual identity. He went on strike halfway through a performance in order, in essence, to convert the group into a kind of identity politics. The criticism was: 'Who were we?' Mostly men. The initial structure was three men and one woman – that obviously had its own built-in 'caucus' – so it became a group of three straight men and one gay man. 'What were we?' – what was our alignment? It was a very good question that was eventually answered. Somewhat to my regret, I wasn't there on the famous night of the 'strike' but it was a very good question and I think it was a contradiction that a lot of small companies faced in that period.

The period where my politics and my practice as a playwright walked most easily hand in hand together was in the period after I wrote *Destiny* – my play about the rise of the National Front – and I became very involved with the Anti-Nazi League. I did a lot of speaking and writing, and I worked for *Searchlight* magazine, and I think it was true that I found it liberating to have a political purpose. It meant, perhaps, that I could feel less obliged to wear my politics so obviously on my sleeve in my plays.

PB   Looking back, do you see *Destiny* as a crucial, perhaps *transitional* play in that mid stage of your writing, in that structurally, it seems to me, there are elements of the agitprop genre in terms of the direct address to the audience but in your treatment of Turner we have an English neo-Fascist presented as a 'human being'?

DE It's always dangerous doing interviews – how much is retrospect? I think, however, I had decided that the play wanted to fulfil two functions. One was that I wanted it to say to the liberals that the National Front were Nazis. To call the National Front 'Fascist' was regarded by many people as typical far-Left 'grandiosity'. The second task was to say to the Left, 'Look, these people have a real hold – they're addressing something really important.' It does have some agitprop aspects: it ends with Hitler appearing and so, to that extent, it is transitional.

PB *Destiny* was the first play that took you out of the circuit of small-scale political theatre and put your work on to a national stage.

DE It was originally written for Nottingham Playhouse, who turned it down – the first draft wasn't really very good. Then I rewrote it for Birmingham and famously the Board complained to the Artistic Director for Programming, partly on the grounds that they thought no one would come, but also because of a certain reservation about its subject matter. Then it went around the houses – it was initially turned down by the RSC – then Ron Daniels took it to Trevor Nunn and they agreed to do it in the Other Place. This was a play that I had written to be produced in a large, urban, main-house stage, so I wasn't very interested in the play ending up in a small tin hut in Warwickshire. But beggars can't be choosers, so it went ahead and Trevor [Nunn] took the bold decision when circumstances unexpectedly determined that the Royal Shakespeare Company needed a play for the start of their London season at their then London base: the Aldwych Theatre in London. My play fitted, so it was done inside the *King Lear* set on a major West End stage. It was a very brave decision and it did change the audience for the play and probably my future writing.

PB Was the 'romance' that you referred to earlier in terms of political allegiances on the radical Left part of a belief that theatre could, and should, intervene as part of social and political debate? If that was the case, what were the implications for dramatic form?

Destiny seems to explore a dramatic form that could incorporate some of those agitprop elements but which was also trying to deal with issues of characterisation and plot, which one might see in more conventionally structured plays.

DE Yes, that's right, I left journalism in 1972 and the first thing I did was to do 'England's Ireland' with Howard Brenton and others. There were various ideas within that group about writing contemporary history plays and putting history within the context of the immediate past, which was obviously very influential upon *Destiny*. For example, the idea of the Prologue that's set some years before, which helps bring people up to date. I was also inspired by the fact that Enoch Powell had burned his major's uniform the day after Indian Independence (1947) and that gave me the idea for the character of Rolfe. What that was addressing was that the collapse and the end of the British Empire had the same place in post-war Britain as the Treaty of Versailles had had in Germany in the 1930s. There was also a dramatic structure within the play where the timescale went backwards and forwards, so that in the last scene of the first act the timescale starts going backwards. So one's saying that here's this man in the 1970s with this problem and we jump back to 1968 where this political party is celebrating Hitler's birthday, which happens to be the same date on which Enoch Powell delivered his 'Rivers of Blood' speech. You can see the far Right party's change in tactics in attempting to be much more popular – to appeal to the sort of man in the previous scene. That was interesting structurally; I don't think people had quite done that before. It was a way of trying to put scenes together thematically so that a scene poses a question to the next scene afterwards – ideologically rather than in terms of strict narrative. But the real narrative coup is having an election, having a race – an outcome. If you recollect, I'm not very interested in the outcome of the election – the Tory candidate wins it – the least prominent of the characters – the actual result of the election isn't the important thing but it obviously gave the play a strong spine.

PB I always felt when I was teaching *Destiny* as a play to undergraduate students that there is a dialectical structure based on a political dialectic of a thesis and an antithesis?

DE Yes, that's absolutely right, I think that was central to the play, it was a dialectical play.

PB If we turn to *Pentecost* as another major 'marker' play in terms of the journey of our conversation together. If you were endeavouring to map something of the journey that you had travelled politically and aesthetically as a writer in between that point on the map that is *Destiny* and that point on the map that is *Pentecost*, is it possible to try and offer some reflection on that journey?

DE Yes, I think one of the staging points in that journey would be *Maydays* in that, of course, in the period after *Destiny*, Margaret Thatcher's Conservative government was elected (in 1979) and whilst that government was clearly not Fascist, the election of Thatcher was not good news for the Fascist far Right. Through her invocation of a sense of British nationality and the imperial past, she clearly did provide a home for those who might have been attracted by the far Right and she did so by an ideology that owed a striking amount to defectors from the Left both in this country and America. So I became very interested in and read a lot about the 'New Right'. During a year in America, I became very interested by those on the Left and liberals who had moved to the Right in reaction to what they viewed as the excesses of the 1960s. I became very interested in Eastern Europe and the Soviet Union and political dissidents, having been on the fringes of the Trotskyite Left, which had a 'nothing to do with me, guv' attitude to the Soviet Union (because the Soviet Union had expelled Trotsky and you can't blame Socialism on one country). I found that viewpoint increasingly unrealistic. Also I found the idea that Margaret Thatcher was a 'flash in the pan' increasingly untenable. So for me clearly the Left was not speaking to current realities, including the feasibility or otherwise of a Socialist state or states.

Then I started writing for *Marxism Today* and spoke to those intellectuals such as Eric Hobsbawm and Stuart Hall, who were wrestling with the same problems. I think I came round to the view that the great mistake that the Left had made in the 1960s and 1970s was not seeking to revitalise social democracy. This was probably one of the most successful political systems that there had ever been in terms of managing to combine increasing prosperity with the preservation of – indeed, increasing – liberty through the social reforms of the 1950s and 1960s. I also felt that we had made a mistake of almost the historical proportions of the pre-Popular Front era of the 1930s, when Social Democrats were viewed as the other face of Fascism by the Soviet Union (and therefore by the Communist parties in the West).

Then of course in 1989, which is not just about the collapse of Soviet Communism but also about a crisis in Social Democracy: the Labour Party in Britain was then currently unelectable and the strains on the Welfare State in Scandinavia and Germany were beginning to be evident. So I did think that we on the Left had to begin to deal with the collapse of the Soviet Union and personally I dealt with it in three plays. *Pentecost* is interesting because in some ways it's a kind of grand 'background' play, because although the background is the collapse of the Soviet Union and Eastern Europe, the foreground of the play (which continues, of course, to be increasingly relevant) is how societies work with very different groups of people. This raises questions also about what Western societies should be like and issues of cultural diversity and multiculturalism. Therefore in a way the second part of the play has become more pertinent than the first. When it first came out, the first half of the play (which looks at how the West was exploiting the East) looked more relevant then.

PB   At the climactic point of *Pentecost* the commandos storm into the church and a number of the asylum seekers and refugees are killed. Also some of the political activists are killed along with the character of Oliver. At the end of David Greig's play *The American Pilot* there's a stage direction which says: 'The gunfire continues. The bombing continues. The End.' In terms of where you position yourself in relation to *Pentecost* as a barometer of your political sensibility at the time and indeed now, does the bleak subtext of the end of *The American Pilot* where the American commandos storm in and kill innocent people resonate for you?

DE *Pentecost* of course has a dreadful ending, followed by a sort of 'where there's life, there's hope' kind of second ending. I hope it's rather more than that, of course! I do feel that the dialectic of *Pentecost* was really observing the fact – and I like to think that I saw this rather early – that 1990 was the zenith of the Delors vision of the abolition of the nation state. People did assume that the countries of the former Eastern Europe would rush to the West to embrace that vision, whereas what happened was entirely the reverse. What happened was that Eastern Europe re-sorted itself into tiny and tinier 'statelets' and Western Europe thought, 'Oh, that's a really good idea.' With Catalonia, Wales, Lombardy, Bavaria – with varying degrees of success – thinking it was a splendid answer: 'We'll too try and find the largest homogenous group that we're happy with and then draw a line around it.' This is what happened in Latvia and Slovakia and so on. Therefore what I was trying to do was to say that Communism strips the untidy bark off the naked trunks of humankind and clothes them in a uniform, whereas the new nationalism raided the fancy-dress box of the past.

In this the new nationalisms were trying to reinvent languages that were more different from each other than they needed to be – and indeed, more different than they had been before. It was also that the future lay in a conversation between cultures: the notion of hybridity. Also the metaphor of English as a second language being unsatisfactory and imprecise but that nevertheless it *is* a way of communicating. Some people slightly misread the storytelling scene as saying, 'We've all got the same story.' Actually, the stories aren't the same (the end of the *Ramayana* isn't the same as the ending of the *Odyssey* or the end of the Christian story) but they've got interesting common elements. However, they also have equally interesting differences and you can have a conversation between them – they're not mutually exclusive. That's what the storytelling scene is trying to say. You can't look at the world in a linear, single, 'central subject' way, but you've got to suddenly say,

'Let's look at the world from a different angle.' The original idea with *Pentecost* was the idea that we'd be seeing the world through the asylum seekers' eyes in the second act of the play.

PB   Is it possible to locate where you think the most possible, realistic potential is for a continuing radicalisation of human beings and for our making of new kinds of society? Is there a voice or voices in the play? Might it be in the notion of hybridity that you've already referred to?

DE   Well, I think that culture is important. On the other hand what is clear is that any contemporary refraction of [Marxist concepts of] base and superstructure just doesn't work any more. Culture may not go all the way down but it goes a very long way down, and we therefore have to look at spaces in which the potential to divide people can be resolved. A Pakistani man still earns £300,000 less in his life than a similarly educated white man. However, it is clear that the ways in which Pakistani and Bangladeshi communities are choosing to address that is through a very different language from the way they chose to in the 1970s. I don't think it's enough to say that the hiljab is the twenty-first-century equivalent for 'jeans' – another protest against school uniform. I don't think that the Koran is just a contemporary translation of Marx's *Kapital*. There is something different going on and everything that raises barriers between groups is bad for finding ways for us to look at ourselves and our society and to live together. I do observe that the number of spaces where that can happen is narrow.

One of the perceptions that *Destiny* provides, I hope, is that the trades unions provided that in the first place although not without a great deal of struggle. Also, of course, the fact that the trades unions are much less important and that that kind of industrial environment is much less prominent now, means that the workplace is a less workable site for that kind of cross-fertilisation of ideas to occur. So culture becomes a much more important arena and while there are limitations to the 'Chicken Tikka Masala syndrome', I think that food is a very good example of the ways in which multiculturalism works in both directions and benefits both sides. You can also see that in terms of music and design. Certainly I think that what people who work with young people find is that the least effective way to encourage young people to try and see the world is through other people's eyes. I'm not suggesting that you therefore take young Asians off to football grounds or march young whites off to Bangladeshi restaurants. Rather you provide some third site where they can be together and expand their horizons, and drama of course is an obvious example of that. Drama works so I think that culture is an important site. However, if you're saying how does working with young drama groups in Burnley, Oldham or Huddersfield translate into anything like the scale of organised political action in the 1970s, well, I think that there are some spaces that will open up in terms of political discourse but to say that it's anything like the 'Big Idea' of the past would clearly be grandiose.

PB I think that's a very important and significant change and development – the absence of meta-narratives or the 'Big Story'. That is, the kind of historical frame in which to think about ourselves as human beings and the possibilities of continuing to build a more just human society. I was very touched, surprised and encouraged that when I went to see the performance of Tanika Gupta's *Gladiator Games* at the Theatre Royal Stratford East I was one of the few people in the audience who was over fifty and one of the few who was white. The fact that the vast majority of the audience were young black British and British Asian citizens who were there in very large numbers and whose response to the play's themes of racial violence and discrimination was intense and, at times, audible.

DE Yes, I've said this a lot, there was a period after *Behzti* when the Birmingham Rep programmed a lot of black and Asian work. It was hugely successful and the one that was most striking was *Little Sweet Thing* by Roy Williams, which was saying that there is something wrong about a black urban culture where there are two weak white people who admire but are being bullied by young black people. They then turn into them culturally – turned from being nice weak people into strong nasty ones. Also the recognition from the audience at the Birmingham Rep, which was three-quarters full and three-quarters young and black, was very striking. Really hard questions were being addressed. In what space can young Asians and blacks – particularly in areas where the BNP are strong – discuss the problems of gun crime, discuss the problems of drugs within the Asian community without fuelling prejudices? Culture can provide that space – theatre can provide that space.

PB I wonder whether you're able to look back from this vantage point of over thirty years of writing plays and writing about theatre and society, and identify any principal themes that have been crucial to you as a writer?

DE I'm now fifty-eight and my first professional production as a writer was when I was twenty-three so that's a long period to think about themes and so on. I think that the overall theme for me – as I mentioned in our earlier conversation – is of coming to terms with the failure of Socialism to live up to the ambitions of its founders. Each new generation comes to terms with that in different ways. But also, why did the idea of a more equal society and – more and more – a society that enables people to emancipate themselves and discover themselves prove to be so unrealisable? How can one get over the waves of disillusionment and avoid the kind of retreat into cynical despair or the defector's march to the Right? To me *Maydays* is a counter-factual autobiography. It's about defection from the Left to the Right in three generations and the central character, who had been a 1960s activist and who defects to the Right, is based on how I might have made that move – written perhaps partly to avoid my doing so. He looks into a mirror and says various things that he'd never think he'd hear himself saying and I can kind of relate to that. Not that I ever have – but I can identify with the temptations to give up on the undoubtedly difficult things to argue, difficult things to commit to and difficult things to believe in. I think, my God, things are even ten times more difficult over the last five or six years, when the most powerful vocabulary of radicalism, dissent and revolt is Islam. Looking back to the days when one was coming to terms with the criminality in the leadership of the 'Black Panthers' that issue now looks relatively easy compared to what one is having to try and come to terms with now.

I think that there is an overall theme, which I write about, which is political disillusionment. I write about people who believe in political things and the difficulties and problems they face when those things are fundamentally challenged. I am surprised at the number of times that Christmas features in my plays and in that there is a feeling for certain things that one might call 'English'. There is a sense of looking at the particular historical traditions of English Radicalism with all of their contradictions. The new community play, for example – it's a kind of 'Napoleonic' era comedy – is about the contradictions between the community and individual emancipation. The tensions between living in a community and the social and sexual constraints of that: one can see all of those themes there – and especially for women and indeed a particular female character. Most community plays tend to be dominated by women yet dominated by male characters and so we (Stephanie Gale, my co-author and I) wanted to reverse that! I've also got a radio play that I'm working on which is really a love story about memory. Those two pieces are quite different from what I've done before.

PB A very difficult question, given the language that we have and the means by which we have to talk about and analyse capitalism. To what extent might one have to accommodate the notion and reality of capitalism in a way that twenty or thirty years ago might have seemed unacceptable?

DE Well, yes, of course, that's true if one's serious about these things. No one has found a way of running a totally state-owned economy that works satisfactorily in relation to its competitors. In 1989 little old Polish ladies realised that although they might be equal to other people in their society, in more absolute terms they were poorer than little old ladies in Germany. I think that there was the possibility in the 1980s of really transforming social democracy: the struggle for feminism and environmentalism in particular. Why don't we have a Green political movement to speak of, why don't we have a Green political party that has the same relationship to social democratic government as is the case in Germany? It's partly the electoral system of course, but clearly there was a chance for the integration of those concerns into the Labour Party back in the 1980s. Labour, by the time of John Smith's death in 1984, had not taken to its heart these issues which the far Left were engaged in. They knew some of the words, but they certainly didn't know the tunes that the far Left were singing, whereas the far Left had not taken the issues of power seriously.

The undoubtedly thrilling political experiments from the mid-1960s onwards, which would have brought culture into the centre, didn't get into the political mainstream until it was too late. That was a real missed historical opportunity. What does that mean? It is possible to have a Welfare State and an egalitarian society and not have a dictatorship or a gulag or arbitrary police powers, but it appears that having an element of the free market is necessary. What is different between Sweden and the former Soviet Union? One thing is that Sweden doesn't have a gulag but it does have a reasonably thriving private sector as well as a very considerable and efficient public sector, so I think here we have the 'horses for courses' idea. I'm not sure that I can put my hand on my heart and say that I can imagine the circumstances in which a state-owned telecommunications service could have dealt with the massive changes that have occurred in telecommunications over the last twenty years. Having said that, I think that there's no question that the privatisation of basic utilities and public transport has been either neutral or a disaster.

Where do I position myself now? I'm a left-wing social democrat in a tradition that goes back through the twentieth century; I'm very much reminded of the Fabian tradition within British Labour and left-wing politics. I always hesitate now when people ask me, 'Are you still a Marxist?' Well, no, I'm not a Marxist in that it's not serious to say – as did the original Communist Manifesto – that 'Workers of the world unite, you have nothing to lose but your chains'. I'm not a Marxist because I don't believe that solution is workable. Am I a Marxist in terms of do I think that Marx is right and that he gets righter and righter and righter in terms of his analysis of capitalism, imperialism and globalisation? In that sense I still am, but thinking that there remain severe and dramatic limitations. As a 'child of the 1960s', I take great comfort from the fact that feminism and environmentalism are Marxist legacies, they came out of a left-wing movement and they wouldn't be as they are if they hadn't.

PB If you were articulating any type of optimistic perspective upon British theatre at this time [July 2006], what would you say was the most creative and productive way that it might function and speak to the times that we live in?

DE I don't know . . . All I know is . . . I think back upon the radical theatre of the 1960s, which itself was a product of the Royal Court generation from 1956 with *Look Back in Anger* and *Saved*, a bit of a dip then as a lot of the energy passes into television, people like Mercer, Potter, McGrath and so on, back in the 1970s with my generation when television started to dry up, I think a little dip in the 1980s when we were of in a state of shock (in the Thatcher period) and there was some great television work such as Troy Kennedy Martin with *Edge of Darkness*, Alan Bleasdale's *Boys from the Black Stuff*. I think that there was some great energy in the novel in that period – the upsurge of women playwrights in the 1980s – another dip in the late 1980s and early 1990s and then the emergence of the 'Brat Pack' in the mid-1990s: Sarah Kane and Mark Ravenhill. I actually have a lot of time for Jo Penhall, David Eldridge and Martin Crimp. I think that a lot of the work that came out of that period was exciting. The unusual thing about the 'Brat Pack' was that they were very inter-generationally generous – we were awful about the preceding generation and the women at the Royal Court in the 1980s were pretty rough on us. There's more space, of course, the market has expanded, and there are many,

many more playwrights around. There are new distinctive cultures like Scottish playwriting, especially with David Greig. Two things are exciting: one is that 'new waves' keep coming. The second is that a significant number of those new waves carry on.

One of the striking things about the 1956 generation was how many of those writers became burned out or were burned out in various different ways. It's very exciting that a number of new writers are not 'one-play wonders' but are continuing to write and forging careers. One of the great tragedies to me is what might Sarah Kane have gone on to write had she lived? I think that clearly political theatre came back after the 'Brat Pack' but I think it was partially a political project of itself. This is especially the case with Mark Ravenhill where there is a sort of eulogy for a lost time of political certainties. It's a bit like CND that had to keep treading water for twenty years but then emerges again when needed. It does seem to me that 'political' playwriting is robust enough to keep on going – new things keep on happening. When politics suddenly becomes a 'live issue' again, people are reminded that there is a language and a vocabulary, there's a culture that enables that to flourish again. That's what excites me and I am very struck when I go and see black and Asian plays that theatre is a site where important things are being discussed.

I felt that very much with my home theatre in Birmingham, the Birmingham Rep. The idea of theatre as a site of a particular sort of discourse is crucial and exciting, and that's why there are sometimes difficulties for Islam and sometimes difficulties for certain Christians. I'm optimistic that in theatre you can still ask questions about the undoubted crisis of black urban gun crime and talk about, for example, why are our sons going to join fighters in Afghanistan? You can talk about sexuality and sexism in various communities. Theatre provides a space to say things you couldn't say elsewhere. If you think right back to *Look Back in Anger* in 1956, that play was clearly saying things that you couldn't say anywhere else at the time. That has to be the continuing basis of hope and optimism for British theatre.

Speaking in Tongues – Politics, Race and Cultural Identity in the Plays of David Edgar

David Edgar remains one of the leading voices of the British political Left of the 1960s, 1970s and 1980s. His substantial body of plays and non-dramatic political journalism represents an important record of a period of major change within British social, cultural and political life. Of all the writers discussed in this book he traverses the widest and longest period of creative activity. From earlier landmark plays such as *Destiny* (1976) through to the recent revival (Chichester Festival Theatre, 2006–07, directed by Jonathan Church and Philip Franks) of his hugely commercially successful and critically acclaimed *The Life and Times of Nicholas Nickleby* (originally commissioned by the RSC, 1980) his dramatic voice remains ever present on the British stage. *Destiny* was a major play for David Edgar. It signalled a crucial transitional stage in his early-to-mid career from his early agitprop work into the development of his later style. This is recognisable by its strong sense of structural symmetry fused with an extensively informed political understanding.

On graduating from Manchester University in the late 1960s, his first paid employment was as a junior reporter on the *Bradford Evening Argus*. Edgar's formative adult years at Manchester and Bradford were a period of profound political activism and significant social and cultural change. This was not only in Britain but also in America and across Europe in the decades before the eventual fall of the Berlin Wall in 1989. That iconic moment symbolised a global, political *fin de siècle*. Edgar's major plays, especially *Maydays* (1983), chart the period from the post-war years of 1945 through to the collapse of Soviet State Communism.

Destiny seeks to place the re-emergence of neo-Nazi racist political parties in post-war Britain into a historical context of Empire and its loss signalled most potently by the awarding of independence by the British to India in 1947. The play succeeds in offering a rigorous post-mortem of the social, cultural and political corpse of Empire and imperialism. With this is also exposed all of its associated issues and themes of racial discrimination and aggressively militaristic nationalism. *Destiny* also reveals a reactionary mistrust within sections of the English lower middle class of all peoples east of Dover and south and west of Penzance.

In *Maydays* the frame of historical, political and geo-ideological reference expands into a breathtakingly panoramic vista of post-war Britain and the European political landscape of the same period. The play's narrative journey takes us to and from 1950s Soviet-occupied Hungary through to the Russia and Britain of the 1960s, 1970s and 1980s. *Pentecost* in turn explores the complex, tragic reverberations of the Balkans war in the 1990s. It is interesting to consider *Pentecost* alongside David Greig's *Europe*, which also explores the traumatic consequences of the end of Soviet Communism and the rapid intervention and impact of free market economic expansion in central and Eastern Europe. In terms of former authoritarian regimes breaking down and the subsequent fracturing of ideological landscapes and individual lives, Mark Ravenhill's *The Cut* also offers significant contrast and comparison.

Playing with Fire (2005) brings the wheel full circle, so to speak, with its examination of the paradoxes and problems facing the established political parties in terms of the challenges presented by a multicultural society. These challenges are exacerbated by the active presence of far-Right, neo-Nazi parties such as the British National Party. The BNP were especially active in the post-industrial towns and cities of northern England where *Playing with Fire* is set. The play itself, premièred at the National Theatre, was motivated by the disturbing large-scale race riots in Burnley, Oldham and Bradford in 2001.

Anticipating Destiny – David Edgar – the General Will Theatre Company and Agitprop

Whilst working in Bradford, David Edgar began to write agitprop plays for a political theatre company called the General Will. This was a group that embodied many key characteristics of radical and revolutionary politics and culture from that period. Agitprop takes its name, of course, from the fusion of two different words: agitate and propaganda: literally, theatre which would agitate political debate and provoke revolutionary political change. Agitprop theatre goes back to the post-1917 Communist Russian Revolution. In this period theatre was used by the Communist authorities to promote the aims and values of the Revolution. This propagandised vision was of a Communist state engineering a radical redistribution of wealth and expansion of economic and social justice. This was a form of theatre that was essentially made by ordinary workers without any professional training as actors and performed in non-standard venues and locations. These would range from the tailboards of lorries parked on street corners or waste grounds to bars and trades union centres. Worker delegates from Communist parties in other European countries such as Britain and Germany visited Russia and returned ready to employ similar kinds of drama in their own urban working-class environments.

These small disparate theatre groups had by the early 1930s coalesced into a loose affiliation known as the Workers Theatre Movement (WTM). These were a range of small, inexperienced groups, again based almost exclusively in the large cities and urban sites of London, Liverpool, Glasgow and Leeds. With names such as the Red Megaphones, they employed a direct and hard-hitting form of political theatre. In cruder variations of the agitprop genre it was frequently the case that in order to achieve its consciousness-raising, propagandist ends, the capitalist character, for example, was customarily a two-dimensional caricature of greed and exploitation. Equally the character of the worker was predictably diligent and heroic. Within England a number of these WTM groups underwent another process of transformation and reorganisation to become known as the Unity Theatre. The Unity Theatre in London was housed in a converted chapel and became famous for the range and quality of its productions. Many of its amateur, untrained actors went on to become household names in post-war British film, stage and television, such as the fine comic actor Alfie Bass and the dramatist Ted – later Lord – Willis. Whilst some characterisation still veers to the slightly schematic, what is also significant about *Destiny* is Edgar's intention to delineate a psychologically consistent, individualised form of character.

It is important to provide this brief historical context as it epitomises the kind of theatre that David Edgar embarked upon in his early writing career with the General Will. Edgar observed his enduring respect and affection for agitprop immediately after his major success and emergent national reputation with *Destiny*. In an interview for the academic theatre journal *Theatre Quarterly* in 1979 he reflected:

> I do like agitprop, and I'm fond of my agitprop plays. I'm fond of
> that period. There may again be a period when agitprop will have
> more relevance than I believe it does now. But I don't think I'll ever
> go back to it, because the sort of subjects that I want to deal with
> now won't take it. (*Theatre Quarterly*, IX, no. 33, 1979)

Destiny (1976)

Destiny was first produced by the Royal Shakespeare Company at the Other Place, Stratford-upon-Avon, in September 1976. The production then transferred to the Aldwych Theatre in London the following year. At that time the Aldwych was serving as the RSC's London production base. It had originally been intended for the Birmingham Repertory Theatre and was then under consideration at the Nottingham Playhouse. It represented one of the first modern British political dramas to be produced by one of the country's two major subsidised national companies, the other, of course, being the National Theatre. Following its transfer it became the first play of its kind to be produced in London's West End. For a writer whose previous work had principally been for the political touring circuit (pub theatres, trades union centres, church halls and small arts centres) this represented a major and hitherto unimaginable change of scale in terms of audience and high public profile.

The play asks controversial and challenging questions about the nature and rise of Nazism and Fascism, and its particular English version through the formation of the National Front (NF) in 1967 and subsequently the British National Party (BNP). Prior to the Second World War (1939–45) Sir Oswald Mosley's Blackshirts in the 1930s had been the principal and very visible presence of Fascist politics in Britain. They were famously defeated by a coalition of local Jewish residents and left-wing activists when Mosley and his followers planned to march provocatively through London's East End ('The Battle of Brick Lane'). Mosley's British Union of Fascists explicitly aligned themselves with Hitler's Nazis in Germany, Mussolini's Fascist Party in Italy, as well as Franco's Fascist Spain following the Spanish Civil War.

Crucial and central to *Destiny* is the rise in popularity of the National Front in certain parts of Britain in the 1960s and 1970s. This was especially, but not exclusively, in Birmingham and the West Midlands where David Edgar was brought up and has his adult home. The fictionalised geographical setting of the play as the small West Midlands town of Taddley is therefore doubly important. It was in this geo-ideological area of England that the extreme Right had their first democratically elected success in 1964 through the success of the racist-motivated Peter Griffiths in the General Election. Even more crucially, it was the Conservative MP and Cabinet Minister Enoch Powell whose parliamentary constituency was in Wolverhampton, who gave his infamous speech in April 1968. In this notorious speech Powell used the inflammatory image of 'Rivers of Blood' flooding the towns and cities of Britain if immigration were not strictly controlled and repatriation introduced. With disturbing irony, it had also been Powell some twenty years earlier who had orchestrated the British government's campaign to recruit a new workforce from the former Caribbean colonies. What was further explicitly and eerily significant about the timing of Powell's speech was that he gave it on the day and date of Hitler's birth.

Powell's speech followed the Race Relations Bill being passed in the same year, formulated by Harold Wilson's Labour government and supported by the Conservative opposition. This collusion by the mainstream political parties is therefore also central to the play's genesis. The cynically pragmatic, populist strategies of not only the Conservatives but also Labour in tacitly agreeing to the 'need' for immigration controls implicitly reinforced the racist, xenophobic scare-mongering propaganda of the extreme Right. These attitudes and values that promote a disturbingly dystopian nightmare vision of the 'Eng-er-land, Eng-er-land' chant of racist football thugs, run the dangerous risk of becoming institutionalised and, correspondingly, 'acceptable'. This deeply depressing scenario continues to have serious implications today in the prejudices, lies and half-truths about asylum seekers and 'illegal immigrants'. In her perceptive, empathetically honest account of inner-city existence for young multicultural people in modern Britain, Tanika Gupta's play *Fragile Land* reveals the traumatic impact upon those peoples defined as 'alien' and a 'threat' to public safety owing to the colour of their skin and/or their ethnicity.

An essential element of what David Edgar achieved through *Destiny* was to show with rigorously informed objectivity that the dangerous presence of racism in British society was not to be located exclusively or explained completely by the Swastika-wearing skinhead thugs of the National Front. What Edgar makes undeniably clear is that its ugliness and hatred exists within the very institutions of the British political and military Establishment. Beneath the supposed respectability of England's 'Old School Tie' public schools and the prestigious officer training of Sandhurst lurk the shadows of intolerance and discrimination.

The structural narrative of the play is significant in that it opens chronologically in 1947. Edgar reveals the historical circumstances and origins of racism and racist politics within post-war British society. The use of the direct address by an individual character at the start of each of the scenes has the function of the Brechtian *gestus*. The *gestus* is a pre-emptive, foreknown summary of the dramatic events to come and the dramatic dialectic that they serve. It also creates a dramatic tension between the notion of the actor-as-character (an agent of individualised action) but also as the actor-as-objective-commentator upon the wider historical and political landscape of the play. In this important sense the device 'privileges' the actor-characters by enabling them to have a relatively historically wide-lens perspective upon the private, individualised actions and motives of characters. This is achieved through them being enabled to comment and reflect upon themselves in the context of the public, political dimensions and consequences of a human-centred, human-driven history. This contributes to a Brechtian disruptive distancing of the audience's perspective and understanding of the interface of public and private histories. Edgar's narrative structure consequently facilitates a focus upon the dialectic or tension between the agency of subjective individualised motive and action in contention with a viewing of complex historically objective and externalised events. From this collision, individual human beings participate as causal channels of events and change, but are also paradoxically recipient subjects of those wider changes and events.

In other words we are helped to see that Turner's apparently inevitable journey towards a political position identifiable with Fascism is more problematic than Turner simply and innately personifying that political doctrine. Instead, the audience is enabled to construe his prejudiced, parochial patriotic values as the complex, interactive product of individual experience in conjunction with the loss of Empire and the consequent move-ment of British subjects to England from the former colonies as 'immigrants'. Alongside this evolution of Britain as an increasingly multicultural society came the relentless post-war decline of Britain's mass-manufacturing-based economy and its rapid replacement in the 1970s and 1980s by property developers and venture capitalists. Interestingly, in David Greig's three-play epic drama about Scotland, *Victoria*, it is the character of Euan, a young, ambitious entrepreneurial developer, who is constructed as the new face of Scotland's likely political, economic and cultural future.

Whilst incorporating some of the key elements of a Brechtian epic dramaturgy such as the direct 'third person' address to the audience, Edgar is also committed to depicting characters such as Turner especially as more than the ciphers of less dramatically sophisticated political drama.

There are no simplistic caricatures in *Destiny*. In Edgar's treatment of his characters, events and themes, even the politically righteous slogans of the radical Left are placed within the metaphorical 'quotation marks' which enable them to be viewed and critiqued as statements of political belief rather than unarguably true or correct.

Within the tapestry of modern and recent British social, cultural and political life, Edgar creates Turner as a credible character. His experience as a white, socially conservative, lower-middle-class man reveals the interface between the private-subjective and the public-objective realms. As is clear from the opening scene of the play, Turner 'knows his place' in the scheme of things. It is 'a place' or status which, as a sergeant in the British army, affords him superiority over the lower ranks of infantry men and corporals. Significantly, in terms of the play's wider concerns and remit, it also gives him superiority over the indigenous Indian peoples such as Khera, the eighteen-year-old Sikh servant in Scene One. This secondary sense of status is viewed by those many thousands of other 'Turners' as 'innate' and 'intrinsic' beyond questioning. Herein, of course, are some of the poisonous seeds of racism sown: racial and ethnic differences are 'natural' and have a preordained hierarchy. *Destiny* opens with an off-stage, disembodied voice, which on its completion as the framing of the play's concerns as the consummation of a 'tryst with destiny', is revealed as that of Nehru, the first President of the newly independent India. He had been a leading freedom fighter along with others such as the revolutionary pacifist and political campaigner Mahatma Gandhi. Significantly, Tanika Gupta dedicated her play *Fragile Land* to the memory of her uncle, who had also been a radical activist in India's struggle for independence and who was executed by the British authorities for his political activities.

The opening scene of the play offers a very good example of the way in which David Edgar presents a microcosm of the English class system and its transposition into the very different geo-political climate of the Indian subcontinent with its own religious and cultural traditions. This includes, of course, its own socially hierarchical and discriminatory caste system where there are four castes or levels of social and religious status. These levels were historically defined by the darkness of skin colouring with the lowest caste, known as the 'Untouchables', delineated as those with the darkest colour. Colonel Chandler represents the English, public-school-educated upper class with all its associations of privilege and, at best, benign Tory paternalism. It is through an example of such tolerant 'accommodation' of the indigenous Indian population that Chandler subtly but tellingly creates the social, cultural and fundamentally political dilemma central to the scene.

The British are preparing to leave India and Turner is delegated to supervise and co-ordinate the packing and transportation of various goods, items and cultural treasures that they will take with them. Chandler senses with the impeccable social credentials and sensibility of his class that this is an important moment, a sort of historical and diplomatic rite of passage. He orders Khera to fetch a bottle of whisky and some glasses to commemorate the event. Chandler's decision is an evidence of 'so far, so good' in terms of the power relations and social hierarchies of the British Raj. Chandler has subsequently, however, to the barely constrained bewilderment of Turner and the angry incredulity on the part of Major Rolfe, offered a drink to the young Indian servant. Rolfe is Chandler's immediate, middle-class social intermediary and inferior, and so desperately seeks to contain his criticism of Chandler's decision. Khera meanwhile has readily agreed to this act of paternalistic benevolence. However, social customs equating to the power relations that they often are, Khera is then instructed to give his glass of whisky to Rolfe who has punctuated his own harassed arrival with 'Some bloody wog's whipped the battery from the Land Rover'. That Rolfe, a major in the British army, can employ such an offensive and demeaning term in both Khera's and the colonel's presence communicates Khera's 'invisibility' within a British society and military informed by the hierarchies of class and racial prejudice with stunning dramatic concision.

It is only when Khera is left alone at the end of the scene that he purposefully pours himself his own whisky, revealing his educated intelligence and political awareness beneath the condescending stereotype of Chandler's 'half-devil . . . half-child', an image appropriated from the poet Rudyard Kipling. Khera is neither devil nor child in any proportion, as is abundantly clear as he drinks his whisky with a toast in Latin: 'Civis Britannicus sum'. It is of course hugely significant that Khera makes this toast to and in the context of a large oil painting of the Indian Mutiny of the previous century.

Scene Two then follows on immediately with a thirty-years-older Chandler providing the cross-over *gestus* into this scene in which the values, traditions and power of the old Tory 'One Nation' vision of benign but privileged social hierarchy is facing up to the imminent spectre of Thatcherism and the New Right. For all of its transparently self-evident faults, inequities and prejudices, the tradition that Chandler embodies is one with an intrinsic assumption of not only a one-way-traffic class deference from the lower to the upper classes. By its own rules and customs, to continue with that analogy, it has also embodied a dual-carriageway mutual obligation from the privileged to the disadvantaged: albeit expressed through paternalistic, charitable dispensation. Such values and attitudes were to be forced off the carriageway of social and political custom by an aggressive economic Darwinism of brutally competitive self-interest. Effectively, Chandler and his kind were to be mugged and consigned to the past. If money made the world go round, it was not only the reactionary assumptions of social class and moral obligation that would be jettisoned but also liberal/Left values of policies driven, however imperfectly, on the conviction of 'each according to his need'. The self-interested individualism of the New Right was to reach its zenith within three years of the play's première with the election of Margaret Thatcher's Conservative government in 1979.

With Chandler's death, carrying with it the death knell for his class and generation, his parliamentary seat of Taddley becomes available. David Edgar uses this carefully constructed scenario to provide the dramatic site for the exercising of a political debate. In this dramatised debate of conflicting political, class and ethnic interests, Edgar expertly reveals and articulates all the nuances, deceptions, compromises and betrayals of the English class system. Furthermore, the pragmatic struggle for power between the mainstream Labour and Conservative parties is set against the strategies of the extreme Right. In the play those racist and neo-Nazi attitudes and actions are embodied by the fictional Nation Forward party. Their principal political intentions, like those of their real-life counterparts the National Front, lay ultimately outside the ballot box as much as within.

Turner, who reappears once more in Scene Five, is now a struggling antique-shop owner and a member of the politically parochial and powerless right-wing Taddley Patriotic League. Both he and the TPL will become affiliated to, if not taken over by, the more politically organised and brutally combative Nation Forward. Nation Forward is itself, however, infiltrated by the interventionist threat of an international neo-Fascist network embodied by the suavely intimidating but impeccably respectable Cleaver.

In Turner, Edgar creates in convincing and credible dramatic terms a kind of modern suburban, petit-bourgeois Everyman who is an economic victim of the compulsory purchase of the buildings in which his shop has its premises. There follows the inevitable collapse of his business and livelihood. He faces a subtext of violent threat and intimidation if he attempts to resist this real-estate *fait accompli*. Turner sees these events as the inevitable result of an old social order passing (that of Chandler) and an influx of immigrants 'taking' 'English' livelihoods away. This ill-informed misreading of events and the need for a scapegoat are at the malign core of the cancer of racism and anti-Semitism. It has been rehearsed and enacted throughout history, most terrifyingly in the Nazis' blaming of the Jews for the collapse of the post-First World War German economy and their horrifying 'Final Solution' to this 'problem' being the extermination of six million Jews. What is also tragically ironic is that the person sent to deliver Turner his ultimatum is non-white. In a subsequent rewrite, Edgar converted this Afro-Caribbean character into a Jewish one. Either way, from Turner's perspective he personifies the 'alien' threat to his livelihood and well-being. Nevertheless, the owners of the real-estate consortium that are his actual enemy are 'respectable businessmen' including a certain Major Rolfe who sits on the company's board of directors.

Other characters from the opening scene of the play appear and are developed throughout this fine play. Khera reappears as a leading trades union activist in a strike that should receive the Labour Party's and Labour candidate's support. However, with a self-interested pragmatism to which Edgar was to return in *Playing with Fire*, they withdraw their support in the mistaken view that it will prevent them from winning the seat made vacant after Chandler's death. With biting irony the prospective Labour candidate is enjoying a meal out at the 'local Indian' restaurant when he confirms his decision not to support the unionised actions of Khera and the others.

Rolfe also reappears, but as a grimly determined older retired army officer, who, we discover at the end of Act Two, is grieving for the death of his son whilst serving with the British army in

Northern Ireland. This is another example of a British colonial military presence as problematic and flawed as had been India. Rolfe does not regret the passing of Chandler and his kind, whom he sees as the embodiment of a politically inept, dated and morally exhausted political and social system. It is therefore to the 'right of the Right' that Rolfe has travelled. He had disclosed in a speech to Kershaw earlier in the play that his vision for a new party of rigour, discipline and ultra-traditional values lay within a network with clear neo-Fascist intentions. This network includes and is defined by a shadowy group of powerful businessmen and a British army brigadier. Their political vision is non-democratic, extra-parliamentary and realisable by military force if necessary:

> **Kershaw** You're seriously suggesting – army into Government?
> **Rolfe** *shrugs.*
> **Kershaw** In England?
> **Rolfe** All right. What happens? Wage control collapses, unemployed take over factories, council tenants massively refuse to pay their rents, in name or not, another General Strike, the pound falls through the floor, the English pound, the English river's burst its banks . . . So what d'you do? You either let the deluge, deluge, or you build a dam against it? Mm? (p. 334)

The image of rivers breaking their banks is potently resonant of Powell's 1968 speech. This precedent reinforces the chilling possibility of those such as Rolfe and his collaborators achieving political power and influence.

The overall structure of Edgar's iconic political play is one in which the epic interplay of scenes is driven and connected by the twists, turns and contradictions of political expediency. This is further complicated by the ruthless direct-action strategies of neo-Fascist movements such as Nation Forward. More disturbingly, given their cloak of social and economic respectability, lies Rolfe's network of powerful men lurking in the shadows 'off stage' of British public and political life. This dialectical interaction and displacement of individual characters and the bigger cycles of political struggle and mass political movements is returned to by David Edgar in *Maydays*.

The Life and Adventures of Nicholas Nickleby (1980)

The epic nature of Dickens's landscape of early-nineteenth-century English social, cultural and political life required a similarly epic dramaturgy. David Edgar proved himself once again a master of scale and proportion. Dickens's novel is one of his earlier works (1838–39) and, like his other novels, was published in serial parts. Its thematic texture and scope are melodramatic and painted with all the vivid colours and shades of that particular literary and dramatic genre. Accordingly the characterisation of the good, virtuous and the just in the novelist's hands is strongly communicated although never piously or self-righteously so. Actively alongside Nicholas-as-hero are two characters delineated in terms of their marginalised positions within early Victorian society. These are the eccentric but right-minded Newman Noggs, who had been brought low in his earlier life by unjust hardship and subsequent alcoholic dependence. The other compatriot is Smike, a victim of both Victorian moral hypocrisy and the terrible ordeals of barely surviving Dotheboys Hall, a place of torment disguised as a residential school. The principal villain of the piece is Nicholas's self-seeking uncle, the financial entrepreneur Ralph Nickleby. David Edgar's dramatisation marvellously captures this vivid world where Nicholas and his family have been made destitute by both their father's premature death but also by his failure in commerce and business. The style of the original RSC production, and indeed the subsequent, successful revival at the Chichester Festival Theatre (2006–07 season) directed by Jonathan Church and Philip Franks, relies upon direct address in the style of Mike Alfreds and his company Shared Experience.

They had begun to establish a reputation for fast-paced visual theatre, which they maintained into the 1990s, employing minimalist staging and storytelling narratives. Their approach worked through their choice of adapting non-dramatic literary forms such as *The Arabian Nights* and Zola's novel, *Nana*. Through this form of narrative, storytelling theatre, the actors are enabled both to drive the narration directly to the audience and to comment, with Brechtian undertones, upon their actions and predicaments.

This is reinforced through the skilful employment and visible manipulation of simple stylised pieces of staging, which enables any location to be summoned from the dark misery of Dotheboys Hall through to the burlesque limelight of Vincent Crummles and his travelling troupe of actors. This combination of Dickens's unique powers and genius as a master storyteller along with Edgar's lively and skilful dramatisation communicates the rich theatrical texture of the original novel. The enduring if sentimental and nostalgic appeal of a narrative in which the archetypal 'innocent abroad' ultimately triumphs over the cruelties and misfortunes of life has a timeless appeal.

Given the sharper political and social commentary of plays such as *Destiny*, *Maydays* and *Playing with Fire*, it might be argued that in *Nicholas Nickleby* David Edgar has been offered a different sort of dramatic canvas on which to paint. Of course, Dickens was not without his own radical and deeply felt analysis and exposé of social inequality and injustice. His own witnessing and experiencing of his father's imprisonment as a debtor in the notorious Newgate Prison in London left an indelible mark upon his life.

When watching the Chichester revival of the play in 2006, I was challenged to consider how the patriotism that surfaces at times throughout the play communicated in the context of a contemporary Britain in the final period of a Tony Blair premiership and foreign policy. Was the risk run of applauding the ingrained, reactionary evocations of 'Victorian values' and right-wing nationalist aspirations of Thatcher and the Falklands war in the early decade of the play's original production?

Whole Company
　　See each one do what he can
　　To further God's almighty plan:
　　The beneficence of heaven help the skilfulness of man . . .
　　. . . Where so many blessings crowd,
　　'Tis our duty to be proud:
　　Up and answer, English yeoman, sing it joyfully aloud!
　　Evermore upon our country
　　God will pour his rich increase:
　　And victorious in war shall be made glorious in peace.

I am not suggesting of course for one moment that David Edgar's play sought to promote a dated and ultimately post-imperial idea of a divinely ordained national prestige and international destiny. Nevertheless even with the self-reflexive irony of Edgar's dramatic intentions, it's worth observing how thin the boundary is between the critiquing of such reactionary popular cultural forms with their latent attraction in popular cultural reception. This is especially so for a twenty-first-century Britain facing a critical endgame scenario in Iraq and having recently (at time of writing, June 2007) commemorated the problematic Falklands war.

Maydays (1983)

Maydays is a hugely ambitious play in terms of its aims, themes and subsequent historical scale. As John Bull observed in his *New British Political Dramatists* (Macmillan, reprinted 1991),

> The play is a vast sweep through a post-war socialist history of Europe. A variant of epic in structure, one scene develops from another, as lights cross-fade, and trucks are moved in and out. The effect is to suggest a continuity of action that plays against the historical and geographical jumps made by the narrative. (p. 221)

There are potentially three character-narrative threads within the piece, Jeremy Crowther, Martin Glass and Pavel Lermontov. It is effectively Glass who acts as the thematic, structural spine through this landscape of early political idealism, radical political activism and ultimate betrayal and disillusionment.

Crowther opens the play as a young man delivering a rousing May Day political speech to Communist activists gathering in 1945 to celebrate the end of the Second World War in Europe. They also celebrate the huge and unexpected landslide Labour General Election victory:

> **Crowther** Comrades, we have been asked a thousand times what we mean by socialism. As throughout the continent the toiling masses rise to liberate themselves from tyranny, to fashion with their own hands their own New Jerusalem, we can at last say: *this* is what we meant. (p. 191)

Crowther first encounters Glass when the latter is a seventeen-year-old pupil at a minor public school in Scene Three. The teenager has been ordered to stand and remain in the pouring rain for the offence of wearing a CND (Campaign for Nuclear Disarmament) badge on his school army uniform. It is 1962, the beginning of the radical, counter-cultural 1960s but after the armed Soviet Russian entry into Hungary in 1956. This was an event that is to prove iconic and symbolic within the play, as much as that real event challenged and changed many on the British Left in the late 1950s. It is this brutally dramatic intervention into Hungary that provides the geo-ideological location for the journey of Lermontov, an officer with Russian Military Intelligence. These three characters and their journeys move ineluctably through the textual, thematic and ideological fabric of the play. They all meet eventually in Act Three, Scene Six. Lermontov is a victim of the Soviet regime's brutally punitive treatment of dissent. His transformation from an agent of the regime to one of its dissident critics began after he witnessed an act of individual political courage by a young Hungarian resistance fighter. Later on in Act Three, Scene Six, Lermontov refuses to be used as a public relations 'trophy' by the network of extreme right-wing business-men and journalists that includes Crowther and Glass. This network is redolent of that associated with Rolfe in *Destiny*.

One of the challenges in terms of multi-character developments and narratives in a play of such epic proportions is that individual characterisation might be subjugated to the demands of the bigger political picture. This can reduce the possibilities for character complexity and subtlety. An accompanying dilemma in *Maydays* is the dramatic tension between the subjectivity of the activist against the relentless demands made upon the individual by a mass political party. This is especially, though not exclusively, the case on the revolutionary Left in relation to Martin Glass. This dilemma is directly mirrored in that character's political and existential angst. The character's surname carries some interesting connotations. Glass as an entity has some dominant characteristics and qualities. It has a transparency that enables clear viewing. It may have magnifying elements, which facilitate more detailed and extensive viewing and sight. It may also, however, be fragile and therefore liable to break or mark. All these qualities help define the character of Martin Glass. Continuing the glass–Glass analogy, he is the central prism through which the audience and reader view the complex ideological world of the play. Glass is also a character whose resilience is ultimately marked, damaged and fractured through his opaqueness. This quality of personal openness and political plurality is crucially an Achilles heel within the territory of revolutionary political activism. It both defines the integrity of his beliefs but also marks him out to the James Grains of that world. Glass is viewed by Grain as needing controlling and ordering. Glass must be made to conform to uniformity of belief, strategy and action. What finally cracks and fundamentally breaks Glass is this stifling ideological and individual conformity. There are two incidents, one from Act Two, Scene Four and the other from Act Two, Scene Five, that embody and express his dilemma and predicament. It entails the crushing of his deeply held political convictions which results in him ultimately moving to the extreme right politically.

Firstly, James Grain, the dangerously self-certain, authoritarian leader of the far-Left Socialist Vanguard Party, thrusts a knife into the young activist as savagely wounding as any street fight encounter:

> **James** (*suddenly angry*) Martin, it's very simple. There are things you won't give up. You still have this antipathy to working in a group that's led, if just in part, by manual workers. There is something in you that fundamentally distrusts the concept of a leadership, particularly if it's on the surface less articulate than you.

One might ask whether it is Grain's ego and status that is challenged rather than that of the party itself. Through Glass, Edgar is challenging the extent to which someone like Grain manipulates and conflates notions of his leadership and authority with the 'true' revolutionary position of the working class.

Martin's angry, wounded response to his encounter with Grain, who has expelled him from the Socialist Vanguard Party, is expressed to Amanda in the following scene:

> **Martin** Do you know what struck me? Very forcibly? I've spent four years of patient toil, trying to make SV the Government. And I looked at him, as he put the knife in me, with all the tact and understated charm of Jack the Ripper, and thought: come on, do you really want this man to run the country? James Grain, the man who put the 'rot' in Trotskyism?
> **Amanda** And the 'rat' in apparatchik.
> **Martin** Yes.

As a title *Maydays* carries within it a number of key connotations. Firstly, May Day was the annual day in May given the status of a public holiday in Britain and across the world to commemorate the struggle of the working classes for equality and justice. The International Socialist Congress had first established this symbolic status of the day in 1888. Within the Soviet Union and its satellite states such as Hungary and Czechoslovakia, May Day was the day on which there would be a powerful propaganda exercise of the demonstration of the military might of the Soviet Union. This would entail a mass parade of troops, military weaponry and nuclear missiles across Red Square in Moscow. Even more potently in terms of the focus of Edgar's play, its title carries additional meaning outside the historic struggle of the workers and the dispossessed for equality and justice. The other meaning is that 'Mayday' is an international radio distress signal used especially by ships and aircraft. Originating from the French phrase *m'aidez* meaning 'help me', Mayday is therefore associated with a sense of peril and danger. There is also implicitly a need for help and support from that danger or threat. What is under threat in the world of Edgar's play? The individual's right to freedom of speech and thought or the possibility of revolutionary social and political change? With Glass as an emblem of a generation of radical Left political activism in the 1960s and 1970s, the question remains whether it is possible to have a human-centred movement for progressive change which does not necessitate the denial of individual freedom. Pavel Lermontov articulates and embodies this seeming contradiction. Is it inevitable that a movement like the fictionalised Socialist Vanguard Party, whilst promising revolutionary change, demands a denial of individualised conscience to fulfil its apparently egalitarian agenda? How quickly and how easily, *Maydays* asks, does this envisioned Utopia metamorphose into the dystopia of George Orwell's *Nineteen Eighty-Four*?

In Act Three, Scene Seven, the final scene of the play, Martin Glass confronts his former lover and comrade Amanda who is involved in a fictionalised equivalent of the Women's Peace Camp at RAF Greenham Common. This real political demonstration had been established in 1983, the year of the play's writing and première. With bleak irony the former Left revolutionary Glass now owns the land on which the women are demonstrating. They are protesting against the introduction of USA Cruise (nuclear) missiles on to Greenham Common, the British air base in Oxfordshire. Glass is bitterly cynical about the women's issue-based politics, which he views as naïve and self-interested. Amanda is equivalently bewildered and depressed by her former compatriot's political transformation. Politicised feminist activists such as Amanda in that period were leading a campaign called 'Reclaim the Night'. It demanded safety and respect for women against the threat from male violence in public and domestic spaces. In answer to his languid, cynical provocation 'From whom does who wish to reclaim the night?' she answers with undisguised anger, 'Oh, Martin, what the fuck's gone wrong with you?' David Edgar's play might be said to be asking a comparable question of a compromised generation of former political idealism, optimism and radical activism.

Pentecost (1994)

In *Pentecost* the decade or so that separates this play from *Maydays* also represents a decade of huge political change in Europe, which is the setting for this fine play. Whilst the Conservative Party continued in government (although Margaret Thatcher had been ousted in 1990 as Prime Minister) seismic political change was happening in what was geographically eastern and central Europe and geo-ideologically the former Soviet Union of Communist Russia. The Berlin Wall, which had literally and symbolically separated the Soviet Communist East from the capitalist neo-liberal democracies of the West, came down in 1989. The wider global struggle between the political and economic interests of the USA and the Soviet Union, and its accompanying acceleration of the nuclear arms race between those two major global powers, had reached a stage by the mid- to late 1980s. It was clear that the Soviet Union no longer had the economic means to maintain its struggle for political and economic supremacy with the USA. Under the Western free market economic instincts and policies of the then Russian President, Mikhail Gorbachev, the unthinkable suddenly started to become thinkable. Gorbachev also demonstrated his willingness to implement a previously unimaginable liberalisation of the Soviet Union's relationship with the West through arms control negotiations (with two major treaties in 1987 and 1991). These actions under his leadership looked towards a more liberal, neo-democratic and pluralistic interior policy. Gorbachev described this radical policy turnaround as perestroika, which had first been used by a former Soviet President, Leonid Brezhnev, in 1979. Brezhnev had employed the term to rationalise the need for increased automation and productivity within the Soviet economy. In Gorbachev's hands it became synonymous with a radical curtailing of centralist economic policies and participation in non-Soviet, Western European and global markets. Perestroika, in this fundamental sense of Gorbachev's economic and political intentions, was also closely aligned with his government's use of the term glasnost or 'openness'.

The tensions between Gorbachev's desires for economic liberal reforms with a paradoxical commitment to a centralised confederation of Russian states conspired to stimulate a mass movement across such countries as Czechoslovakia, Yugoslavia and Baltic states such as Latvia and Lithuania. These mass movements sought for national political and cultural independence from Moscow's centralised military, political and economic power. Following an attempted military coup in Russia in the summer of 1991, Gorbachev lost his battle with his major political opponent Boris Yeltsin and resigned in December 1991.

With the post-war political map of Europe irredeemably changed, the most traumatic and devastating consequence of the break-up was the emergence of a clamour of competing, often reactionary if not neo-Fascist political nationalisms. The Bosnian war in the former Yugoslavia was the most cataclysmic consequence and expression of this. The Balkans are geographically the central south-eastern territories of the European continent bordering on what was formerly known as Asia Minor (Turkey and the western frontiers of Islam). They had historically, politically and ethnically remained a volcano waiting to erupt.

Indeed, the annexation by Austria-Hungary of Bosnia and Herzegovina (to give the territory its full name) in 1908 had been a major contributory factor to the outbreak of the First World War in 1914. Under the post-war, centralised leadership of its Prime Minister and later President, Joseph Tito, a Communist who had fought alongside the Bolsheviks in the Russian Revolution, Yugoslavia enjoyed a unique status as a non-aligned Communist state with its own non-Soviet constitution.

David Edgar's play *Pentecost*, whilst set in a fictionalised and unnamed south-east European country, clearly has unmistakable and conscious parallels with the savage, bloody civil war that erupted in post-Yugoslavia, post-perestroika Bosnia and also violent ethnic conflicts in the former Communist state of Albania.

The play's title is interesting and revealing. Pentecost was an important event in the early emergence of Christianity. It describes the critical occasion when, as the New Testament account tells it, people of different nationalities and languages were miraculously able to understand each other. This event is profoundly symbolic ideologically in its prediction of the cross-cultural, transnational growth of the Christian religion. It is achieved through the direct intervention of the Holy Spirit descending visually in flames upon the people who 'spoke in tongues' (languages other than their own). In the narrative of Christian belief and theology, Pentecost is the dialectical counter-balance and response to the Old Testament story of the Tower of Babel from which we get the word 'babble' or meaningless talk. In this story the peoples of the world were punished with a multiplicity of languages driving them into separate, non-communicating nationalities and races.

Pentecost is significantly set in an old, abandoned Romanesque church. It is cleverly used by Edgar as both a material, geo-graphical site but also an ideological site redolent with the history and conflicts of the region. The remorselessly savage Babel of the late twentieth century was expressed through the onslaught of the neo-Fascist Bosnian Serbian Orthodox Christian forces led by

Slobodan Milošović against Bosnian Muslims. With grim and unbelievable barbarity, the Serbian forces decided upon a policy of 'ethnic cleansing'. This disturbing euphemism described a chilling clinical process whereby those ethnic Muslim regions and communities would be 'cleansed': ultimately exterminated. Concentration camps and rape camps followed. Mass graves are still being discovered where hundreds and thousands of innocent men, women and children were murdered solely because of their ethnicity and religious beliefs. Sarah Kane's play *Cleansed* took its title from these events. The problematic Pentecost of the play's title does not, of course, describe a miraculously mutual understanding suddenly happening between different peoples and their languages, cultures and histories. Edgar understands too well that any long-term sustained reconciliation between historically warring peoples will necessitate a political strategy and determination. Miracles were in very short supply in the former Yugoslavian cities of Dubrovnik and Mostar. There were no angelic interventions to help protect the innocent women and children systematically murdered.

In Edgar's play it's not miracles that are needed, even if such things existed. Human hands and political pragmatism provide the only provisional possibility for fragile mutual understanding. There is no direct supernatural entry to effect a Pentecost but instead the violent intervention of armed (Russian-speaking) state commandos. At the play's ultimate climactic point they storm the church after it has been occupied by armed ethnic terrorists or freedom fighters. They have earlier kidnapped the Western visitors and tourists as hostages to achieve their own political demands. As the commandos free the hostages, the hostage takers are killed, as is Oliver, an English cultural historian mistaken for a terrorist.

As in *Maydays* and the later *Playing with Fire*, David Edgar set himself the considerable task of creating an epic dramatic landscape and characters through which to explore and discuss major narratives of history, cultures, politics and religion. There is a richly complex mix of individual character development and relationships in *Pentecost*. These are set against the material and ideological layers of European history signified most imaginatively through the wall painting discovered in the interior of the church. The contrast between the substantiality of brick, mortar and plaster and the transience of the centuries-old painting mirrors the interaction between the relative certainties of history's major narratives and the fragility of human existence. What Edgar does especially effectively is subtly to explore the ways in which culture itself (i.e. the wall painting) provokes contesting historical inter-pretations of its ownership and significance. Such notions of ownership and cultural meaning, Edgar expertly suggests, are themselves layered over with ideological and theological vested interest. Culture and cultural products are not therefore the decorative afterthought of history but powerful expressions of it. As in the case of the wall painting, decoding its possible meanings and significance requires care and rigorous scrutiny. What you see is dependent upon where you stand, not only physically but politically and culturally. Edgar interweaves the strands of individual lives within the disorientating, bewildering and often dangerous currents of radical political change and upheaval.

At the heart of the play's thematic and dramaturgical devices is the church with the recent, post-glasnost discovery of its ancient fresco. As is often the case in the narrative structuring of Edgar's major work, this discovery becomes a motif of cultural, ideological and historical debate and slippage. The battle that ensues for the cultural and ideological 'ownership' of the religious fresco will result in the victors being able to assert the primacy and superiority of their own partial interpretation of nationhood, theology and history. This ideological struggle over the identity of the painter, the age of the fresco and its significance inevitably involves outsiders in the case of Oliver and Leo, two contesting Western art historians and critics, and also the propagandist interests of the former Soviet Russia.

What is also contested is the politico-cultural and financial moral and cultural capital of the West as expressed through Oliver, who is English, and Leo, who is American. Importantly in terms of the European history of anti-Semitism, Leo is also Jewish. The vested interests of the new post-Soviet state are represented by the government minister, Czaba, who has his own cynically pragmatic reasons for wanting to verify the circumstances surrounding the painting of the fresco. There may well be both lucrative financial and propaganda rewards to be accumulated for his new regime.

Czaba expresses his own version of pragmatic politics in the following short speech. The high-cultural concerns of Oliver for the safety and preservation of the fresco lead him to assert that it should be moved to a safer museum location outside the country in the West:

> **Czaba** You know, I have theory that big problem with high culture is it makes you think too much of past. You go to opera, see painting, all time they are reminding you of dreadful precedent, how everything goes wrong before. Which is why if you want real change, you put barbarians in charge. People who don't know about walls will all fall down. Who don't know history of Tower of Babel.
> **Oliver** *looks quizzical.* **Czaba** *drops his voice again.*
> **Czaba** I'd say, you have two weeks. (p. 24)

This play sometimes runs the risk, as with *Maydays* and *Playing with Fire*, of seeking to paint too panoramic a canvas of human experience and struggle. What we gain, however, is a dramatic map that dares to document major change in ice-clear detail.

Leo makes an impassioned speech informed and driven by the bitter remembrance of European history and the late twentieth century's continuing capacity for political violence, war and oppression of the dispossessed ethnic minorities. It is a bloody scenario of nationalistic expediency and expansionism, played to a soundtrack of artistic achievements and cultural artefacts. It is important that Leo delivers this speech having become a hostage on the arrival of the terrorist/freedom fighters earlier in Act One.

They have sought the time-honoured sanctuary of the sacred or religious building.

> **Leo** So, people, what you have here is not just the most valuable art-find of the century, but, to coin a phrase, the birth of universal European man.
>
> *He looks questioningly at* **Gabriella**.
>
> **Gabriella** I think I say of modern rational universal man.
>
> **Leo** Well, you do too. Which of course is the most delicious irony. That the folks out there, who want so badly to be universal Europeans, to be part of that, are much more interested in that than they are in you, or even us. So they'll bar their gates to you, and risk our lives, to keep the art . . . And it's not the first time. As Dubrovnik burns, Western intellectuals write polite letters to the papers protesting the destruction of the architecture. Mitterrand destroys a squatter camp to build a library. The camp guards at Auschwitz spend their evenings listening to Mozart on the gramophone.
>
> *Pause.*
>
> And of course, it can be argued that you shouldn't blame the art. But on the other hand . . . there is a view, that somewhere in all that remorseless questioning – there is – as you point out – a kind of arrogance. That somehow it's always Western man who's doing the inquisiting and everybody else who's quisited. So maybe, yuh, there *is* some line, if not from Beethoven to Buchenwald, then at least to the World Bank, the IMF and NATO. (pp. 75–6)

It is one of the enduring qualities of Edgar's writing that he is able to draw the lines, so to speak, between the complex dots or points of British and European history. In this, he reminds us that even the decisions and actions of individuals are a part of a much wider and detailed tapestry of interwoven threads of politics, culture, ideology and – yes – even our own conditioned subjectivities.

Playing with Fire (2005)

David Edgar's most recent play for a major stage, not excepting the Chichester Festival Theatre's consecutive revivals of *Nicholas Nickleby*, was this hard-hitting play produced at the National Theatre in 2005.

It shares all the epic qualities of scale and style that are central to the other plays discussed in this essay. It also represents what might be seen as the third play in a trilogy, the others comprising *Destiny* and *Maydays*. The three plays together take us through a comprehensive dramatised history from the end of Empire beginning in 1947, the first arrivals in Britain from former colonies in the Asian subcontinent and the Caribbean, and the reaction of the far Right to that first stage in the emergence of a multicultural Britain. With *Maydays* especially charting the fall of the radical Left with the complacency and inertia of the traditional centre Left, *Playing with Fire* demonstrates the dangerous consequences left by that vacuum in the strong re-emergence of the British National Party. This is especially so in northern post-industrial towns and cities, and also parts of the East End of London, most notably Barking.

Playing with Fire also examines with dispassionate scrutiny the conflicts, contradictions and pragmatic compromises across a political and multicultural landscape. New Labour's centre-Right obsession with targets and task forces collides with the vested interested and hard-earned politics-on-the-ground mentality of traditional Labour councils. Also thrown into this melting pot are the elements of progressive and reactionary British Asian community leaders and activists, a disillusioned ex-Labour councillor and the member-activists of Britannia, a fictional far-Right racist party: the younger white working-class brother of Nation Forward (*Destiny*). A young white man is killed in the context of increasing racial tensions in the fictional northern town of Wyverdale, even as the central government dispatches a young female civil servant, Alex Clifton, to front a kind of task force to persuade, or force, the ruling Wyverdale Labour Council to 'modernise'.

If that summary of the play sounds like a very big dramatic 'ask' to pull off, it is. In fact, the play has moments of real dramatic power and, as always, Edgar shows himself the supreme writer-as-barometer of the socio-cultural political landscape. Sometimes, however, the play struggles to support its ambitious aims.

Part of the problem lies with a dramatic strategy and structure that necessitate a disproportionate amount of either direct address to audience narrative or versions of such. It's as if the play is compromised by the need to communicate as much information as possible about its characters and their backgrounds. If dramatic characters tell us as audience too much directly, we are left with placards rather than people. Ironically, given the early governing culture of New Labour in 1997–2001, the characters run the risk of becoming soundbites.

Whilst David Edgar undoubtedly attempts to sketch in human detail and smudge, the characters sometimes feel like symptoms of old or new politics, white working-class or white bourgeois attitudes or British Asian (mostly but not exclusively Pakistani) ethnic community politics. It's also significant for a writer whose earlier *Maydays* predicts the final dissolution of the Soviet Union that he gives his New Labour enforcers euphemisms to describe two of the strategies open to them regarding change in Wyverdale. These are the 'Czechoslovak Option' and the 'Polish Strategy' approaches. The invasion of both countries by Nazi Germany in 1938 and 1939 precipitated the outbreak of the Second World War. Equally, the former Czechoslovakia was invaded by the governing Soviet Union in 1968 for seeking a more democratic Socialism. They ultimately achieved their long-sought independence through their non-violent 'Velvet Revolution' over twenty years later.

Playing with Fire looks to examine and offer non-simplistic explanations for the major race riots that disturbed Burnley, Oldham and Bradford in 2001. It is to his considerable credit that Edgar tries to confront all the competing elements with rigour and clarity, and without the explicit intrusion of his own political values. Edgar shows us a microcosm of our wider British multi-racial and multicultural society in which there are no heroes or heroines. Through the character of Alex he appears to acknowledge tacitly the need for reform in the governance of economically and socially deprived post-industrial communities. The notion amongst the entrenched traditional Labour councils such as Wyverdale that a red rosette in itself will guarantee electoral successes is exposed for its parochialism and complacency.

Nevertheless Edgar is no narrow advocate of the target-led, metropolitan bourgeois class of Whitehall. Their New Labour bureaucracy-speak of 'diversity criteria', 'risk assessment' and 'antisocial public space behaviours' is revealed as a new political evangelicalism. It is the twenty-first-century, non-religious Authorised Version of political language, which even the cynical, world-weary councillors of Wyverdale can use to create the *appearance* and *illusion* of change. One is reminded of Mark Ravenhill's similar concerns and scepticism with the mantras of political correctness as an inadequate means of talking about and resolving issues of sexual identity in *Citizenship*.

The final scene of *Playing with Fire* shows Edgar employing a potent non-textual, visual dramatic metaphor in Alex creating a circle of upended chairs as a way of trying to demonstrate in concrete terms the complex requirements of radical social, economic and cultural change. Beginning her, and the play's, long concluding speech, she starts by saying, 'I don't think we're to blame but I do think we're responsible . . . And I'm told, if you want to foster tolerance and understanding, the thing you've absolutely got to do is to provide a site that's new for everyone.' As she slowly begins to build a circle of chairs, she pauses before placing the last chair in place to complete the circle, itself an image of cohesion and inclusion, and observes:

And it's actually pretty simple. You go into a different room. And you turn yourself the other way up. And you stand inside the circle, and you put yourself in range . . . And thereby you give yourself the right to say there must be – there must always be – an alternative to going back home to your people. (p. 139)

As she places the last upended chair down it is as a statement of staying within Wyverdale and beyond the conditions of her original remit and agenda looking to play her part in building change.

In conclusion, David Edgar remains a major figure of British theatre in the period from the early 1970s through to the mid-1990s and today. His major plays provide an unyielding, acerbically honest and rigorous ideological and moral examination of the tumultuous events of the rapidly changing political landscape of Britain and Europe. His is a dramatic voice that is always instantly recognisable both for its eminent stylistic detail but also for its insistence upon asking an important question: is progressive social and political change possible? If so, can it accommodate individual conscience and judgement within a wider search for equality and justice? Our hope should be that, to quote the Marxist activist and theorist Gramsci, the optimism of the will, our will, should we choose, will continue to find ways to survive the pessimism of – our? – experience.

DOWNLOADS

- Try some of the other major political playwrights of the 1970s and 1980s such as Edward Bond, Trevor Griffiths, Howard Brenton, David Hare and Caryl Churchill.
- Try Sarah Kane (*Blasted* and *Cleansed*) for two very different kinds of play inspired by the Bosnian war (a major background to Edgar's *Pentecost*). Also compare and contrast *Pentecost* with David Greig's *Europe*.
- Compare and contrast David Edgar's exploration of race, racism and multiculturalism in plays such as *Destiny* and *Playing with Fire*, with Tanika Gupta's *Gladiator Games*, *Fragile Land* and *Sugar Mummies*.

3 DAVID GREIG

SHORT CUT
- Postmodern politics of Green and globalisation issues.
- Innovative generic explorations of a *heightened, poetic realism*.
- Post-Socialist politics of Scottish and European national and cultural identities.
- Co-founder of Suspect Culture Theatre Company (1990) with Graham Eatough.
- Dramaturge with the National Theatre of Scotland (2006).

PLAYS
(Bold titles are plays discussed in the critical essay)
A Savage Reminiscence (Suspect Culture) 1991
Stalinland (Suspect Culture) 1992
Europe 1994
The Architect 1996
Caledonia Dreaming 1997
The Cosmonaut's Last Message to the Woman He Once Loved in the Former Soviet Union 1999
Victoria 2000
Casanova 2001
The American Pilot 2006

Interview with David Greig

The following is an edited account of an interview that took place in Edinburgh in April 2006.

PB David, could you tell me some of the major early influences upon yourself as a writer for the theatre?

DG I had been studying drama at Bristol University and as I proceeded through that course I formulated the idea that I would direct theatre. When I graduated, I felt that at the time – which was the very early 1990s – everyone was doing their own versions of the classics with radical approaches. Stephen Daldry and Katy Mitchell were starting their careers. I didn't want to do that. I thought, if I'm going to direct, I want to do something different – I wanted to direct new work and I was essentially trying to establish a theatre company whilst being on the dole. I had a carefully calibrated budget for each production of up to £300, which was my overdraft limit. At the same time I felt that I could get it back in box office [receipts] from a pub theatre. Even cheap writers were not possible on this budget! I suppose that the last bit of it was that I had a feeling that if you wanted to say something, you should just do that rather than adapt a classic to say it for you. So I began writing, but really what I thought I was doing was devising – I don't think I was writing plays, really. I think I was 'making shows'. Probably the very first thing I did was a monologue called *Savage Reminiscence*, which I staged at a pub theatre in Bristol and which we then took to Edinburgh. It's a monologue spoken by Caliban after all the other characters have left the island in *The Tempest*. Then with Graham Eatough we formed a company called Suspect Culture together and then we got some acclaim for that and won a Guardian Student Drama Award. Over the course of the year at Bristol I did a piece called *The Garden* – I then did a piece called *And the Opera House Remained Unbuilt* – I didn't think of myself as writing the plays.

PB So you were more of a collaborator in that sense?

DG   No, no I wasn't working collaboratively . . .

PB   You worked autonomously?

DG   It was more that I didn't see the writing as 'the point'. It wasn't *that* which was really interesting me at that time, the work was facilitating my development as a director. Had I been offered the chance to direct a play for a professional company, I would have taken it. What did happen next was that I took four plays to the Edinburgh Fringe that I had worked on and produced through the year at the Hen and Chicken pub theatre in Bristol. By that time I was beginning to realise that I was writing plays as much as directing them. In fact, I won a Fringe First for one of those plays that year, *Stalinland*. After that I began to get professional interest in my writing – I remember a moment where I thought, am I going to be a writer or not? I remember that moment because for some reason that I never truly understood, I had the very strong feeling that if I was going to be a writer I would have to go back to Scotland – to be a writer it would mean my going back to Scotland. From that time I haven't really directed.

PB   How did the dramatic text itself evolve in those early works? Given that you weren't working from a commissioned, pre-existing script – were you working autonomously in finding and developing the script, or was it coming out of interplay with the actors in a more devising way?

DG   Well, that was the beginning of a certain method which I'd call the 'Suspect Culture' method. What I found was that I liked to work with the actors in the rehearsal room and then I would go away home and write at night – I didn't want their (the actors') words. I wanted them to help me to try to find the right situation. But even at that time the play I wrote called *Stalinland* – the piece that won the Fringe First – that was a kind of a commission in that someone else who was part of the team said that they'd like to direct and would I write a play for them? I can't remember why I would have agreed to do it – I can't remember money changing hands. I had this deal early on – this guy was a sort of entrepreneur who ran a venue in Edinburgh (Theatre Zoo). I got free all the theatre slots he couldn't sell to any other companies to put on my own shows and I also got the concession to run the bar.

PB   It was a 'commission in kind'?

DG   Yes, kind of. Anyway, he directed the play and he did a good job on it and it won the Fringe First and so the notion of writing a play for its own sake emerged at that point.

PB   Writers often talk about hearing and finding their own voice. Was there any stage in that early period where you felt, 'Ah, yes, I'm aware of my own voice emerging'?

DG   I would say that it was the play *Savage Reminiscence* – it was a style that seemed to unleash something – that's to do with influences – I think I was still a long way from finding my own voice – I had simply found a voice that worked for me.

PB   What was that style or influence – if it's possible to elucidate for me?

DG   It's very possible – it's very clear to me – this was the work of Howard Barker – the early work that I did is very influenced by him – both philosophically but, more literally – just the way that he writes. It's very interesting the new writing boom of the mid-1990s was actually very Mamet-influenced. Just before then, there was this 'mini-moment' where there was a sequence of writers who were very influenced by Barker – Sarah Kane was very influenced by him – I think you also find it in Mark Ravenhill. Barker has certainly been a very big influence for me – the rotundity of language, a sense of the rhetorical – an understanding that what is to be spoken on stage is to be spoken out loud. Then of course there was also Brecht but in a lot of my early work – and this builds up to *Europe* as well – I had this idea that I wanted my work to sound as if it were 'in translation'. I wanted that the feel of the language had originally been in some other language – that was partly because that's how I read Brecht, in translation.

PB   Of course, thinking of Howard Barker and of his own journey from the earlier work of the 1970s to the work of the 1990s to the present day was a distinctive one in its own terms?

DG   Absolutely, yes.

PB   Were there are any specific plays by Barker that influenced you?

DG   Yes, particular plays that influenced me were *The Bite of the Night*, *Victory* and *Seven Lears* and *Europeans*, but I think that *Victory*, *The Castle*, these were the plays that I really lapped up. The rhetoric of the Barker manifesto was a kind of manifesto to cleave to because at the time, in the mainstream theatre, it was still very much locked into Thatcherite values. For me what Barker did was that he neither succumbed to the liberal Left orthodoxy that I was being educated in – solidarity and support for the miners, for example. He also recognised the exhaustion of that position in theatrical terms with a line that did become inspirational: 'I knew that, I knew that, I already knew that! Don't mouth these things at me – we should be discovering these things ourselves.' He smashed in my head any idea that what I needed to do was to write 'smooth plays'.

PB   What was your understanding as a young man at that time of Barker's position, both philosophically and ideologically?

DG   I can't quite explain it – he was terrifically important for me, that's all I can say – I know I wasn't alone amongst my compatriots in feeling that (*slight pause*) it was meat and blood and bone and viscerality combined with intellect, combined with saying the unsayable and saying unsayable things and doing so with a flourish. Now, it's complicated because I'm also affected by my perspective now on those things – but at the time – he was just *correct* – he was right, it felt self-evident. My perspective of him was that a theatre establishment which was corrupt – corrupt is a hard word – a failed theatre establishment – was ignoring this obvious development. You just had this feeling: oh come on, why aren't you interested in that?

Bristol University Drama Department when I was there was at the absolute zenith of 'High Identity Politics' – all of it was very prescriptive linguistically. It was *very* prescriptive. It's built into my bones now that certain words and phrases were 'offensive'. What's also interesting is that the next generation coming through at

Bristol – have all become – for example, Matt Lucas and David Walliams, Simon Pegg – they're all into television rather than the stage and big, big television shows. I think they kicked rightly against us (and those 'High Identity Politics') and I think you see that in *Little Britain*. Looking back, I liken us to young Maoists – we had rules for what was correct – we were the vanguard – we thought we knew the answers. It's interesting – Barker deflects this and he encouraged that one should write the unthinkable – write the unsayable, the unthinkable and challenge one's audience.

PB Let's go on to talk through some of the plays. What came across to me really strongly about *Europe* was that powerful sense of a fragmented world, a world of material alienation. This was a world characterised by an alienation produced by these major economic, political changes within the economics and politics of Europe: the removal of the old Stalinist ideological and economic systems, the rapid and brutal introduction of free market economics. Your play communicates that change in a number of both implicit and understated ways – the impact of that meta-narrative upon individual lives – the Bosnian war raging – what drew you to that play?

DG My partner and I spent some of the money that we'd made upon the Fringe shows on travelling around Eastern Europe. That must have been 1991 or 1992. We took a couple of months' train journey around the Czech Republic and Hungary, and at the time I was reading work like *The Good Soldier Schweik* and Brecht, but also contemporary Czech writers like Kundera. This world of central Europe was drawing me, I loved being in it, and it threw up questions wherever I went. On my return I wrote *And the Opera House Remained Unbuilt*, then *Stalinland*, then a Lehrstück called *Petra's Explanation*.

Returning to your question, this idea of a central European town was becoming my equivalent of Tennessee Williams's Deep South – this is where I'll set everything – so when it comes to the play *Europe* I'm already inhabiting that world, I know what it looks like. Why was I drawn to this material? There were two things concerned with the genesis of the play – one was travelling through Fife and the old Scottish mining villages there and realising that the trains didn't stop there any more – they just went whizzing by. I suddenly thought: the really violent places aren't the inner cities but these deserted towns. I then tried to imagine myself living in them: I thought it would be intolerable. Why did these places exist, why did people still stay there, why didn't people just fuck off? I don't mean that aggressively to the people of those towns. So that was the central question that came to my mind: why were these towns deserted and who was still living there and why? I used to say – rather flippantly – my plays always start with a question and my question was, 'When a place is dead, why do people remain?' – and that's where the character of Berlin comes in. I guess that the other thing is the image of two people sitting alone on a train platform but the trains have stopped running and so it seemed like a good dramatic journey to take.

PB Of course, a train station is both a place of location and in that sense – a kind of relative permanence, but it's also simultaneously a place of transit and transience – it's a very evocative setting for the play and its themes.

DG Not only was Eastern Europe changing but also all of central Scotland was changing with all the traditional heavy industries that were dying. For example, there was the final closure of Ravenscraig and the coal mines. I used to say that – when it's on in Europe, they should call the play 'Scotland'.

PB It's strange, when I first read the play I heard Scottish accents and I thought: this could be Dumbarton, this could be Falkirk – it felt to me that when an entire continent is in a state of rapid and violent change and conflict, there are no fixed points of reference – everything shifts.

DG Another thing you've reminded me of is why *didn't* I set the play in Dumbarton. If you hear the way I speak, because I was brought up in Nigeria and then I went to a 'posh' school, I don't have a Scottish accent, I have no Scottish voice. I therefore felt very unconfident writing other people's voices. At the same time I felt perfectly confident writing in my own voice: the only problem was that nobody I wanted to write about spoke in my voice! Working men in Scotland don't speak like this – I felt unhappy trying to articulate their experience – almost like a ventriloquist – by trying to make them speak in my voice. By doing it in translation they could speak and yet be exactly who they were and I was not in any way diluting them – that underlay the whole central European thing and why I kept with it as a writer was because it allowed me to release my voice without having to apologise for it.

PB . . . and for there to be an authenticity of voices within the play(s)?

DG Absolutely – of course, one returns to Barker again – Barker allows everyone to speak.

PB What's very interesting for me is that powerful element of rhetorical language in your plays, is that the characters – or at least a good number of them – seem to have what I think one might call a 'privileged insight': both experientially and ideologically. This dimension to your characters could not be communicated or realised through either social realism or dramatic naturalism. Sometimes these characters have a prescience – which can be slightly unnerving. The kind of formal poetic precision with which they speak has that sense of 'This is a Russian speaking English', 'This is a Lithuanian speaking English', or 'This is an Englishman speaking Latvian'.

DG Well, yes, I think that's right. There's a sort of European sensibility that is reinstated by following Barker and Brecht . . . At that time I just felt that the English theatre playwriting tradition was so impoverished and televisual and dull, and I didn't want to be in that tradition. This was a way of separating from that tradition which I associated with social realism and naturalism. That for me was a key separation and language was my focus.

PB Berlin says to Adele in Act Two of *Europe*, 'I don't have a job any more. It's how things are. Terrible,' to which Adele replies,

'Nothing is how it is.' That seems to be close to the core of the play; if one could talk about a play having a soul, then 'Nothing is how it is' might be *Europe*'s rough-hewn signature.

DG Yes, I can see that. It's complicated because for me, each character in a play is a sort of embodiment of an internal dialogue that I'm having, or a feeling. It used to come as a feeling. If you are trying to write argumentatively, this can hamstring you because I don't actually, wholly, believe *anything* I think. When I allow *that* to be character, I can give that full range, which is a good thing, I think. There is a strong sense in all of the plays – because it's a strong sense in me – which is 'Everything is possible – it's you that choose what is – you choose it, you do it' and I'm drawn to characters that feel that way: that sense of fluidity and possibility.

PB If everything is possible then, of course, hospitals are possible, schools are possible but so is Auschwitz. I suppose that's where those major historical narratives of oppositional ideologies, of politically seeking to engage with the 'possibilities' of human history come into full significance?

DG Yes, if people understand that the world is changeable, then they will try to change it. I've been having a very interesting debate with myself, which I can't quite get to the bottom of, which has been inspired by what we might call Green questions. I suppose you could put it down to the question: 'Is there such a thing as progress or is there not?' and a very big part of me believes that we *do* move forward, we may move forward by recognising that something from the past was good. We incorporate that into the present and we move forward and we solve things: that is a very traditional left-wing perspective. Also, however, life experience has taught me – I think it was somehow always a part of me – 'I don't quite buy that.' Somehow, the ideals that I was glibly expounding during the late 1980s and early 1990s – I didn't *feel* them – I *wanted* to feel them but I knew that they were rather hollow-ringing. Somehow, this idea that if you change the *language* that people use to talk about various things, then things themselves are changed, then everything would be all right. For example, a lot of the stuff about sexuality: 'Look, we choose our sexuality.' Of course, sexuality is on a spectrum and people must be allowed to express themselves in that context, but the raw lived experience of people was not that and if it's you and you're twenty-one and you want to have sex with someone but you say something totally different because 'that's what you have to say' – there is bullshit in that. 'We'll fuck up as much as we progress': it's not even a pessimism; it's more that 'life goes on'.

PB I think it was Gramsci who said that he lived by the 'pessimism of experience but the optimism of the will'?

DG Yes, great, I love that. (*Pause.*) One of the most active political projects I'm involved in at present is 'not shopping at supermarkets', being part of a project in the town where I live to establish a food co-operative. To 'not fly': this seems to me to be one of the defining issues of the age to some extent. Under a bundle of things we might call Green or environmental – they're urgent issues of the time – the guiding thoughts behind much of that eco movement is that things were better at some point in the past and that humans are the problem. Yes of course, it may be that there are millions and millions of children in China currently coming into their full flowering who will solve these problems for us and then another problem will be created. That's the cycle. It's interesting to trace back – and it's not something I often do – but I think that 'dialogue' motors a lot of the plays.

PB Yes. Also, in *Europe* Katia says, 'Whatever you can imagine for yourself, Adele, this continent can come up with much worse. You'll soon learn that the best way is to stay where you are, keep quiet and lie low. Believe me; you're better off where you are.' There is that strong sense in the play of the individual, of the intimate, of the interaction of individuals together – and of course, Katia and Adele flee as two women together in an intimate relationship. There is the haunting presence of violence and intimidation. There is also, of course, the burning down of the railway station and the racial attack upon Morocco by Berlin and the others. I sense that there is an impulse within your writing to want to engage with the material conditions of history and people's lives and that, as human beings, we might build hospitals rather than build Auschwitz again. Of course, at the time of your writing *Europe* the concentration camps *were* there in the former Yugoslavia. There seems to be a tension between the personal and the political, which enables the characters to speak as they are, often in a muscular, heightened poetic way.

DG   I'm not sure how this responds to your observation but I can't write characters unless I like them – liking them is a complex issue – I have to love them, feel a great empathy for them. What interests me about a character is: why would I do that? Something that motivates me constantly in life and in my writing is that I just don't believe that people do things in order to be bad or immoral. Auschwitz had a whole number of people involved in its creation but everyone at some stage thinks they're doing the right thing by doing that. That's a horrifying and very wobbly thought. The question then becomes: 'How would I – given those circumstances – have been different? What would have saved me from being the perpetrator of such a thing?' So when Bosnia was going on, it was very shaking for me because first of all I was reading a lot about it and I passionately believed that this war was not about long-buried ethnic tensions whereby people just couldn't wait to fight each other. I thought that this was a society – a *European* society. These acts were *not* inevitable – people were fomenting these actions. Also one knew that the men who were going next door and raping the women and killing the men, these were profoundly ordinary people. What if that was you or me? How can we feel so sure that it's just not there, in the former Yugoslavia, but that our own society is not also capable of that?

PB   Yes, yes, of course. Perhaps we could go on to talk about your play *The Architect*?

DG   Yes, well, with a play like *The Architect* you have someone like Leo who is an idealist in his own terms. It's odd, I think I began the play wanting to take apart his ideas and of course I eventually became very sympathetic to him because – again – he *thinks* he's doing the right thing.

PB It's interesting you saying that, David, because a strong imprint that the play made upon me was that here is a play that begins and attempts to deconstruct, in a forensic way – with a very precise scalpel – this man in order to expose a set of values and a certain viewing position upon the world – but well before the conclusion my strong empathy was with him . . .

DG Yes . . .

PB . . . but it wasn't because you made him so but because you *allowed* him to be who he *was*. He therefore embodies some of the contradictions that are an inescapable part of the liberal-humanist-Left project: its relative successes but also its fairly significant failures.

DG It relates back to some of the stuff that I said about Bristol. I began that play . . . If you'd asked me what I thought I was doing, I'd have said that I was showing up the nuclear family and patriarchy and Socialism for the hollow shell that it was. If you see the play now it reads as a lament for Old Labour and for patriarchy because of course he – Leo – is patriarchal . . .

PB He's paternalistic?

DG Yes, that's right, he's paternalistic and I remember watching it and feeling embarrassed because I still had enough of the sense that I shouldn't be saying these things. I hoped that 'no one would find me out'! What I'm pleased about is that I *did* trust my instinct and commitment towards the characters that I write which means: 'What brought him to this position and what would have brought me to that position?' If you let your unconscious speak then you will to some extent speak the unconscious of the society you're writing within and you may discover that you're a bit more right-wing than you think you are but also, conceivably, a bit more left-wing than you think you are. Now, I believe my *only* job, as a writer, is to try to communicate with that inner truth: to put it out there on the table where we can all look at it.

PB Ibsen seems to be hovering above the play?

DG   Yes, and it's interesting because I haven't read *The Master Builder* to this day . . .

PB (*laughs*)   Amazing! It would have been the most obvious of his plays to read.

DG   It's even funnier than that – there'd been a production of *The Master Builder* at the Lyceum [in Edinburgh] at about the time that I was writing the play – *The Architect* started off with the title of 'Pandemonium' and it was subtitled 'Seventeen Scenes in the Life of One City': very much a title of the period! The architect was merely one character in it but he grew and the play became him and his family – it didn't begin with Ibsen and a conscious nod to him.

I really *did* get told the story that is in the introduction [to the play] about the person who designed Airdrie shopping centre and then jumped off the top: that's what inspired me to write the play's ending. I then discovered during the rehearsal of the play that every town in Scotland has the story of an architect who designed and built some ugly estate or shopping centre and then jumped off the top. Then, shortly after the play closed, I was reviewing a biography of Ibsen. In that biography there is a letter in which Ibsen writes to his friend in Germany about a man he has heard about who designed a church and then jumped from the top of this church spire. Ibsen is inspired to write *The Master Builder*. When he has finished he receives his friend's reply: 'Henrik, every town in Germany has this story of the man who designs a spire and jumps off the top!' It was an 'urban myth' of the time. I wrote what I thought was *The Master Builder* without actually having read it!

PB   Within *The Architect* there seems to be a prevailing sense of loss. For all of those contradictions that he embodies, there is a strong sense of your affinity with him.

DG   Yes, it does. When you speak about certainty, that's interesting. I seem to have more of a problem with certainty than with anything else. I think uncertainty seems to be the condition I'm most comfortable with and I immediately think that the moment you think 'I really believe this', you have to change because that is the dangerous point. The moment that you really think something is true is the moment when it becomes false. Some of the lament that you refer to in *The Architect* is a lament for certainty; if you like, a lament for a certainty: for a plan that could work, that should have worked. How could you have the hubris or the arrogance to build that giant tower unless you really believed in it?

PB Coincidentally your use of the word 'hubris' takes us back to Classical drama. In just the way that Ibsen drew upon the dramatic structure of Classical tragedy and wrote these ground-breaking prose tragedies, you have – even without knowing that specific play by Ibsen – also returned to that kind of dramatic form.

DG What prompts some of this thinking is that to produce art, you can't feel as if you know what you're doing; you can't feel as if you've arrived. You always have to feel that you're 'becoming' – that there is some place further down the line where you may realise your abilities. When you said that you needed to question in order to be human, I think that's right for me. For me there is only the question because that is the motor, the engine that produces our aliveness, our thought and our action. We have to imagine the possibility of an answer – although the likelihood of an answer is also potentially dangerous. If there is the question and the answer, and if the answer represents Utopia: that to which we are heading, that to which we can imagine and plan, that which will make the world better, we know from history that these things are terrifying because too few people are involved in their creations.

I've become very interested recently in forests and their ecology because this was the environment in which human beings evolved and they remained the most literally fruitful environments in which we could find ourselves. Forests are ecosystems, which are accretions of growth, and this occurred to me to be something that really attracts me in both human art and culture. That is, that there could be a city or it could be a religion where these things are accretions or conglomerations of things around a simple idea. For example, no individual created New York – it is a conglomeration of millions of ideas and millions of energies and yet New York is in itself an incredible entity above and beyond its individual citizens. Buddhism – there are many possible Buddhas – every day there's probably a Buddha wandering around whom you could make a religion from – but only one entity has thousands of years of ideas accreting around his central philosophies. That accretion is all we can trust.

PB . . . and with *Victoria* – this seems like very good timing to move on to that play – might it not be reasonable to suggest that across those three plays that constitute 'Victoria' is an accretion of human lives and experiences? Again, sometimes within the context of the individual and the intimate, the interpersonal, sometimes within the context of the bigger historical meta-narratives: the Spanish Civil War, the American oil industry . . .

DG Yes, absolutely. It also connects the other way in that *Victoria* is about Utopias and there is a driving ideology behind each play that is shown to be problematic. So you have the driving ideologies of Fascism and Communism in the first play, in the second play, theatre there is that incipient kind of Thatcherism – what Utopia oil and wealth might bring. In the last play you're living both with the death of the previous two ideologies whilst at the same time a new one in the form of Green or environmental thinking is beginning to present itself. I suspect that this latter is the closest to where I am today and yet it's interesting that the character who has the best speeches about that in the play is Euan. He says we should take apart this mountain, it's nothing but a scraping of land on top of a rock. As usual, through Euan in this case, I'm more interested in trying to articulate those things I don't understand rather than those that I feel I do understand.

PB What do you think Euan's human imperative is? What is his driving ideological or other motivation? Euan's 'Utopian' vision is in fact very pragmatic, but I don't think it's entirely pragmatic and he's not entirely without 'vision'.

DG That's a really interesting question, actually, because I do like the character of Euan. What does he think he's doing that's good, you might say? I suppose he would say that he's very clear-sighted. He would put it the other way round – he would say look, the people that fuck everything up are these Greens who say you'll fix everything if you do this. Or these Socialists who say you'll fix everything if you do this. Euan says, 'I have a clear practical understanding of the reality of life: we have many mountains, I could sell *this* one!' Euan considers it's only his hard-headed practical personal energy and vision that keeps these other lazy bastards going – which is, of course, a very Thatcherite thing!

PB (*laughs*)   I was going to say, David, what then prevents him from becoming/being an unreconstructed Thatcherite or indeed a venture capitalist?

DG   I think he is. It's complicated – more and more you find that you meet capitalists or unreconstructed Thatcherites and individually they're quite interesting people – perhaps even more interesting than unreconstructed Lefties, although the Left have become so marginalised from the mainstream that they become interesting as contrast. Meeting an unreconstructed Thatcherite as against meeting someone who wholeheartedly believes in New Labour, I know whom I would find more interesting – and it would be Euan. (*Pause.*) I remember when I got this commission from the RSC – I thought, wow, you've hit the big time now – you've got a call from the RSC! I thought that there were basically two approaches that one could take to this. One could either write a monologue or you had to write a three-part play with twenty-odd actors in each part. God, in some ways I wish I'd chosen the monologue because it would have got put on much quicker and I would probably have done a lot better with it, but I went the other way. If you do a big ambitious play like that, there are going to be mistakes, you're going to fuck up, some of the things won't quite work. I think that's also true of it: that the sheer scale of it means it's quite unwieldy in parts – but it does have a cumulative effect – it's not one that audiences are hostile to – they were very much into it – it's got a story.

PB   I'm using the term in quotation marks but it's also fairly self-evident that this is the most 'Scottish' of your plays? In terms of the commissioning process from the RSC, was there ever an implicit or explicit expectation that you provide a play about cultural and national identity?

DG   No, quite the contrary, interestingly. In fact, one of the things that Adrian [Noble, the Artistic Director of the RSC at that time] said in a meeting was that this play couldn't be part of the repertoire because he wasn't going to have fifteen Scottish actors as part of the company. I think they *didn't* want me to do a play like that – I don't think they'd have minded if I'd done it with four actors – but they didn't want a big statement about Scottish identity, no. It *is* the most explicitly Scottish of my plays except the missing play – because it hasn't been published – is a play called *Caledonia Dreaming*. This was, interestingly, written around the same time as *Victoria* and is just definitely about Scotland and Edinburgh, and Scotland at that moment, particularly that time just before Devolution. But you're right, yes, *Victoria* does have that sense of concern with Scottish cultural and national identity. It's about the Western Highlands, isn't it? It's also a certain 'flowering of voice'. Do you remember when I said before about the confidence to let certain characters speak in my voice? In *Victoria* I have working-class Scottish characters on stage and I allow them to *be* working-class Scottish characters without – *translating them*.

PB   I think that the play also asks questions about those soft-edged, liberal, folk cultural notions of 'Scottishness' and Scotland. The play invites us to question those stereotypes?

DG   Oh yes, yes . . .

PB   . . . which brings us back to Euan, interestingly – what if Euan were the embodiment of the best that Scotland might be – or the best of what it might mean to be Scottish at that time? Is he an embodiment of an aspiration, of directness, of pragmatism, which might enable the people who constitute Scotland perhaps to start to live less in whatever idealised historical notion of their past and more in the present . . .?

DG . . . I think that's a very strong thought and insight – yes, I would concur with that. At the time, just before Devolution, one of the McIlvanney brothers wrote that what the Scots most like to do when they hear a party going on is to bang on the door to be allowed in and then, as soon as the door is opened, they suffer a crisis of confidence and say, 'Oh, I'm so sorry for bothering you' and then they go away. This is what had happened in the 1978 Devolution vote where we'd had the chance to 'go to the party' but we'd shied away. I think you're absolutely right, there's a real thing that existed in Scotland at the time that *Victoria* looks at – there's a sort of 'dreaminess' – a kind of idealism. It's the part of my national culture that I most dislike, the sense that we'll not try – it's not possible to change, things are as they are – 'they' do this to 'us'. It's 'them' – whoever 'they' happen to be and you come to realise that 'they' is a kind of crutch because it lets you off the hook for doing anything yourself. I still come across it in my village where we led a campaign to take a piece of land into community ownership. The times that you encounter this – people create the most extraordinary walls inside their own heads. Thinking 'things are not possible', the council won't let you do that – as if the council is some kind of giant monolithic creature – of enormous power. I know it's the ability of a middle-class education to think in this way, but none the less the culture is that we don't have to try to change the situation because it's *their* fault and they're doing it and we're victims of *them*. (*Laughs.*) In fact, you began this interview thinking that I was an old-school Leftie and I've turned out to be a concealed Thatcherite Conservative of the worst sort!

PB I take your point; it's a very good joke! I'm not quite sure where that places me, though! If we could go on into *The American Pilot*, one of your recent shows that I saw in its revival at the Soho Theatre? The final stage direction of the play is 'The bombing continues. The gunfire continues. The end.' I thought that might be a useful way of entering our talking about the play and its themes and concerns?

DG This play has some very tangible roots that I can identify clearly. One is, I know the moment that it came into being more perhaps than any other play that I've written. Some plays have to be fought for line by line by line, other plays simply arrive – they come to you. I was sitting in a restaurant whilst I was in the middle of writing *Pyrenees*, which I was very blocked with. I was halfway through it and I was reading a Heiner Müller piece called *The German* and it was a piece from the perspective of a Russian soldier at the Front in 1914 and it begins with the line: 'We saw him coming – the German' – with 'THE GERMAN' in capital letters – 'he was awesome, his power was extraordinary'. At this point the Iraq war was incipient by about four or five months – it wasn't here yet – but everyone knew that it was coming. In that moment I just saw the whole play – I saw the whole thing: a pilot lands – the villager sees him – he is 'THE AMERICAN' in capital letters – we saw him coming – the American – he was beautiful, the American. I thought this is really annoying, I'm supposed to be writing *Pyrenees*, I'm halfway through it, but I thought if I don't do it now, I'll lose it. So I did – I wrote it in two days – and I then sent it to my agent – I hope that it will happen again one day – I'm lucky it's happened once!

So in that sense *The American Pilot* is (a) an immediate response to the Iraq war and (b) has a direct literary route. It's also mysterious and complicated, and had an odd journey to production because it wasn't commissioned. It was very hard to find a place to put it on and the Royal Court specifically turned it down – which was problematic for me – and that left me homeless with the play. It didn't actually go on until the Iraq war was really quite well advanced. In retrospect, I'm very happy about that because had it gone on at the time it would have been seen as a direct response, whereas now it's a lot more nuanced. The other side is there was an incredible prescience to it, which often happens where if you imagine things you tend to imagine stuff that will then happen because we're all human. If I can imagine something then someone else can. The play was written a long time before the videoing of execution of hostages by terrorists. By the time that play was on it seemed as if I was responding to these issues, but I was in fact just imagining what it might be like. What might one set of people decide to do, given a certain set of circumstances? I think that the delay in the play's production allowed it to float free of some of its immediate concerns.

PB So, presumably, it was the RSC who were prepared to 'run with it'?

DG Yes, well, I'd been offered a commission from the RSC, which I was still to fulfil, and so I said, what about this for your commission? I'm naturally very pleased that they were prepared to go with it.

PB These questions about 'engagement' and 'certainty' within your writing perhaps become even more pertinent with a play like *The American Pilot*?

DG They remain the major questions that I'm engaged with. The project that I'm involved with at the moment – I'm doing a new Suspect Culture show, which will be called *Futurology* – and which will be premised on the idea of the near future and particularly the sense of apocalypse that is hanging once more over our everyday discourses – peak oil, global warming, eco catastrophe – that sort of thing. The next play that I'll write is very, very consciously about Iraq, although through the prism of – it's a sort of 'follow-up' to *Macbeth*. It's what happens after the end of *Macbeth*. There have been a large number of productions of *Macbeth* since the Iraq war started but I thought, you've got it wrong. It struck me that what was really crucial is not about the overthrow of the tyrant but what happens *after* the overthrow of a tyrant? Discovering that the tyrant turns out not to be quite the figure you thought he was. Of course, as well, the fact that the literal, historical Macbeth bears no relation to the monster that's portrayed in Shakespeare's play. My starting point is to write about an English commander arriving in hostile territory full of good intentions, hoping to govern but ending up mired in atrocities and catastrophe. One of the things I need to do in researching that play is to find out what I *don't* know about him so that I can start to write about who he is. I want to look at him – that man – someone in his early thirties. This new breed of a New Labour person, not to 'slag him off' but to really try and get inside his skin. Come on, this guy arrives in Basra and wants to sort the place out, build hospitals and schools: good old 'British fair play'.

PB The play that you're describing, which I'm intrigued by, becomes an interrogation of the nature of tyranny?

DG The concerns remain the same. A sense of the fact that the world we live in is changing and – I expressed it in a newspaper interview once – the trouble with me for audiences is that I keep changing all the time. Some people might have really liked *Outlying Islands* and thought, this is an interesting playwright, I really want to go and see his next one. The next one they'd have seen would have been *San Diego*, which is about as different from and opposite to *Outlying Islands* as you could possibly get. Very few audiences who liked both would then have come to see my next play – I think it was *Pyrenees*. There were numbers of those in Scotland who thought that this was a terrible let-down after *San Diego*, which they had fully been expecting me to return to. People don't like prolixity in an author, they don't like diversity. I used to think they would – if you like, an equivalent might be that you really love Franz Ferdinand and then the next album they bring out is Country music and then the next album they bring out is Heavy Metal – you'd start to get anti with them.

The problem therefore with my work is that you look at it and think – where the hell is it? – I can't 'take a line' through it – I don't know what to expect from this guy. For me, it all comes from the same place and, you know, it's a big wide road. I'm going forward (*laughs*); I'm just veering around a lot. I had a slightly 'grim moment' last year when I realised that I was no longer 'up and coming'. In a sense, of course, that might seem great because you think, you know, perhaps 'you've arrived'. But I thought, 'Oh God – what if that's it? – What if I don't get any better than this?' The only reason to write another play is to learn from what you write . . . There's a brilliant quote from Whistler who was asked 'Why do you paint London in the fog so often?' to which he replied, 'Because I haven't got it right yet.' For me, there's this sense that the *next* play will somehow really show what you can do. The only thing I *would* say that connects to British theatre more widely is that I sense at the moment the exhaustion of the new play genre that briefly flowered in the 1990s. There was a genre, a culture of new writing, a body of directors who directed new writing. It was also quite London-based. It's not produced much powerful stuff for quite a while. You can already feel that directors are moving back to the classics. They're also going back to site-specific work and so at the moment the play as a form – 'new play' – is certainly in a little abeyance and this is where I hope I have some purchase. I started before the 'New Writing' of the 1990s and I've never truly felt comfortable or part of that world.

I think for me, I hope that the British theatre is moving back to a little away from linguistic naturalism and Mamet-style 'stage pictures', and opening up once again the possibilities of that moment to which I'm most wedded. This was when New Writing was Gregory Motton, Paul Godfrey, Sarah Kane and Martin Crimp. It was these fragmented poetic writers who were putting visual poetry on to the stage. It's time for a renewal in that regard. The pendulum will swing back again to plays – fashion also takes place, of course – it just goes back and forth – so trying to discern where playwriting is at the moment is not easy. I'm not even sure where I am. I'm not sure where I am in writing at the moment. I'm very interested in narrative. If you get really good narrative, the play remains much more ambiguous, more open-ended, more returnable to than any idea or concept you can bring. I'm trying to follow simple narratives – the Blues is a big thing that's really interesting me just now – in the sense of distilling meaning – of coming down to saying things in the simplest way possible.

Inhabitants of the Tide Mark – Towards a New Political Poetics in the Plays of David Greig

David Greig is one of the most important new playwrights to have emerged in contemporary British theatre over the last ten years or so. There is an emerging distinctive hybrid poeticism within his style, fused with an acutely scrupulous dramaturgy. There is a political sensibility, which epitomises a generation and period in which the relative certainties of earlier dramatists such as David Edgar and Trevor Griffiths have become subject to scrutiny and even rejection. In the context of his initial arrival on the national playwriting landscape he was viewed and located principally in terms of a young Scottish writer. However, with the obvious exceptions of *Victoria* and *Caledonia Dreaming*, his plays are much more concerned with wider issues of politico-cultural identity and alienation within the liminal borders of postmodernity. His first major play to draw critical attention to him as a significant dramatic voice within contemporary British theatre was *Europe* (1994). There is a strong sense in which many of the characters in Greig's work are experiencing life from the border or margin, frequently metaphorically, in terms of an alienated, fragmented interiorised angst. This internalised dysfunctional condition is also conveyed geo-ideologically in terms of the rapidly dissolving transnational boundaries of the last nearly twenty years. Indeed, in his *The Cosmonaut's Last Message to the Woman He Once Loved in the Former Soviet Union* (1999) the geo-ideological frontiers of the play's themes take us to outer space itself. Simultaneously, feelings of profound internal trauma and dislocation define the Russian cosmonauts whose space mission is irredeemably doomed, even as the earthbound characters are disorientated by the absence of an emotional and psychological gravity as relationships collide and fall through inner space.

David Greig has also established a dual reputation as the co-founder with Graham Eatough and Nick Powell of the innovative theatre company Suspect Culture. Like Tim Etchells and Forced

Entertainment to some extent, Suspect Culture, who are a touring theatre based in Glasgow, develop performance projects from initial ideas and concepts through a developmental creative process leading to eventual performance. Their work has defined an important site within contemporary Scottish performance, incorporating as it does the notion of site-specific installations such as the *Cranes Project* (2003) in which a lighting installation on cranes in Dublin's city centre was choreographed to an original sound-scape broadcast on FM Radio. Other major projects by Suspect Culture have included *Airport* (1996), *Mainstream* (1999), *Casanova* (2001) and *Lament* (2002).

Along with other dramatists such as David Harrower and Chris Hannan, David Greig represents an important orientating presence in terms of viewing and evaluating the emergence of a new wave of Scottish playwrights over the last decade or so. This renaissance in contemporary Scottish playwriting undoubtedly reflects, and has also contributed to, a significant sea change in Scottish political life with the vote in favour of a devolved Scottish parliament in Edinburgh in 1997 and the formal establishment of that institution in 1999. In the early part of the new millennium that evolving sense of a renewed – if not exactly new – Scottish national identity has been reinforced through the founding of Scotland's first ever National Theatre. There has been a major continuing debate about the prioritising of state funding to the National Theatre of Scotland (NToS) at the expense of the wider distribution of funds across regional and touring theatre in Scotland. Two newspaper articles from March 2006 highlight these issues most cogently. In 'Glasgow's rangers' by Sarah Jones (*Independent*, 16 March 2006) the journalist questions the decision by the founding staff at the National Theatre of Scotland to reject the opportunity of a material base for the company's work, outside of administrative offices in Glasgow's Easterhouse. The first production of the NToS was *Home*, which was ten different theatre productions around the themes of that generic title in ten different locations. The first artistic director of the fledgling company is

Vicky Featherstone, formerly artistic director of one of Britain's leading touring companies for new writing, Paines Plough. The rest of the creative team comprises the Scottish playwright, Liz Lochhead, John Tiffany, formerly of the Traverse Theatre, Edinburgh and also of Paines Plough, and David Greig himself in a developmental and programming role in relation to new writing in the repertoire. New writing will certainly be a major feature of the NToS with a new play, *Black Watch*, commissioned from Gregory Burke to a new version of Schiller's *Mary Stuart* commissioned from David Harrower. The NToS is set to receive £4 million annual funding until 2007 with the arts political rhetoric at least that, building and baseless, the theatre will be truly 'national' as Jones concluded in the final paragraph of her article:

> Featherstone aims to work with all of Scotland's theatres, concentrating on boosting developmental art forms and the creative talents of Scotland's existing theatrical practitioners while bringing in international artists and exporting Scotland's own. No existing company could provide such an all-inclusive programme, and it will allow many companies to do work which would have been impossible without the NToS's clout. (p. 46)

Aside from the fact that these optimistically concluding sentiments sound as though they might have been dictated by the marketing wing of the Scottish Arts Council, a rather more sobering counterbalance may be found in another article, this time the banner headline article in the previous week's issue of *The Stage* (9 March 2006). With the provocative headline 'SAC "culls" top touring groups' the article's author, Nuala Calvi, proceeds to reveal how the Scottish Arts Council (SAC) has been accused of 'culling' the funding of four established touring groups, along with financial inroads into the financial supporting of the Edinburgh Festival Fringe. It is also significant, perhaps, that two of the four companies are ones with traditional Socialist political roots and reputations – 7:84 and Borderline Theatre Company – whilst the other two, Theatre Babel and Gaelic Theatre Company Tosgare, embody both genuinely innovative work on a small scale and incorporate non-Anglicised Scottish language in their work. The political theatre company 7:84 was set up in the 1970s by one of the major figures in British political theatre of the last forty years, the late John McGrath, to take radical touring theatre to remote parts of Scotland, usually playing in non-theatre venues. The company took its unusual name from the then current statistic, which was that seven per cent of the population in Britain were in control of eighty-four per cent of its wealth. In the article, General Manager of 7:84 Ruth Ogston states:

> We are in shock and so deeply sad that and angry that the company's work over 33 years has been wiped out under new criteria that ignores audiences. We will be appealing this decision . . . but fear that the company – and the Scottish touring circuit and vast audiences – are not being respected enough for that decision to be revoked.

The company was expected to fold, given that it was told by the SAC that its funding was to be stopped completely and that it would not be able to apply for further additional funding until April 2007. The increase of £4 million that fifty arts organisations were to share in 2007–08 matches the budget awarded to the NToS and it is hard not to see a 'cultural devolution' of resources paralleling the wider national political devolution of (selected) resources and decision making. Of course, there may have been other hidden criteria relating to the artistic scope and quality of the work done by companies such as 7:84. It is hard not to construe some connection between the 'new Scotland' devolved from New Labour anxious for cultural soundbites like 'diversity', 'community' and 'participation' and these funding decisions. 7:84 has been engaging in such activities for over three decades, albeit to a political agenda a solar system away from both the London and Edinburgh administrations. Whether or not the election of the first ever Scottish Nationalist (minority) administration in May 2007 will further influence such funding decisions is, of course, open to speculation.

David Greig has always actively distanced himself from the simplistic and reductive politics of national or nationalist identity. In *Victoria* (2000) he explores through the three separate, but linking, plays a geo-ideological and cultural excavation of layers of Scottish and wider European and global politics through the twentieth century. In doing so, Greig critiques any simplistic or sentimental excursions into a 'Scottishness' of romanticised, historical myth or victimhood. David Greig spent his childhood and much of his early teenage years growing up in Africa, where his father's work had taken the family, rather than Scotland. This enables him to sustain a more critically suspect eye upon issues of national and cultural identities.

Europe (1994)

David Greig originally considered himself a director rather than a writer and his earliest significant projects whilst at university were in that context. Nevertheless, it was with his play *Europe* that the seeds were sown of the evolving distinctively muscular, heightened-poetic-realism voice intrinsic to his work. *Europe* inhabits the same genealogy and geo-ideological territory as David Edgar's *Pentecost*. The seismic change in the redefining of Europe's geographical frontiers and also the Pandora's box of violently competing claims and ambitions of ethnic and nationalistic ideological agendas provides the context and setting for both of these dramatists' plays. Sarah Kane's *Blasted* (1995) and *Cleansed* (1998) are other major disturbing dramatic echoes of a civil war fought on atavistic doctrines of nationalism, ethnicity and religion in the former Yugoslavia. The existence in the mid-1990s of rape camps and nationalist neo-Fascist strategies of ethnic cleansing on mainland Europe fifty years on from the Nazi death camps and the extermination of six million Jews signalled a recurring nightmare of that past. *Europe* is located in the darker shadows following the new dawn of enlightened free market global capitalism in the newly re-emerging eastern and central European states. What in fact happened was that a political and cultural vacuum was created, which was noisily and aggressively filled by the previously suppressed and marginalised far-Right nationalist groups. Far from generating a democratic sense of tolerance and plurality, ancient prejudices resurfaced, with those defined as alien or other susceptible to violent intimidation and oppression.

Some of the characters' names are redolent of the wider geo-ideological landscape that they inhabit, for example Morocco and Berlin. Meanwhile the character named Horse signals the potentially bestial dehumanising effect on the poor and unemployed through the dismantling of the old Soviet bloc. The character Fret evokes the deepening unease that erodes the fabric of a former political, economic and cultural fabric. This rapid unravelling exposes the dangerous subtexts of prejudice, alienation and despair beneath both the derelict buildings and ideological apparatus of the past.

The setting for the play is a 'small decaying provincial town in Europe' but its meta-setting is that shifting, transitional geo-ideological signing of Europe reconfiguring in the last decade of the century. The play has an undeniably Brechtian resonance and texture to it, structured into two acts with the scenes within each act simply numbered with a generic *gestus* defining who the characters are and where they are. It is significant that the play opens with, '1 Morocco', and that this is bleakly signified through the overwhelming sound effect of an international express train hurtling through the night. The first human character we see is Morocco, a dark-skinned non-European, carrying a heavy suitcase. The visual and metaphorical signing of the world of the play is thus achieved with potent visual and aural economy. Transit and transience are signified through the deafening roar of the train. The train is a dramatic icon of the new, fast-changing world that spits out its human cargo in places of indeterminate identity and significance. It is a train that no longer stops at the anonymous town that is *Europe*.

This explosive opening scene is followed by all the actors in the cast assuming the anonymous roles of a Chorus, which seems to embody the nameless, citizen-less, stateless disenfranchised of this new Europe. This is a world rapidly colonised by Western European and American multinational companies. It is a world where labour costs are lowest and unemployment is greatest. There is a haunting poetic quality about the choral dialogue, migrating from one unknown human being to another, sometimes alighting upon two or three voices in unison. The theme of the border and connotations of the margin and marginalised is communicated powerfully in this scene. The numerals next to each line of dialogue indicate the characters speaking those lines, known only by a number:

1   History has washed across us
2   In armies driving first west
3   Then east
2   Then west again
4   Wave upon wave has crashed about us,
All   But we've remained
5   A rockpool on the shoreline,
6   Inhabitants of the tidemark,
7   The place where driftwood is deposited,
8   Beyond the cleansing reach of the waves

The central sub-location is that of the train station, which appears to have become redundant. The station is still looked after by Fret, who is wrestling with the crucial question as to whether the trains are stopping at his station any more. If not, what does that say about the world beyond the tracks and what are the implications for the scattered humanity left behind? Adele, a local young woman, is watching out for any incoming trains. Meanwhile two characters in transit, Sava, a man in his late fifties, and his daughter Katia try to snatch some sleep made elusive by hunger, exhaustion and the cold. Adele's husband is Berlin, a local man and a personification of dangerous dilemmas post-Berlin Wall unified Germany. Berlin is an active and vociferous member of a far-Right neo-Nazi faction. He is angry that there is no work for local people and that aliens and foreigners are descending upon the town. Thematic and narrative seeds are sown by Greig for what will be a climactic harvest of racially motivated, xenophobic violence. This mirrors the continuing violence that flourishes in former Yugoslavia, Albania and the post-industrial cities of the former East Germany. The growing conflict between Adele and Berlin embodies the tensions and contradictions between the optimism of the neo-liberal social democracies of a better tomorrow against the pessimism of the brutal street politics of those seeking a scapegoat for their plight in the 'foreigner'.

Adele needs to believe that the new Europe is one of new freedoms and the breaking down of barriers. Her husband angrily rebuffs her naïve idealism even as he becomes increasingly undermined and emasculated by her growing friendship with Katia. This friendship quickly grows into an intimate lesbian relationship where the hope of escape beyond geographical frontiers mirrors their need to cross beyond the borders and checkpoints of homophobic prejudice.

A warm and comradely friendship also grows between the two older men, Fret and Sava. They seek to navigate a pathway into a security of reminiscence of a past world, a past Europe. For all the past miseries, cruelties, privations and autocracy of the old Europe, it seemed nevertheless to embody some notion of permanent identity and continuity. Greig employs a carefully constructed pathos to pre-empt the imminent tragedy that has all the dark inevitability of Euripides. Sava seeks to assure his friend of a means of survival, even as Berlin and the other racist, nationalist thugs are about to destroy them and the rail station with home-made fire-bomb grenades:

> **Sava** It's just imagination, Fret. If there's one thing I learned in the yards about staying awake on a long night it's keep the old imagination under control. Don't let the old mind invent things to

frighten itself. Don't conjure up demons. Don't talk to ghosts.
(p. 81)

In the following, final scene of the play titled 'Europe', Katia and
Adele are speeding towards at least the possibility of escape and
change. Their relationship deepening emotionally into sexual
consummation, Adele is still trapped in naïve dreams of what
'Europe' might now mean beyond the confines of the past. In a
way that's filmic rather than theatrical in its structure and effect,
Greig expertly intercuts the dialogue between the two escaping
women with a monologue from Berlin. He reflects upon the
aftermath of the bombing of the station, the savage beating of
Morocco and the deaths of Fret and Sava. The dialogue between
Adele and Katia is like a catechism of the past. The ritualised
naming of Vienna, Paris, Milan, Moscow and St Petersburg evokes
a tapestry of Europe's cultural achievements, whilst Berlin's
monologue functions as a dark counterpoint of Europe's contrasting history of nationalist wars and anti-Semitism over two
millennia. The racist terrorist attack has finally brought the
previously anonymous, forgotten provincial town a reputation
redolent of this darker, destructive past horrifically resurrected
in twentieth-century Europe. Greig chooses 'Salzburg' and
'Sarajevo' for the two final cities to be named, the former the
home of Mozart. Sarajevo was the location for the assassination of
Archduke Ferdinand in 1914 and was also an epicentre of some
of the worst fighting of the Bosnian war. The play closes with an
expertly crafted interlocking of the major and minor chords in the
complex motet of Europe:

Berlin For one day, for one week . . . maybe even for a month.
Everyone knew the name of our town. And now they know. They
know that even as they travel to some older . . .
Adele Salzburg.
Katia Sarajevo.
Berlin Or more important place.

Adele   Just imagine.

Katia   Shh . . .

Berlin   They know that, in our own way, we're also Europe.

(p. 85)

The Architect (1996)

The Architect was first performed at the Traverse Theatre, Edinburgh in 1996, giving very clear evidence of the development of David Greig's dramatic voice within a short time-frame. This play offers a more sophisticated narrative structural sense along with extensively developed characterisation, especially in the principal characters. These are less impressionistic and schematic than those in *Europe* and subsequently excavate deeper volcanic layers of suppressed anxieties and guilt. The play's title not only describes the central character's profession but co-signifies an optimism of the social and political vision of the post-war generation converted into the bricks and mortar of the built environment. As the play unfolds, the very problematic foundations on which that vision and its implications are grounded are exposed. It's not only the foundations of buildings on mass public housing projects but also those of the liberal democratic project itself that are shown to be unstable.

The central character of the play is Leo Black, a very successful public-project architect. He sees his work as a concrete expression of direct socially productive intervention within modern society. It is clear from the opening of the play that there is a destabilising subtext of doubt and alienation beneath his proselytising zeal. As he tries to communicate his architectural vision to his son Martin, a subtextual oedipal dysfunction acts as a fissure between them. It becomes clear that as Leo tries to enthuse and inspire his son with a shared vision, Martin's debilitating cynicism and *fin de siècle* weariness cause a coruscating alienation between father and son. When Leo seeks to coerce Martin into working on his latest scheme, his son's response communicates the bitter disillusion that permeates not only Leo's relationship with Martin but also infects and colours Leo Black's married and family life:

> **Martin**   I could be in charge of making the models look real. Cover the walls in graffiti or something . . . put little models of dossers under the bridges . . . Use my know how . . . Could I do that?

Another character enters who represents the material world of those tenants who are obliged to live with the daily consequences of the architect's and urban planner's social engineering. Sheena, the tenants' representative from Eden Court, has arrived with a petition from its residents urging that the planned reinvigorating of this failed Utopian housing project be stopped and Eden Court demolished. Failing to secure his support for their petition, she reflects as she leaves at the conclusion of the scene:

> **Sheena**   You know, it's funny to think it was you that built them.
> **Leo**   Is it?
> **Sheena**   Not you in particular. I just mean it's funny to think someone thought them up. You know, a person? You always feel as though they just happened. You're not insulted are you? (p. 105)

The spirit of Ibsen hovers over this play. *The Architect* is clearly a play in the liberal progressive tradition that originated largely in the work of the major dramatist of modern prose Realism.

Ibsen's drama is the 'drama of resolution' in that his plays serve to propose the character and cause of repressive, hypocritical, bourgeois social and moral values. These are then critiqued and counter-argued, often using a central protagonist caught up within their web of deceit and corruption. Ibsen's plays therefore propose a socially progressive, humanist resolution to the problems emanating from that corrupt status quo. This resolution requires radical although not revolutionary social and political change. Given that Ibsen's *The Master Builder* has direct parallels with Greig's *The Architect*, it is remarkable to discover therefore that

Greig had not read Ibsen's masterly analysis of individual corruption reflecting a wider social malaise prior to writing his revisiting of these themes.

Greig's play travels with considerable maturity through this territory and presents without reductive dramatic treatment the interior lives of characters who are traumatically alienated both within themselves and also in their relationships with each other. A dysfunctional corruption stalks the psychological and material environment of the play in a way that is reminiscent of Ibsen's *Ghosts* without any literal parallels in terms of plot and character.

To his credit, Greig never tries to define or explain the nature of this social, ideological and psychological disease except to offer the audience two signposts in the mapping of the play's thematic territory. These cairns or journey markers are individual alienation and the limitations within liberal humanism and its vision of social progress. *The Architect* examines the ways in which the complex causal interplay and interaction exist between human beings and their psychological and genetic imprint with the ideological and social environment that they construct. At the heart of the play also are a crisis of confidence in and the credibility of concepts of social engineering and progress. The failure of so many well-intentioned inner-city and urban housing regeneration projects of the post-war years to provide communities with the decent housing and facilities that they envisaged is evidence enough. The urgently needed post-war clearance of traditional back-to-back terraced slums and their replacement with high-rise skyscraper developments created not the 'Eden' of Leo Black's socially progressive optimism but too often a purgatory of inner-city alienation, crime and decay.

In Act Two, Scene Nine of the play, Greig employs the same kind of filmic montage technique he used in *Europe*. Characters in different situations are nevertheless thematically, simultaneously present, albeit through cuttingly contrasting perspectives. For example, Martin and his boyfriend Billy are in a gay bar where a stereotypical pub quiz is taking place simultaneously with a post-coital scene between Leo and his wife Paulina. Alongside the camp frivolity of the bar, the couple share perspectives upon what is clearly a rare sexual encounter between them. The domestic tragic pathos of Leo's 'I'm glad it happened. It needed to happen' and Paulina's 'It was interesting . . . It was an experiment' coexists with the superficially edgy fun of Billy and Martin at the quiz. The dramatic counterpoint between the abyss of alienation and marital and mental breakdown alongside the postmodern surface of Martin's and Billy's relationship is powerful. As the scene progresses, Paulina enters into a disturbing litany of profound psychological breakdown and disintegration, foregrounded by her banal, matter-of-fact admission that Paulina 'feels like it isn't my name any more'. She then begins to name a cabbala of objects and images from her domesticated bourgeois world: 'Dressing table. Bedroom. Husband. Living room. Sofa. Carpet. Wall'. The inclusion of 'husband' and later 'Paulina' alongside the inanimate motifs of the family home conveys with stylistic economy and psychological potency her inner alienation. She and Leo have become commodified objects eerily equivalent to those that populate their home.

This spiralling descent into ever deeper despair and frag-mentation erodes like a cancer as characters are consumed into its fatal destructive power. Billy commits suicide, jumping off one of the high-rise balconies of Eden Court. In the final scene of the play, Leo effectively chooses suicide, remaining in one of the empty Eden Court flats which is about to be blown to demolition. Two scenes earlier Martin is in a men's toilet, alone, waiting and abject. There is a tragically ironic resonance to the final stage direction in which 'Leo is alone'. This is surely not only his imminent epitaph but also that of his family and the play's other principal characters. The stage directions 'The sound of a series of explosions' and 'The sound of a crowd cheering and clapping' act as the final iconic, aural and visual landscape of the play. The destruction of both the dream of social progress and urban regeneration along with the death of one of its key, misguided visionaries is applauded. For all of its methodically understated and unremittingly dark tonal gloom, *The Architect* is nevertheless a kind of final love-letter-as-suicide note to the liberal humanist belief in the possibility and sustainability of social, cultural and political progress.

The Cosmonaut's Last Message to the Woman He Once Loved in the Former Soviet Union (1999)

This play was performed by Paines Plough Theatre Company and premièred at the Ustinov Studio at the Theatre Royal Bath in 1999.

Its title must qualify for the longest of any play written or produced on the British professional stage in the last fifty years, presenting a major challenge to theatre poster sign writers and publicists.

Much more seriously, this remarkable play criss-crosses time, place, space and gravity in a way that is haunting and profoundly evocative. Individual narratives and subjective journeys of memory and desire collide with Russian cosmonauts on a 'mission impossible' from which their only escape can be death in the farthest reaches of outer space. The geophysical separation that Oleg and Casimir experience mirrors both their internal alienation but also the weightlessness of an entire historical-political project: the former Soviet Union. Dismantled, disempowered and frag-mented, the dislocation of the former Communist Empire into its constituent nation states is a powerful motif hovering over this play, even as the cosmonauts' space module, ironically called *Harmony*, hovers many miles above the earth. They are also like the redundant gods from earlier cultures and ideologies who once entered via the deus ex machina into human affairs. The gravita-tional impotence of the two Russians reflects the waning and dying influence of the ideological-economic apparatus that has launched them above the earth. Material and metaphorical estrangement define them and the wider territory of this very fine play.

A couple, Keith and Vivienne, enact a mirage of their marriage relationship through the signposts of the domesticated and the known social habits of social coexistence. Significantly, Vivienne is a speech therapist. Her job is to facilitate communication from and with those whose illness or accident has rendered them inarticulate prisoners within the unyielding demands of human language. They are as alienated from their own memories and contact with others by language as the cosmonauts are from the earth. Even as Vivienne sensitively seeks to find a key that will unlock them from their psychological and existential exile, she and her husband are as lost and distant as her patients and the cosmonauts. Keith has an ongoing sexual liaison with Nastasja, a Russian sex dancer and daughter working in a Soho club. Her father is Oleg, one of the two trapped cosmonauts.

Other characters in the play include Eric, a high-ranking official with the World Bank, a powerful global instrument of facilitated if not enforced social and political cohesion. Capital is the means by which this power exists, is consolidated and implemented through the world. 'Money is Civilisation – Civilisation is Money' is echoed from Ravenhill's *Shopping and Fucking*. Having met and got drunk together in an airport terminal lounge, an icon of the transience of life and its pleasures, Eric has been given Nastasja's details by Keith. Profoundly personally disempowered and existentially impotent, Eric enters into and manipulates a relationship of shopping and fucking with the young, emotionally vulnerable Russian woman. Keith meanwhile has staged his own suicide. He has left his car and clothes on a remote beach, even as he tries to make an escape from the gravitational pull of his relationship with Vivienne and a life defined by an addiction to the mass-mediated world of television anaesthetised by whisky.

Vivienne, critically disorientated by Keith's seeming death, tries to trace him posthumously through the fragile evidence of a new tie that he had bought depicting Cezanne's famous painting of *Mont Saint Victoire*. She meets Bernard, a former worker on the European Space Agency Arianne rocket project. When the rocket self-destructed on take-off, Bernard's life had also self-combusted into a near fatal stroke. He and Vivienne tentatively form a fragile friendship, sharing their mutual sense of personal loss and of worlds falling apart: the bereavement of optimism compromised and hope deferred – if not spinning endlessly in an internal space of lost relationships and historical, idealistic projects. Before he suffers a second stroke, Bernard has given all of his remaining time and energy to a lingering act of faith in other intelligences beyond the human and the earthbound. With tragic irony, the automated recorded mantra that Bernard transmits through his computer into outer space is the question, 'Is this harmony?'

All of the relationships in the play are subject to the traumatic impact of alienation both material and metaphorical. 'Is this harmony?' David Greig's play asks this question of its myriad kaleidoscope of characters, relationships and locations of inner and outer space. Its impact upon an audience is one of breathtaking disorientation and emotional and ideological weightlessness. This reflects a prevailing atmosphere of our time. It is 'The Unbearable Lightness of Being', to quote from the title of the novel by the acclaimed modern Czech novelist, Milan Kundera.

The play specifically and intelligently uses double casting of actors in different roles. This emphasises that strong sense of the X-ray, ghost-image resonance of these characters caught between the former meta-narratives of history and political change, and a postmodern mélange of dark, dizzying chaos and indeterminacy.

In the very final scene of the play, the double casting hits home powerfully when Keith, having escaped to a bar in the West Highlands of Scotland, is confronted by the character of Sylvia, an erotic dancer and confidante of his former lover Nastasja. However, it is the same actress who played the part of his wife. This gives added poignancy to the play's final dialogue:

Sylvia Keith?
Keith How did you find me?
Sylvia I looked for you.
Keith What do you want?
Sylvia Only to talk.

Victoria (**2000**)

David Greig began work on *Victoria* in 1996 whilst he was Pearson Writer in Residence at the Royal Shakespeare Company (RSC). The Royal Shakespeare Company at the Pit Barbican first performed *Victoria* in April 2000. In his Author's Note to the published edition of the play he wrote:

> Two images coalesced to spark the play's creation. The first was the image of a woman standing by a tree, smoking a cigarette and waiting for a man to arrive. The second came in a visit to an island off the west coast [of Scotland] where I drank in the only pub. Also drinking that particular night, in that small room, were the owner of half the island and his guests, distillery workers from Glasgow, some hippie-ish refugees from city life and some old crofters who had lived and worked on the island all of their lives . . . the physical presence of history is unavoidable in towns and in cities. But perhaps in smaller places, places more remote from the capitals of nations, history is refracted and revealed in a different way . . .

It's interesting and instructive to visit *Victoria* in the context of the preceding discussion and analysis of *Europe* and *The Architect*. It is not only the geographical location of the play that is so very different: the remote and rural west coast of Scotland. It's also that this change in landscape and setting enables David Greig to explore issues of national and cultural identity in relation to Scotland.

The play's dramaturgical ambition and range are very ambitious. This means that the narrative structures and thematic correspondences across the three pieces' different historical settings are sometimes strained and even a little contrived. Nevertheless, this is the most self-evidently 'Scottish' of Greig's plays (outside of *Caledonia Dreaming*: a Suspect Culture project) and asks some penetrating questions about the nature of precisely what is meant in the twentieth and early twenty-first century about the concept of not only 'Scotland' and 'Scottishness' but, by implication, national, political and cultural identity within contemporary Europe.

Briefly and anecdotally, when visiting Edinburgh in April 2006 to interview David Greig, I was reflecting on themes of contemporary Scottish political and cultural life whilst visiting an exhibition of contemporary Scottish art presented by members of the Royal Scottish Academy. One piece that really spoke to me was a monochrome photograph of an older, contemporary Scottish woman. Her glasses had been given a distinctive red tint. It was called *A Revolution* and was by the photographer Christopher Park.

From a postmodernist reading of popular culture and cultural production the tartan oven gloves in the tourist shop on Princes Street were as relevant and valid a reading of iconic depictions of Scottishness as Christopher Park's marvellous photograph of an older working-class Scottish woman, returning my gaze with an uncompromising, challenging resilience. What I think is indisputable is that the site of cultural and political identity in contemporary Scotland is a vibrantly contested one. On this geo-ideological and historic fault line are many disparate claimants for ownership of 'Scotland'. These include the enduring traditional notions of clan and the wild rural landscape of the north and outlying islands, in vivid contrast with the urban density and diversity of centres such as Glasgow and Edinburgh. Add to the equation the competing political ideologies of Scottish Nationalists and Socialists along, of course, with Labour, Conservatives and the Liberal Democrats. These strands and others all conspire to complicate an ingrained, nostalgic populist sense of a Scotland of the past in tension with the diverse economic and multicultural needs of the present.

Victoria takes a challenging plunge into this melting pot of idealised, romanticised notions of a Scotland looking perpetually over its shoulder to an imagined past of 'glorious defeat' cooking away and boiling over with postmodern contemporary aspirations of independence within a rapidly reconfiguring Europe.

The play is in three chronological parts, 'Part One, The Bride', 'Part Two, The Crash' and finally 'Part Three, The Mountain'.

The three parts carry with them evocative associations and echoes of themes of migration and changing landscapes in both the geographical and geo-ideological sense. Political doctrines and activism explored include the 1930s neo-Fascist ideology embraced by David, the English aristocratic heir to the Red House, the local mansion. It is the visible presence of history's English 'colonial intervention' set in the midst of an otherwise isolated rural Scottish community. The play also explores the left-wing beliefs and political activism of some of the indigenous Scottish characters within this community.

In Part One these are embodied by Euan, Gavin and Oscar. On discovering David's sexual overtures towards Victoria, a local minister's daughter, they conspire to kill him. Oscar shoots him, after which the heir's corpse is found hanging from a butcher's hook in the grounds of the Red House. Interwoven into the thematic tapestry of Part One and running as narrative and thematic threads throughout the other two plays are issues of national and cultural identity, and that of women. These focus upon the historic English strategies of British Union and more recently of global capitalist economics into modern Scotland.

In Part One there is a strong dramatic focus upon the relationship between Oscar, a prospective student, and Victoria, his lover. They represent, in the context of the 1930s, the overwhelming need and desire to travel beyond the geographical horizons of this community, which is also enclosed by its history of parochial social and cultural attitudes. These remain painfully reinforced by an economic dependency on the aristocratic English colonial presence. In the ongoing evolving of Greig's heightened poetic-realist style it is as if the characters in *Victoria* are sometimes seeking to escape the gravity of the printed page. This dialectical tension between an impulse to ground and locate his characters in specific material settings whilst simultaneously to 'ask a question of them' (Greig's phrase) creates a dialogue uninhibited by the demands of conventional dramatic naturalism. This results in a distinctive dialogic texture of which the following short extract from Part One, Scene Five offers a very good example:

Victoria

You and talking.

You just talk.

You could smoke away your life with that talk and still be

Sat here when you're old.

Still the same.

Oscar

You told your father this?

Told your mother?

Victoria

Course not.

They'd have me kept.

Have me married to a theological student and mansed all

My life, like my mother.

Oscar

You half look like her.

See, with your mouth – your eyes.

Dressed in black at the back of the Kirk.

Black rock she is.

Victoria

Twenty years of Kirk and winter and she's had.

Time's took her looks from her.

I'll not be my mother.

The elliptical interplay of poetic, visual image – 'Black rock she is' – and epigrammatic, third-person perspective – 'I'll not be my mother' – colludes to give the character a kind of privileged viewing position of both herself and her relationship with others. It's as if the character has a self-reflexive wing bud on each of her shoulders, straining for that bird's-eye perspective upon herself and her circumstances.

In Part Two, 'The Crash', an aeroplane crashes into the

mountainside just above the village. In time the action is now set in 1966, thirty years on from the pre-war period of the Spanish Civil War and the imminent culmination of the Nazi–Fascist axis of power. Usually identified in the popular imagination, and indeed by social and cultural historians, as a decade of progressive liberalisation and also radical political unrest, especially the Paris riots of 1968, the kind of 'liberation' that the crashed helicopter signifies for the indigenous Scottish community is of a different and problematic kind. The play opens with a new, American, Victoria, a geologist working for an American oil company, and a dazed and traumatised survivor of the crash. Carter, her American business colleague, remains trapped in the helicopter and yet, despite his imploring pleas, she has made no attempt to help him escape:

Victoria
    Rock.
    No lights.
    No houses here.
    The sea.
    Carter,
    This is the place.
    I know this is the place.

Once again the interweaving of the image of 'the rock' emanates and migrates with another simple but powerful image of nature, 'the sea'. Absorbed and distracted in some post-traumatic space inside her head, she fails to rescue Carter, who perishes when the helicopter suddenly bursts into flames and is completely destroyed.

Part Two plays interestingly with the surviving of some of the now thirty-years-older characters from Part One, principally Oscar who himself is now married to Shona. She was a young kitchen maid at the Red House in Part One. They have a son whom Greig wittily and cleverly names Euan, like the young revolutionary activist from the earlier first play. However, with an audacious sense of both the century-crossed currents of social and political change and also the emerging pragmatic materialism of the post-1960s generation, this younger Euan is an entrepreneur. He displays barely concealed impatience for his father Oscar's haunting folk refrains upon his violin or Oscar's left-wing political past. With a historical synchronicity that could strain an audience's suspension of disbelief, the recovering Olivia is staying and recuperating with Oscar and Shona. The tensions between Oscar and his son are not only generational but also born of radically opposing values. The dramatic tension generated helps to maintain a dramatic urgency necessary in narrative terms for this middle play:

Oscar

You should make a record of this.

You could make a lot of money.

Out of real music.

Euan

Folk's out.

Glam's in.

Whatever you are, Father.

You're not glam.

Oscar

And I suppose you are.

Your world is glamorous.

Jet set.

Euan

Not at this precise moment, no.

Oscar

To go to America is glamorous.

Not here.

Not to be among ordinary folk.

Working.

Euan

I work.

Oscar

For yourself.

Euan

You don't change, do you?

Same tune.

Crack in the vinyl.

Over and over.

Meanwhile, this place's sliding off the map.

You're all talk.

Oscar

In the village they're saying – if they've found oil,

Offshore,

It'll mean work. Oil, generational tensions and the parochial and local in complex opposition to the national, transnational and global capitalism.

Proper work.

You could come back – you could involve yourself. (pp. 102–3)

This dialogue again conveys the imagistic and emotional sub-textual economy of Greig's maturing dramatic idiom, but also serves to pursue the dialectical conflicts and tensions within the work.

In Part Three of *Victoria* Greig draws together some of the narrative and thematic strands of the first two plays whilst also trying to avoid a simplistic, reductive sense of dramatic closure. Within the helter-skelter of individuals and their business and personal relationships David Greig continues to demonstrate an acute sensitivity for the layers of personal and public histories in those individual lives. Once again, he employs the technique of multi-location in geographical and historical tension when, in Scene Sixteen of the final part of the play, Victoria and David (a wealthy young woman and young male graduate) are in bed with the now deceased Oscar's book. It is his long-hidden account of his left-wing political activities in the Spanish Civil War in the 1930s. In terms of the political and personal tensions between the older

Oscar and his entrepreneurial son Euan there is an added poignancy to the narrative intercutting of human memory, experience and political idealism tested in the furnace of war. The Young Euan – that is, the revolutionary friend of Oscar from Part One – recounts a potent memory from the Spanish Civil War, made even more moving by the audience's knowledge that he has died saving his friend, Young Oscar:

Young Euan
> My first day in Madrid, Oscar.
> I saw a tram full of barbers.
> Barbers.
> Going to the front.
> They hadn't even taken off their aprons.
> They still had combs in their hands.
> . . .
> Are they members of the Communist Party?
> Or are they anarchists?
> But I was proud to see them.
> Proud of myself and proud of us.
> . . .
> On their way to defend the city.
> Oscar,
> Even the barbers are prepared to fight for Socialism.
> We have to win.

By the conclusion of the play, such political commitment and courage towards resisting the oppression of Franco's Fascist forces seems from another solar system, let alone a different place in twentieth-century history. This is reinforced with some biting irony when Kirsty, a marketing consultant in collusion with Euan, Oscar's son, invokes the dead man's memory and life as part of their charm offensive with the local community. This is to secure excavation and quarrying rights of the mountain above the village for Euan's own company, Sutherland Granite Aggregates:

What I am here to say is that we have considered the objections of
the environmental lobby and we have taken some of their worries
on board. It is as a direct response to these worries that we have
included a new element to our proposal. The Oscar Sutherland
Business Training Centre. Mr Sutherland has decided that if the
proposal for a second quarry goes ahead, then he will build for the
community a training centre, fully staffed, and will give out a grant
of five thousand pounds to young local people with business ideas
that can be located in the West Highlands . . . Mr Sutherland feels
such an initiative will do justice to the memory of his father, whose
life was dedicated to increasing opportunity for all, and to the
community in which he himself was brought up. (pp. 170–1)

The smoothly cynical deployment of media-friendly words like
'community' and the uncritical celebration and advocacy of
business and private enterprise have their roots in Britain in the
Thatcherite era of the 1980s but have been politically rebranded
and owned by the New Labour project. To suggest, as do Kirsty
and Euan, that Oscar's revolutionary Socialism can be reworded
and sanitised as 'increasing opportunity for all' reveals Greig with
his finger very firmly on the pulse of early-twenty-first-century
capitalism and its methods of concealing its own economic self-
interest under a guise of 'opportunity', 'choice' and 'community'.
In *The American Pilot* Greig extends his dramatic focus to
investigate the impact of United States military-economic policy
on another isolated community, this time in a fictionalised Third
World country.

The American Pilot (2005)

This play was first performed by the Royal Shakespeare Company
at the Other Place, Stratford-upon-Avon, in April 2005. I was
fortunate enough to catch the short revival of that original
production at the Soho Theatre, London in the spring of 2006.

One of the characters in *The American Pilot* is Sarah, a villager in
an unspecified, fictional Third World country, which is waging a

'terrorist' war against a brutal military dictatorship, itself supported by the United States of America. Sarah is the wife of the Farmer (interestingly, without any 'individualised' name) who has found the American pilot. The pilot's plane has crash-landed into the mountainside above the remote village where the people live a life of material hardship accentuated by the dangers and privations caused by the armed resistance to an oppressive regime supported by the USA. The play has a very similar Brechtian parable structure to Greig's earlier *Europe* and, in Scene Six, Sarah observes with a hard-wrought wisdom born of suffering and hardship:

> **Sarah** If God has given you a time of war, don't daydream about visiting the city. God gave us an American pilot. God asked that my daughter be taken away from me. God decided that I should be left alone. This was God's plan for me. It is painful and unnecessary to dream of a life in which it could have been otherwise. (p. 62)

In the context of *Victoria*, another remote enclosed community threatened by the deus ex machina intervention of wider economic and militaristic forces and interests lies at the heart of this play. For Sarah, the wider ideological and imperialist global interests of the United States of America are conflated in terms of a God and destiny beyond her control and means. 'God' of course may be seen as inevitable but benign. However, in the light of the continuing war in Iraq (at the time of writing, May 2007) 'God' may equally be in fundamentalist Christian terms the 'God on our side' who legitimates and ordains the questionable military invasion into another country. This God also provides a moral imperative to the otherwise morally problematic motives regarding the attempted securing of massive oil reserves and production. 'God' may also be the fundamentalist Islamic authority for not only armed resistance to what is seen as a morally corrupt and economically expansionist West, but also for the murderous ethnic and doctrinal factions of both Sunni and Shi'ite Muslims in Iraq and the immediate region.

It is the Trader who significantly understands the function and transnational and cross-cultural significance of trade and commerce that counterbalances Sarah's poignantly misguided, fatalist acceptance of God's will. He offers a far shrewder recognition of things-as-they-are:

> **Trader**   The margin exists in the deal and the deal exists in the world as it is – not in a dream of the world as you would like it to be. The margin exists in this world, not the next. (p. 66)

The Trader's cynical realism enables him to acknowledge that it is not 'God' who controls the world to resolve its problems, but economic self-interest. In the early years of the new millennium this continues to equate to the power of capital, which is the politics of oil. He knows that it is this *realpolitik* which both enters their isolated community and also controls that wider world beyond the boundaries of custom and tradition. With very astute and clever stagecraft Greig takes the classical notion of the deus ex machina (or 'god that descends') with the literal 'falling from the sky' of the American pilot. Equally, at the violent and shocking conclusion to the play, it is highly trained special American Assault Forces who also enter the world of the village 'from above': abseiling down into it to rescue the pilot at the cost of the savage, premeditated and brutally non-differential killing of everyone except him and Evie, the daughter of Sarah and the Farmer.

Within the framing device of the entry of the pilot into the village, the main body of the play proceeds to explore the conflicting views amongst the villagers about what should happen to Jason Reinhardt (the pilot's name). This debate is driven on by the arrival of the Captain of the armed resistance to the regime and also Matthew, his interpreter. The interplay of the personal and the political and the private and the public is exceptionally well handled by Greig. The playwright had conceived of his play well before the American and British invasion of Iraq in March 2003 and could not have anticipated either the direction that war would take or the way that terrorists or insurgents would react against the 'liberators'. *The American Pilot* therefore has an uncanny prescience about the events that were to follow its original conception. The videoed public execution of Reinhardt intended for global transmission on the media and Internet is hauntingly predictive of the savage beheadings of Western hostages in Iraq and their transmission across the world media. This event is prevented when Evie, the idealistic young daughter of the Farmer and Sarah, intercedes on Reinhardt's behalf. Her intercession has something of the quality of a moral or spiritual plea for both wider human values of non-violent resolution to political conflicts. With tragic irony, given the eventual massacre of the village by the American Marines, Evie invokes the power and values that constitute the United States of America:

Evie
America is on our side.
He told me this.
America is watching us.
America sees us, Captain, just as surely as if we were
On television.
All the attacks.
All the awfulness.
America has seen it.
All the hunger.
All the fighting and stealing.
America has seen it.
He told me this.
We had no hope left.
We were full of dust and sorrow.
We were lost but America sent him to tell us, we don't
Have to be alone any more.
We can save ourselves.
We can be found.
We can be American. (p. 60)

The Captain is nothing if not a realist and pragmatist. Whilst not, of course, convinced by Evie's idealised vision of the USA as saviour of her community, his hard-won political instinct – 'We're a poor people, in a poor country, and we can muster only a very small, very poor army. In the scheme of things, we're nothing' (p. 57) – recognises the potentially powerful propaganda opportunity. If his rebel army and their cause can be associated with a kind of contemporary, non-violent, Third World 'Joan of Arc', the world might support the justice of their political cause. He plans accordingly to take Reinhardt down into the valley for a peaceful handing over to the American-backed military-government authorities: videoed and transmitted live across the world.

Matthew, the translator, has no optimism about the Captain's strategy and warns his commanding officer against this course of action. The Captain speaks with all the weariness of someone whose original political optimism and ideals have been similarly exhausted. For him, using Evie as a symbol of innocence and moral and political legitimacy might achieve some fragment of successful resolution of a war for justice that they stand no other chance of winning: 'My dreams have been of a half-mile gained in the valley. A trench defended. Evie is water on a dry field to me, Matthew' (p. 65). The Trader also has a crude but accurate economic grasp of the global-media value of Evie's idealism being transmitted around the world. She and the village will become a commodified product that can be 'sold' in the same way that 'Jesus', McDonald's and the 'American Dream' can and are 'sold' around the globe: 'Visions attract people. If she gets on television saying that stuff – we could have the world on our doorstep. Television brings people' (p. 69).

With strange postmodern synchronicity the Trader is simultaneously an echo of Euan in *Victoria* for whom the community and landscape are something that is ultimately a commodity to be sold at a profit. Furthermore Brian, in Mark Ravenhill's *Shopping and Fucking*, whose mantra as a gangster businessman is 'Money is Civilisation – Civilisation is Money', also echoes that view. There is an important sense that even if the historical political narratives of Marxism and Socialism are now considered redundant in relation to issues of globalisation, poverty and injustice, a lingering residue of political and ethical critique remains resonant amongst some contemporary British dramatists.

The final stage direction for *The American Pilot* is 'The bombing continues. The gunfire continues. The End'. This bleak postscript for the play and its themes may also be viewed as a postscript for our times at the time of writing in the early summer of 2007. Political violence and terror of the state-sponsored American and British kind, as well as that of Al-Qaeda and Hezbollah, remain harrowingly dominant. The last scene in global politics may be playing out before some apocalyptic 'final curtain' comes down. The optimism and youthful visionary idealism of Evie and all that she represents seem desperately fragile, vulnerable and untenable in our early, second-millennial world.

Nevertheless after seeing a matinée performance of *The American Pilot* at the Soho Theatre in 2006, along with the numbing sense of shock at the play's darkly savage conclusion, I also carried with me a fragile optimism through the tourist crowds around Piccadilly Circus and Leicester Square. Fifty years on from the nascent optimism of the British theatre in 1956, here was a writer and a play that embodied the enduring, pragmatic optimism and vision of George Devine for what theatre might and could be.

DOWNLOADS
- For other plays by new Scottish writers see the plays of David Harrower, Stephen Greenhorn and Chris Hannan.
- For powerful influences upon the early development of his dramatic voice, see some of the plays of Howard Barker, especially *Victory* and also Ibsen's *The Master Builder* in interesting contrast to Greig's *The Architect*.
- For the influence on the dramatic parable structure of *Europe* and *The American Pilot*, see Brecht's *The Good Person of Setzuan* and *The Caucasian Chalk Circle*.

4 MARK RAVENHILL

Interview with Mark Ravenhill

This is an edited transcript of an interview that took place at the offices of Paines Plough Theatre Company, London, in May 2006.

PB   I want to begin, Mark, by asking you why you first started to write for the stage and whether there were any particular influences upon you in terms of particular writers for example?

MR   For a long time I'd thought about writing but my main interest initially was in directing. It was only really in about 1994 that I actually seriously sat down to write plays, so it's hard to say what finally pushed me from directing to push ahead and write a play with the full intention of pursuing a theme and seeing the play through. Undoubtedly, that play for me was *Shopping and Fucking*. I'd thought about it a lot and I think that the murder of James Bulger was certainly a major event for my generation in the 1990s. There seemed to be, following his death – it seemed to shift something in the national consciousness – a re-questioning of traditional ideas of what was good and evil and the subsequent debate surrounding that. The murder of a young child resonated very strongly – there was also a strong sense that the [John] Major government was coming to an end and I think all of that led to a new energy in theatre and pop music and art – and all sorts of things. I think I picked up on that kind of energy at work. There were also personal experiences for me in the background to the play as well. It had only been about eighteen months previously (to my writing the play) that I had lost someone very close to me and I think that personal bereavement got me down to writing more seriously. So I think it was a combination of things. It wasn't that there was any one playwright or play who inspired me although I had been going to see plays for a long time and plays have been a very big part of my life for all of my life, so I think that there were a whole range of influences there.

PB   Sure . . . your talk about that shift in public consciousness and a shift in public opinion in what constitutes good and evil seems to me crucial, especially in relation to *The Cut* where Paul describes himself as evil. In *Shopping and Fucking* when the character (Brian) says 'Money is Civilisation – Civilisation is Money' that kind of indicates a world where certainly conventional moral values of any kind, even liberal ones, have disappeared or have become suspended or marginalised – could you respond to that in terms of your earlier references to good and evil relating, for example, to the James Bulger case?

MR Yeah, I think the vast majority of the theatregoing audience tends to be the liberal intelligentsia. In a kind of a post-ideological era they have tended to fudge any kinds of questions about morality without any kinds of political guidelines as to what morality might be or mean. I think that that liberal sense of values just gets woollier and woollier, and is simply a mixture of liberalism and postmodernism. With this, it makes any definition of moral values just cease to exist. Therefore, I think that one of the things that I'd like the play to do in different ways is to get the audience to question and challenge what their values are: moral values and questions of good and evil, which are very complex. I'm not saying that the play is a 'morality play' but I would like to challenge that liberal, postmodern consensus of either, 'There are no moral values' or 'Oh we're not quite sure if we've got any'.

PB Yes, I think it's very interesting, Mark, that in your latest full-length play *The Cut*, the characters are located in an unspecified but presumably contemporary Western European society. Here, we have the central character Paul who is a combination of a senior civil servant and interrogator who has administered this form of torture known as 'The Cut'. He is kind of trapped within what we might say is either a moral – or maybe it's an ideological – crisis about both what he does and who he is. I wonder if you could offer some thoughts in relation to him and the play?

MR Yeah, I think at the beginning of the play I was interested in kind of reversing the usual situation because I thought by now that the person who was carrying through this form of torture was racked by a kind of liberal guilt. This meant that it was a huge punishment, therefore, to have to perform this form of torture whereas the person having it done to them has kind of fetishised it and ritualised it as a badge of pride – as I think quite a lot of people who have suffered some form of oppression do. So I think it's a classic reversal of a master–servant relationship where the master is anguished about the role of the master whereas the servant is begging to remain as the servant. They don't actually break the cycle, they continue in their roles but their attitudes are changed – so that's what propels Paul in the play. He's not actually breaking the cycle but he's just racked by the liberal guilt about his role in the regime and it's destroying his relationship with his wife and by the end of the play he can't accept the new regime's offer of a form of forgiveness – he wants to be punished.

PB Does that kind of liberal guilt ultimately propel him into what is fundamentally a very reactionary moral position, in that he insists upon his own sense of being evil: of deserving punishment, which in a way is a very conservative moral position? Does that strike with your own thoughts or were your intentions different?

MR I'm not sure what my intentions were. By the end of the play he's in a position to say 'I am evil' and yes, he wants some form of punishment. I don't really know how I feel about that – it's certainly very clearly what he wants – that that form of forgiveness wouldn't be any kind of solution to his suffering but only punishment could bring a solution. He's certainly reached a point where he believes in moral absolutes.

PB That's right and in a sense it's a world, as you say a mental world, an ideological and moral world, in which there is no 'grace'. There is nothing to soften the blow of judgement: 'an eye for an eye and a tooth for a tooth'?

MR Yeah, I don't know exactly where all that comes from – it's certainly what that character wanted in that scene and there *is* something 'Old Testament' about it.

PB It's only just occurred to me in the context of this conversation but I wonder whether there is any point of connection between Paul and the young male prostitute Gary in *Shopping and*

Fucking whose ultimate desire is to enact a fetishised act of sex and violence?

MR   Yeah, I think that actually the closer connection is between the young man in the opening act of *The Cut* and Gary, because they both fetishise their own punishment and their own suffering. I think it's something that people often do and it's something that is very challenging for that liberal consensus which wants to say 'We can make you better, we can free you'. But actually it's much more than just one step for those people to let go of their sense of being oppressed, because it's often the only identity they have as once that's taken away, there's nothing left. That's absolutely terrifying for those people.

PB   Of course that's where Paul finds himself – or chooses to be – doesn't he? At the end of the play he is living an equivalent identity to John?

MR   Yes, it would give him a clearer sense of identity if he could be someone who was punished – a very clear-cut identity.

PB   Yes, of course there's a very real sense of a Judaeo-Christian morality hovering somewhere . . .

MR (*laughs*)   . . . Yes, there does seem to be, doesn't there? I hadn't thought about it that way but there does seem to be, yes . . .

PB   . . . I guess in a sense because historically, culturally, the world that we live in has those roots within that broader religious and ideological territory, they are so powerful and enduring. I have to say, talking as we are about liberalism and liberality, I have been thinking a lot about how the extent to which that form of liberal humanist project has come to an end and the implications that has for theatres and writers and the kind of society that we live in.

MR   I certainly think that it's come to an end of a very substantial phase although it's not finished completely and obviously that's why it's so confused and so alarmed. It doesn't seem to be able to understand itself and the means by which it's thought that everything could be read through its liberal humanist frame. There are things which just don't fit that code and values at all and that's where the comedy of *Product* comes from because my character is constantly trying to read it, read, read it, through this classic narrative. You've got this model of a Hollywood narrative and he wants to try and just squeeze this Western idea of a love relationship into a classic action adventure model. It keeps on slipping and it just won't fit and that's where a lot of the comedy and the dramatic tension of the piece come.

PB Yes, I enjoyed reading it on the page and look forward to seeing you perform it this evening. It is very darkly, savagely funny, isn't it, and the kind of clash between the politics – the ideology – of the narrative in terms of Islam but then the wholly inappropriate – 'Hollywood means' by which that narrative is communicated is hilarious.

MR Yes, and that was quite conscious for me from the beginning to actually have that and it is about our inability to understand Islam through any of the language that we have.

PB Of course, in terms of language in a formal sense and also language in terms of the media. The communication of information and values through this very sophisticated technological media world that we live in – it does beg the question how are even we going to begin to come to any kind of understanding about fundamental Islam?

MR Yeah . . .

PB . . . because everything is refracted through the channel of communication. Outside of Al Jazeera – which of course the United States allegedly tried to bomb out of existence – that seems to be one of the few non-Western but journalist-respected news channels that we have to receive and hear an Arabic viewpoint from. Was it a challenge to take on a one-man show?

MR No, not really, it was certainly a very different kind of experience – certainly the initial stuff for it was I just wanted to see how simple a piece of theatre you could make. I'd been inspired by – I love it as piece of writing but not necessarily the writing – the idea of Wallace Shaw in writing *The Fever*, which was to write something that could be performed in someone's living room, he could do it anywhere. It's also a fantastic piece of writing. He'd said in an interview that he wanted to write something that he could do anywhere. I thought, yes, I'd like to do that as well, that would be great; you wouldn't necessarily need anything in terms of sound or lighting cues or in terms of props. You could just turn up and do it. So it took me a few years and then really I was searching to find a way to write about this marvellously complex thing that we've all been thinking about for the last few years. That is the relationship between our culture and Islamic culture and it just seemed so overwhelming. Then I thought, well, often the thing to do when you've got something that big is to pair it up with something very small, which can become a way in, and my idea was just to have me speaking, which is so small and specific that it might be a route into the impossibly big issue of two whole cultures meeting. That's what really got me started and so I just wrote it, tried it out as a late-night event, carried on writing a bit more. Then I took it to Edinburgh as a forty-five-minute piece and then this year an international tour has been organised for it and so now it runs at an hour. The actual acting of it – it's a good discipline for me – it's very precise work – you just have to chip away at it every day and put it together as a performance. Rehearsals are very detailed.

PB I mean I guess in a way, as a writer, you're involved in a dramaturgical way upon your own process as a writer?

MR Yes, it's a good test of the writing. I asked Lucy Morrison to direct it. I needed someone who could be honest with me and also that we could use the rehearsals to try out the script and then go away, rewrite, return to it; a very immediate way of testing your own writing is to have to perform it.

PB It's interesting that we've been talking about morality and questions of morality which are authoritarian, conservative, reactionary by contrast with the liberal postmodern value framework. Certainly within fundamentalist Islam, it seems what's unmistakably clear is that it is a profoundly conservative, binary moral code where there are some events, actions and behaviours that are unquestionably wrong and those that are morally good.

Therefore it strikes me again that where Paul's journey takes him might not be so far from the Taliban: 'I have done wrong, punish me, without grace, without forgiveness.'

MR Yes, I see – of course – liberalism has its own taboos and 'no-nos' – any form of racism or sexism or homophobia so it's kind of . . . it's not liberal about illiberal things – there's a kind of intrinsic contradiction there.

PB I've increasingly started to wonder whether there's what I would call a 'tyranny of liberalism'?

MR Yeah, I agree . . .

PB . . . and certainly with the current governing culture – and I don't imagine in the event that David Cameron would be elected that a Tory government would be any different – it seems that what we have is the veneer of liberality and liberal humanism and yet it's supported and enforced by the most authoritarian and centralised government apparatus . . .

MR . . . no, that's right, that's absolutely the accepted code of government now, it's one of the things that I wanted to write about in *Citizenship* because the kids and the teachers exist in that environment where that form of liberalism is especially evident in the school environment. Everybody knows the language and yet there is all kinds of slippage and actually the kids become very literate in that form of liberalism and so in the classroom, talking to teachers, they can absolutely speak the language of 'diversity and equal opportunities' and all that stuff. Yet in the playground there are all codes of other language and as much as a school might try to instil a liberal environment, it's still incredibly hard for the teacher that is gay to talk honestly about their sexuality because there are both parents and kids who couldn't handle it. Therefore, there's all sorts of gaps between the liberal vision that the school aspires to be and the reality, and that's where quite a lot of the stuff in *Citizenship* comes from. Yet you're also able to see moments when everyone is able to suddenly fit into the formal language, which is almost like a very mild form of cultural revolution that has gone on where everybody can do the 'double thing'.

PB   It's one of my concerns that changing or trying to change the ways in which people talk and describe themselves or others doesn't necessarily engage with the reality . . .

MR   Yes, that's right . . .

PB   As you say, Mark, the world of the playground and the world behind the bike shed has its own dynamics and its own forms of language, and it sits probably very uneasily with a kind of public language. The idea that somehow, through the control of public language, human behaviour or attitudes will change . . .

MR   Yes, that's right, the key thing for me is the end of a scene between a pupil and a teacher where the teacher says, 'You know, as a school, we celebrate diversity, you report bullying, everything will be all right' and the boy says, 'But I'm not all right' and the teacher implies 'Well, you should be' – once they've got their policies in place – look we've 'done the policies' – 'what more can we do?' – And then a kind of panic sets in – to imagine that having 'We celebrate Diversity' above the public door of the school means that everything will be OK. Those kinds of words have become almost like talismans . . .

PB   Again, as you say, because this is all becoming so drilled into our political and social culture, many people will become increasingly familiar with the language . . .

MR   Oh yes, the people who really learn that language by heart are schoolkids and people from within institutions – you'll hear from people who've been in 'rehab' – junkies and stuff – trotting out stuff like 'My Key Resource Worker has negotiated' . . . I hear it on any bus in Camden – it's almost like a kind of patois – this new vocabulary – everybody's learning it! (*Laughs.*)

PB   (*laughs*)   I remember Tony Garnett saying in an interview with me that his production company World Productions had very deliberately resisted using the drama (the making of *The Cops*) for positive images of class and ethnicity etc. and he memorably said, 'Political correctness makes very bad drama and even worse politics.'

MR   Yes, yes . . .

PB   Given this kind of landscape and going back to *The Cut*, we have at the end of the play a very strong sense of the revisiting of cycles of political authoritarianism, political oppression without any noticeable sense of any real change or progress. Does that reflect your own current thinking and position in terms of the possibilities of political action, political intervention, and political change?

MR   Um, yes, I think it probably does – of course, it's not that I sit down and write a chart of what's going to be in the play. I don't know how it is for every writer but the characters in the play can surprise me, they do surprise me at times. Yes, I think that it's a play that could only have been written a long way into that New Labour government – I wrote a substantial part of it back in 1995 – just as I think that *Shopping and Fucking* could only have been written at the absolute tail end of those Tory years. I think that the sense that the new regime has ended up almost exactly where the old regime had ended is a very strong feature of the play and in that respect it's a very bleak play. I write these plays and then I read them and I say 'Oh!' – it must have come from me somewhere but it's not consciously – and I'm quite shocked, but I think that on a day-to-day basis I'm much more optimistic about the possibilities of political action. But with that play, at that moment, that seemed to be the overwhelming mood of that play: change has been tried a number of times and it always seems to prove to be a total failure.

'We all need stories so that we can get by' – Sex, Shopping and Postmodern Politics in the Plays of Mark Ravenhill

Mark Ravenhill is, along with the late Sarah Kane, probably the most well known and controversial of the new generation of young writers in British theatre from the mid-1990s on until the present. Ravenhill's *fin de siècle* notoriety was guaranteed with the public controversy surrounding his first major play. This was a play with a title that marketing executives and entrepreneurial sex shop owners would have given their Rolex to have come up with: *Shopping and Fucking*. Inevitably the play's title and the scene where Gary, the young working-class rent boy, lives out his 'porn-fantasy as real life' through a ritualised act of violent anal rape, has placed a problematic screen in terms of this fine play's serious wider themes and concerns. A similar phenomenon happened forty years ago with Scene Six of Edward Bond's seminal *Saved* (1965) in which a baby is stoned to death in a south London park. The deployment of the term 'In-Yer-Face Theatre' by Aleks Sierz in his book of the same title contributes to the notion that a kind of uncompromising sensationalism was the primary characteristic of the emerging writers of the 1990s and their antecedents such as Bond.

Ironically, the play was received by virtually all the major newspaper theatre critics without censor or disclaim. It did materialise, however, that under a hardly remembered Victorian law – the Indecent Advertisements Act of 1889 – the word 'fuck' is banned from public display. This provided an unexpected field day for the play's publicists. Whilst questioning the legitimacy and relevance of such outdated legislation, what better way to draw attention to the play than the enforced requirement of highlighting the title through the device of a splintered fork or asterisks replacing the offending letters? Of course, Max Stafford-Clark's producing Out of Joint theatre company and the Royal Court Theatre as venue would have been equally delighted at the fulfilment of the old saying 'All publicity is good publicity'. Large audiences of often new theatregoers from the metropolitan gay subculture where *Shopping and Fucking* is located included the Royal Court Theatre for the first time ever on their itinerary of a good night out.

Across Mark Ravenhill's major work is a contemporary political and moral sensibility that is often in active resistance to what he perceives as the listless vacuity of many postmodern narratives. Ravenhill's major debut play is set in a retro-Pop consumer-capitalist world where, to quote the gangster businessman Brian, 'Money is Civilisation – Civilisation is Money'. With savage irony and a class A cutting-edge humour Ravenhill critiques a world and society where shopping has become a fetishised pleasure activity equivalent to a good night out with the boys. Similarly, sex is like the convenience food that the characters consume: a commodity subject to crude economic transaction and (sometimes rough) trade. There's much more to Mark Ravenhill's plays than shock value alone. He is as much a subversive social and political commentator as were two other earlier radical gay writers: Oscar Wilde and Joe Orton. Ravenhill recognises a world in which traditional political and moral certainties have either disappeared or been terminally compromised. In early major plays such as *Shopping and Fucking*, and *Some Explicit Polaroids*, mid-career pieces such as *Mother Clap's Molly House* and in his more recent work *The Cut*, *Product*, *Citizenship* and *Pool (No Water)*, Ravenhill serves as an astute and savagely funny observer of our times.

My discussion and analysis begins with *Shopping and Fucking*, *Some Explicit Polaroids* and *Mother Clap's Molly House*, and then focuses exclusively on his most recent work at the time of writing, *The Cut*, *Product*, *Citizenship* and *Pool (No Water)*.

Shopping and Fucking (1996)

In *Shopping and Fucking*, Ravenhill takes us on an after-hours journey into the lives of five principal characters centring upon three young people in a problematic but nevertheless ongoing relationship of mutual need and dependence: Mark, Lulu, Robbie.

Robbie and Lulu are lovers of Mark. Of the two other main characters one is a young rent boy called Gary, a pick-up for Mark who has failed to last more than a matter of days at a rehabilitation centre for his drug addiction. Equally spectacularly, Mark has also failed to sustain his attempts at sexual celibacy, paying to lick the fourteen-year-old's anus, only to discover that it is bleeding. A pub-quiz part of postmodern urban folklore of the London scene is that these characters were named by Ravenhill after members of the major pop 'Boy Band' sensation Take That and the retro-pop singer Lulu. The remaining major character is Brian, an older London gangster and businessman.

Lulu, an out-of-work actress, is desperately seeking to get a job to support both her and the perennially neurotic, unstable Robbie. Brian interviews her for a job allegedly in television advertising. Believing that she is auditioning for a mainstream sales job, Lulu reconsiders this naïve assumption when Brian asks her to take her top off before trying the hard sell on kitchen tableware. Far from sell dinner plates and soup bowls, Lulu secures the sales job of dealing three hundred Ecstasy ('E') tablets at £10 per tablet on the London club scene. Her sales targets and life expectancy are dangerously undermined after recruiting Robbie to the sales team. He allows the allure of sex-for-drugs with a steady stream of handsome gay guys and his own Ecstasy-fuelled elation to result in giving away the entire stash of drugs. He also gets beaten up. Brian's business acumen and gangland modus operandi means that Robbie's Utopian dream of sharing and caring and trans-cending the injustices and suffering of a cruel world is viewed by Brian as a life-and-limb-endangering deficit. Lulu and Robbie are faced with raising the £3,000 they owe Brian to a painfully tight schedule. This schedule is not as painful, however, as having their legs broken and worse should they fail. The two show com-mendable initiative in setting up a mobile-phone-based sex chat line from their flat.

Still short of their target, the opportunity to stay alive and on two working legs is provided when Gary offers the remaining money if they'll help him enact a sado-masochistic fantasy. Deeply disturbingly, it's a fantasy that has its violent roots in Gary's own experience. He has been repeatedly sexually violated by his stepfather, who has anally penetrated him with a knife. Whilst Robbie is prepared to play the role of the dominant sexual predator and have sex with Gary, he refuses to penetrate him with a knife despite the teenage boy begging him to do so. Gary reprimands him: 'I thought you were for real.'

Like some surreal mix of a Ray Winston East End villain and a Zen Buddhist master, Brian rewards the trio for their commercial acumen in raising the money they owe him by the deadline. He gives them back their bag full of £3,000 in used notes, repaying them for their entrepreneurial success. Brian nurtures and expresses his feminine, sensitive side through his completely adoring absorption in the sentimentality of Disney's *The Lion King*. It is for him a parable of family life, filial bonding and moral vales. He is equally consumed by his admiration for the young people who have successfully navigated a journey leading to the appreciation of the power of money and its absolute moral ascendancy in the world.

Ravenhill's use of bitingly funny dialogue is carefully interwoven with a serious-minded treatment of events and characters who are the victims of a world in which, as Brian has Lulu, Mark and Robbie repeat like a Sunday School Christian catechism: 'Money is Civilisation – Civilisation is Money'. Ravenhill's play that has been so completely associated with an eroticised thrill of transgressive shock can be more fully seen as a postmodern parable of a Grimm fabled world where everyone knows the price of everything but the value of nothing. The traumatic impact upon Ravenhill of the premeditated murdering by two pubescent boys of the innocent and vulnerable three-year-old James Bulger in Liverpool brings his play into the terrifying territory of the real and the present. The desolate railway line where a little boy was tortured and killed is more unimaginably horrific – and yet so anonymously urban – than the worst and darkest woods in *Hansel and Gretel*.

Robbie's assertion that 'we all need stories so that we can get by' is more than some simplistic, postmodern mantra. It is more than an equation of story and narrative as being the only secure cultural rendition for individual and communal lives. In a montage world where all constituent cultures and identities amass in some value-free, valueless coalescence, the story is a limited lifebelt. It is nevertheless an undeniably powerful motif within the play, which opens and closes with one told by Mark to Lulu and Robbie. The play's structure has a clear sense of parabolic storyline where, in Mark's final story, the 'buying and selling', 'shopping and fucking' of his opening story is replaced with one in which the sex-slave owner releases his sex-slave commodity.

It is a morally problematic world where the most Utopian freedom imaginable is to forgo the pleasure and gratification of sexual ownership. The violence that underpins Brian's world and the narratives of sexual violence that killed James Bulger and scarred the real equivalents of Gary for life cannot be simply accommodated as the darker textures and colours in postmodern life-as-decoupage.

Some Explicit Polaroids (1999)

Some Explicit Polaroids followed Faust is Dead (1997), Handbag (1998) and Sleeping Around (a co-project with three other writers) (1998) and explores a world in which issues of personal choice, political commitment and activism, and moral and ideological angst define the territory.

At the opening of the play Nick, a former revolutionary Left political activist, has just been released from prison after serving a fifteen-year sentence. This was for an act of near fatal political violence on Jonathan, a venture capitalist who also plays a significant supporting role in this play. Nick arrives at the flat of a former friend and revolutionary Socialist Helen who is now, we discover, a committed Blairite New Labour activist. Far from advocating violent political overthrow of the neo-liberal democratic system, Helen is serving as a local councillor. Her political objectives have migrated from the 'Eat the Rich' violent activism of 1970s 'class war' to trying to secure a reliable bus service for her poverty-stricken constituents on a local housing estate. The play's opening scene skilfully demarcates the personal interwoven with the political. Also it shows the ways in which the optimism of the revolutionary Left in the 1960s and 1970s has now given way to, at best, a community-orientated politics of pragmatic social democracy.

Helen is very hesitant about providing Nick with the temporary shelter and material help that he needs. It is through the character of Nick that Ravenhill offers us the 'viewing frame' into the dislocated world of the play, a world inhabited by Nadia, a lap dancer whose response to being beaten by her boyfriend and to all of life's difficulties is to espouse the banal mantras of Californian 'self-growth' spirituality. Then there is Tim, a gay man who is HIV positive and has purchased (with very definite shades of the 'story game' in *Shopping and Fucking*) a young Russian rent boy, Victor, who seeks any and all of the consumerist 'trash culture' available to him. On the edge of this world is Jonathan, Nick's political nemesis from nearly twenty years previously, who has a seriously expensive cocaine habit. Though a 'respectable' businessman and the epitome of aspirational Thatcherite values and success, Jonathan is nevertheless seeking to blackmail Helen as she tries to further her political career by entering Parliament as a New Labour MP.

Ravenhill's play was inspired by a satirical political fable from earlier in the twentieth century, *Hoppla, wir leben! (Hurrah, We Live!)* (1927) by the German anarchist poet and dramatist Ernst Toller. Toller's play deals with precisely the same kind of political compromise and betrayal that Ravenhill explores in *Some Explicit Polaroids*.

In Toller's play a former revolutionary political activist re-enters the world, only to find that the sacrifices he had made in terms of his political activism including his subsequent loss of liberty have been brutally and cynically betrayed by his former comrades.

These erstwhile revolutionaries have become indistinguishable from the corrupt capitalists and capitalism that they had previously criticised and violently resisted. Toller's play was itself informed by his own traumatic experiences of the radical Left and anarchist political activism. He had been involved and subsequently imprisoned following the 1919 post-First World War 'Munich Uprising'. Like his anti-hero Thomas, Toller also eventually committed suicide.

As with *Shopping and Fucking*, the title of Ravenhill's play carries with it some strong connotations and subtextual resonance. The 'explicit' nature of the Polaroid photograph suggests an eroticised blackmail, whilst the Polaroid camera itself is a means by which private acts may be 'captured' and 'processed' instantaneously. The camera develops and prints the photograph within minutes of its being taken. Crucially this is without the need for any intermediary. The Polaroid denotes a world of closeted, private, transgressive experience. Its ephemeral witnessing is reinforced by the fact that Polaroid photographs are poignantly transient images of the human condition experience. Unlike other conventionally processed photographs, Polaroids fade and discolour relatively quickly. They are therefore a powerful material and aesthetic sign of memory and mortality. This is most potently communicated with considerable pathos in the relationship between Tim and Victor, played out against a kind of contemporary, post-Victorian Gothic melodrama of 'diseased desire' and 'desire-as-death'. With all the wit and cool elegance associated with Ravenhill at his most insightful and engaging he conveys an authentic portrayal of emotional devastation, loss and bereavement. He also explores the contradictions inherent in the possibility of an altruistic love existing in tension with love-as-sexual-gratification. As Victor mourns after Tim has finally died and reappears as a ghost to his former Russian 'toy boy': 'Why do you only say I love you when you feel orgasm coming on?'

Some Explicit Polaroids is a major development of many of the themes and their dialectical counterpoint established by *Shopping and Fucking*. It also demonstrates the emerging maturity of Ravenhill's political and moral sensibility, as well as the continuous fine tuning of his dramatic voice. Whilst he always avoids the easy or sentimental, this play captures for the first time perhaps a deeper connectedness with those darker and harrowing aspects of our humanity. This is especially so in a sense of a profound disorientation and crisis in the navigating of journeys of personal desire and intimacy, but also in the shipwrecked remnants of radical political optimism by the late 1980s and the 1990s. Whilst there is still a strong sense of characters-as-montage, there is nevertheless a growing recognition of those aspects of social and political necessity and individual personal desire and needs, which challenge a style of characterisation that had retained an ironic, schematic detachment up to *Some Explicit Polaroids*.

Mother Clap's Molly House (2002)

This play was first commissioned and presented by the London Academy of Music and Dramatic Art in February 2000 and was then given its professional première at the National Theatre in 2001 directed by Nicholas Hytner. It transferred into the West End at the Aldwych Theatre in 2002. It is a play with songs, the music written by Matthew Scott.

Ravenhill's work finding its way to the National Theatre at that early-to-mid stage in his writing career provided him with a platform and entrepreneurial infrastructure that his work to that date had not received. This is reflected in the epic nature of the piece which, although it borrows from Brecht, nevertheless stays more firmly in the postmodern territory of metropolitan sexual politics. The postmodernity of the piece is expressed both in its characterisation and also, in Act Two, through the cutting and pasting of historical time periods (early to mid-eighteenth century and the opening year of the millennium) within one contemporary London location.

The title of the play is taken from the Molly Houses, effectively gay brothels, of eighteenth-century London where gay men could

meet and entertain and enjoy themselves without fear of prose-
cution for sodomy. 'Molly' was a euphemism for gay male
prostitutes and conveyed a sense of effeminised masculinity that
affronted the dominant moral hypocrisy of the time. Mother Clap
was the colloquialism of Margaret Clap who kept a Molly House
or, in the Old Testament language of the judiciary, a 'Sodomitical
House'. This historical character is transposed into that of
Margaret Tull, widowed by the premature death of her husband
and seeing in the running of her own Molly House a profitable
fusion of libertarian leisure with financial profit.

The play's use of direct-address songs to the audience is clearly
influenced by Brecht and used by Ravenhill to comment upon the
wider themes in the play with humour and satire. The play's
themes include the continuing emerging power of the mercantile
bourgeois class in the later post-Republic period and the stifling
conformity of their social and moral values. With their proto-
capitalist business activities legitimised and sanctified by the
work ethos of Protestant Nonconformism, pleasure – especially
homosexual pleasure – becomes relegated and marginalised to the
far boundaries of public life. In the case of homosexuality, or
sodomy as it was named and condemned, it was beyond even
the remotely acceptable boundaries of moral taste and was
criminalised.

Ravenhill's play seeks to expose the double standards and moral
hypocrisy of that social class and its dominant values and attitudes
by blowing them out of the water with a heady mix of rich
theatricality and vibrant dramatic language. Whilst it undoubtedly
packs a punch, the play has too many targets in its sights and
therefore fails to hit any of them consistently. This results in a
reiteration and repetition of the play's concerns. For example, the
commodification of gay sexuality through the agency of the Molly
Houses is presented as simultaneously and ironically promoting a
provisional liberation for gay men at that time. However, this
seems demonstrated rather than proven. The jump from a rather
simplistic House Heaven of the 1720s to the House music of a gay

sex party in 2001 is insufficiently plotted and supported both by the narratives of history and the play itself. The characters have neither the sculptured, sharp-edged assemblage of Lulu, Mark and others from *Shopping and Fucking* but also lack the more conventionally layered depths of Paul and Susan in the later *The Cut*.

Mother Clap's Molly House works best in Act One with its focus upon the social, cultural and moral context of its historical period. The songs are explosive in their uncompromising assertion of the primacy of sexuality and its expression through same-sex desire and their critique of moral authority and hypocrisy. There are also some cleverly inventive postmodern games of dressing, cross-dressing and a playful exploration of the performance and metaphorical, ideological dressing of sexual identity. However, the attempts to fuse the transgressive and subversive role-playing of that period's gay subculture is not effectively or convincingly welded into Act Two's principally twenty-first-century concerns and perspectives. The play lacks the more dramatically focused ideological definition and counterpoint of *Shopping and Fucking*. It runs the risk of conceding to the surface reality of people and sex as commodities that the earlier play so potently exposed. Margaret Tull, the 'Mother Clap' of the play's title, expresses both some of the unresolved contradictions in the play's treatment of its themes and the sentiments of a postmodern Mother Courage as sex entrepreneur towards the end of the play:

> In't time for them games no more, is it? Old woman Tull – that's her wanting, that is. And I dun't want no more of that foolish bitch no more. And Mother Clap. She's gone too. Goodbye to her. Dun't need me mollies a-skipping and a-fucking around me no more. Good game while it lasted and it filled me purse fit to bursting. So now we can move on. Away from this world. And on to the new. Whatever we are. Just the four of us. (p. 105)

The Cut (2006)

Mark Ravenhill's first major full-length play since 2002, *The Cut*, was originally produced in February 2006 at the Donmar Warehouse, London with Sir Ian McKellen in the central role of Paul. Directed by Michael Grandage, the play is structured along the lines of three consecutive and chronological acts. Through this structure the emotional and psychological subtext of the characters' lives and relationships are explored in the context of a contemporary, non-specific, neo-Fascist state. It is for this regime and its government that Paul, a man in his late middle age, is the senior interrogator and torturer. He administers the fatal 'cut' to known and suspected terrorists: that is, enemies of the regime. The play's title is the final, fatal, punitive action of Paul inserting a scalpel into the still-conscious victim. In Scene One Ravenhill cleverly sets up a dramatic situation in which Paul makes it evidently and progressively clear to his intended victim, the young political activist John (played by Jimmy Akingbola) that he has become afflicted with a disabling and suicidal guilt about his role as torturer and administrator of 'The Cut'. Ravenhill's darkly satirical humour (one *might* say cutting . . .) informs this dramatic predicament in which John desires and demands the incision in equal measure and proportion to Paul's avowed unwillingness to carry out the action. One might say 'transaction' for Ravenhill seems to be exploring with his own forensic clarity the problematic binaries of oppressor and oppressed through this premeditated, sadistic punishment. Required and implemented by the regime, it is also desired as a perverse mark of authentic, political martyrdom by the victim himself. This clearly mirrors the sado-masochistic, psycho-economic transaction of Gary and his 'tormentors' in *Shopping and Fucking* ten years previously. However – and this takes us even more deeply into the complex territory of desire-as-torment or the torment of desire – in *The Cut* it is not only John who is addicted to this sado-masochistic eroticisation of violence but also Paul. He consensually enters a kind of guided fantasy game with John, as did Gary and Robbie in the earlier play. This is after a recent victim of 'The Cut' had tried to kill Paul with a gun that he had smuggled into his office. John leads Paul on this guided 'internal journey' in which:

> **John**   . . . there's no society. All the prisons and the universities have fallen down or been exploded. Or maybe they never were . . . and so there's nothing. Don't fight. Don't try and feel your body . . . because it's all nothing. There's only truth. There's only you. Darkness is light. Void is everything. You are truth. (p. 18)

John concludes his narrative of oblivion-as-freedom by telling Paul that he has a gun pointed at him, ready to kill him. John believes that the imminence of death will help evoke the sense of existential freedom that Paul longs for even as he reveals that he has no gun. When Paul opens his eyes he is devastated with crippling disappointment and disbelief: 'Listen, son, don't fuck around. If there's a gun then have a fucking gun, okay? Okay? Okay?' When John responds to Paul's almost pre-coital frustration about the absence of a gun by observing that the fantasy ending in death is 'not healthy', Paul's explosive response is: 'Healthy? Healthy? Healthy? Fuck you. Fuck you. Sorry. Sorry. Sorry.' Foucault and Freud hover above these dramatic events like the Greek Furies in a tragedy by Aeschylus. They disturb and pervade the air of this intriguing play with an overpowering sense of ideological and moral fatalism. In the immediate aftermath of this sequence Paul pressurises John to confirm his nihilistic, existential philosophical position. John resists. Untroubled, Paul perseveres with thankful appreciation that John has been able to articulate Paul's long-standing fears:

> **Paul**   . . . I admire you. I revere you. To say what's been in my head, what I've never been able to . . . the articulation. Because, as you said, I was afraid and I have been lied to. For generations.
>
> And there in the dark. In the moment. I saw. I'm worthless.
>
> I'm a piece of shit. I'm a speck of shit on a lump of shit on a piece of shit. I'm nothing.

And I don't want to carry on.

And I do have . . .

He produces a gun.

Paul pleads with John to kill him. A problematic dialectic ensues in which they both seek the freedom and release that death will bring. For Paul this would be the ultimate expression of his innate, corrosive self-loathing. For John death is the liberating release consummating his political *raison d'être*. Paul tries to persuade John to accept the regime's offer of release, so that he will not be a culpable witness to Paul's intended suicide. However, it is John who ultimately succeeds in securing his death with an exhausted Paul acknowledging that John has 'broken him'. Scene One ends with Paul thrusting the scalpel into John's willing open body with all of its Freudian homoerotic associations of phallic penetration. John's dying words to his murderer are 'Thank you', which he repeats three times with ritualistic insistence.

The middle bridging Scene Two is deliberately located in Paul's domestic domain of home and wife. Initially home and wife seem to be a reassuring alternative to the deadening, claustrophobic sterility of his public persona and office. Nevertheless, Paul has acknowledged to John in the previous scene that the moral crisis he is struggling to contain made him sexually impotent. This perforation of the domestic and the professional with the private and the public is in the process of detonating like a silent, life-shattering explosion. Paul's sexual and existential impotence is clearly seen to be only one dangerous symptom of a deeper, darker intermarital disaster area.

The domestic activities of preparing and serving food are delegated by Susan, Paul's wife, to a servant, Mina, with a great deal of posturing and patronising commentary on the part of the wife. The social dysfunction of the failure of food being prepared and consumed to time and order is yet another symptom of a profound moral and ideological disease, which permeates the social, political and interpersonal relationships of the play. One is

powerfully reminded of the way in which David Greig explores
and delineates corresponding territory in the relationship between
Leo and Pauline in *The Architect*. One of the defining symptoms of
the times in which we live is presented as the permeation of the
individual and intimate by a corruption that is both public and
ideological. Ideology itself may be in a condition of degenerative
corruption and decay. Whereas Paul is increasingly consumed by
savage and uncontrollable feelings of psychological rage and
despair, Susan's whole modus operandi is to function through a
form of emotional and psychological displacement and distraction.
She recounts an afternoon reverie to Paul, which is significant in
terms of its interiorised domestic setting. This is reinforced
through her impersonal third-person recounting of her husband's
professional activities as with Freudian significance she lies
inactive on their marriage bed:

> **Susan** I try to imagine what you do. I try to picture it. I lie on my
> bed in the dark in the afternoon. And Mina is breaking something.
> She's always breaking something in the next room. And I try to
> block her out. It's better now I've got the pills. And I block her out
> and I try to picture what you're doing. (p. 30)

Paul responds with angry impatience to this quasi-serenity and
passivity in his literal and sexual absence. He sublimates his anger
at his wife's implied criticism and rejection of himself by
denouncing those like her and their student son Stephen as part of
a wider opposition movement to the regime which his professional role embodies:

> **Paul** Writing. Discussions. Just fucking do something. For the
> losers. Take them some clothes. Go through the wardrobe and take
> them some clothes. Bake a fucking fruit cake. Bake a hundred
> fucking fruit cakes and go out to the villages and give out the fruit
> cake. And help instead of lying on the fucking bed in the afternoon.
> (p. 31)

Susan's clinical strategies win through with her premeditated distancing of herself from a husband in the grips of a critical physical and mental breakdown, which she can only look upon with chilling detachment and even contempt. Towards the very end of the scene an existentially disenfranchised and alienated Paul pleads with Susan to spend the night together in the marital bed and 'just lie tighter for a night'. Her response is to re-invoke domestic, dining propriety by enquiring as to whether he has a 'greasy fork': a darkly iconic metaphor of displaced, contaminated phallic sexual potency.

In the third and final scene of the play, having travelled from the interior of Paul's office and his public role through to the domesticated torment of the family home, the location now finally moves to an unspecified room. It immediately transpires that Paul has been arrested and imprisoned by the new opposition government who have overthrown the previous regime. In this scene there are moments of understated and oblique affection on Paul's part towards his revolutionary student son, Stephen, who it is clear has significant status in the new regime. Stephen offers to secure Paul some form of pardon and possible release. His father faces the very serious charges for his former role as interrogator and executor of torture. Paul resists any offer of pardon with the same ferocious intensity that he had earlier sought death. Stephen tells his father that his mother has given evidence at a tribunal alleging that she was unaware of her husband's former role as interrogator and torturer. Paul responds by cynically commending the pragmatism of saving your own life even if this necessitates lies as truth. Stephen refutes his father's implicit judgement of his mother. Paul views his son's defence of his mother as an embodiment of the fatalistic, futile reactionary cycle that he sees crippling any possibility of personal or political change:

Paul So – this is the bright new future. This is the new world. Kids who can't tell the difference between a lie and the truth. Oh son. Oh son, I would weep but there's no more fucking tears. (p. 49)

This powerful play concludes with Paul confirming his refusal of any accommodation or forgiveness by the new regime. Instead he focuses with pathological obsession upon the nature of evil and his own status as a human, individual embodiment of evil: 'I want punishment.'

In my interview with Mark Ravenhill we discussed the ideological and philosophical implications of this notion of 'evil'. It's a term more commonly associated traditionally with religious moral systems. Consequently within the Judaeo-Christian tradition the term evil has carried with it a reactionary connotation of individualised 'sin' or an innate capacity for wrongdoing. In the case of the infamous abduction and murder of James Bulger the tabloid press translates this further into ideas and images of the demonic. *The Cut* is not making such religious pronouncements about any of the play's characters. However, in a modern world that has witnessed the mass extermination of six million Jews by the Nazis, profound questions about the human capacity for violence and premeditated cruelty remain unanswered. The more recent neo-Fascist Serbian ethnic cleansing of the Bosnian Muslim population and their instituting of rape camps where Muslim women were brutally violated (which Sarah Kane wrote of in *Blasted* and *Cleansed*) reinforces the question: does the traditional use of evil with supernatural connotations adequately describe such depraved human barbarity?

Despite Stephen's final attempts to persuade his father that a suitable confession to the Orwellian-named 'Ministry of Forgiveness' would secure his release and freedom, Paul reconfirms his earthed, world-weary stoicism:

Paul It always happens. Sooner or later. Sooner or later when the forgiveness is done there'll be scourging again and I'll be here. I'll be ready for it. It's what I deserve. I'm evil. (p. 52)

This sense of predestined inevitability runs through the play like an indelible bloodstain and takes Ravenhill's work further into the challenging territory pre-dated in the thematic seeds of earlier plays such as *Shopping and Fucking* and especially *Some Explicit Polaroids*. What distinguishes *The Cut* from the earlier work is Ravenhill's construction of dramatic character and also a significant change to a more conventional, less episodic Ibsenesque dramatic narrative structure. In those early plays there was a postmodern montage and assemblage about character, narrative and settings. In *The Cut* Ravenhill recognises the need for an alternative form of dramaturgy and idiomatic language to accommodate the evolving and more complex issues that he is addressing. The major London critics were mixed in their response to the play at its première. It's fair to say that all were united in their praise for Ian McKellen's excellent virtuoso performance as Paul and Michael Grandage's tense and atmospheric production. Both helped to draw out and consolidate the latent thematic gravity of the piece. Interestingly, both Michael Billington in the *Guardian* (1 March 2006) and Charles Spencer in the *Daily Telegraph* (9 March 2006) identified their view of the influences upon Ravenhill in writing the play. Billington opened his three-out-of-five-star review with a rather dismissive 'it tells you more about what Ravenhill has been reading, rather than actually experiencing'. Spencer was even more bitingly dyspeptic in opening his review with 'Mark Ravenhill's play is so up to its ears in debt to Harold Pinter that I'm not sure whether the Nobel Laureate should be merely flattered or demanding a slice of the royalties'. Nicholas de Jongh in the London *Evening Standard* (1 March 2006) was particularly vituperative, regretting the passing of Ravenhill's *Shopping and Fucking*, which he rather condescendingly remembers as 'sharp, specific and shocking' in contrast to the new play, dismissed as 'soft-edged, vague and obscure'. It's most interesting not only in relation to Ravenhill's work but also wider concerns within this book and contemporary British theatre that Billington concluded his review with the request:

> But, at a time when state power is increasing in specific, well-charted ways, Ravenhill's play offers us symbolic generalities.

What one craves is a modern Brecht who deals with living, correctable injustices. (p. 36)

I don't agree that Ravenhill only offers 'symbolic generalities' and neither can I share his interpretation and evaluation of Brecht's theatre as offering 'correctable injustices'. Brecht, after all, protected his own professional interests and personal safety in supporting the brutal suppression of a workers' uprising by the East German Stalinist authorities that simultaneously financed and sponsored his Berliner Ensemble. What is important is the question of what defines theatre as 'political' in terms of the interplay between dramatic form, aesthetics and ideological intention. This is especially important in the post-Soviet, post-Marxist landscape and the crisis facing Socialist thinking, which David Edgar so expertly explores in his play *Maydays*. *The Cut* by implication examines this political and ideological dilemma from a position of bleak, cynical pessimism, which has been previously rehearsed, it's true. I also believe that the play yields and reveals rich veins of a new stage in the evolution of his dramatic voice.

This evolution in Ravenhill's work is further evident in his short one-man piece (in which he performs the sole male speaking character) *Product*, which had premièred at the Traverse Theatre at the Edinburgh Festival in August 2005, directed by Lucy Morrison. I was able to see that production's revival at the Theatre Upstairs, Royal Court in May 2006.

Product (2005–06)

Product is a savagely funny satire on both Hollywood and the politics of popular media representation seeking to define and control our perception of both ourselves and others. When that 'otherness' is both Islam and Islamic terrorists in a post-9/11 world, the implications in perceiving that religious belief system and its fundamentalist versions are serious indeed.

Ravenhill employs his undoubted skills as a satirist with a facility for biting humour to full effect. There are two characters in the play: James, a film producer, and Olivia, an actress. The narrative thrust of the piece is James making a pitch in more senses than one of a film script to the actress. Her incentive to hang on to his every clichéd word is the promise of that film's female lead.

There is a camp sensibility about James and his personal style and language register where the proposed male lead is referred as 'a tall dusky man'. This takes us straight into the world of airport lounge 'Mills and Boon' romances or the soft-edged pornography of the 'Black Lace' series of erotic novels marketed at a post-feminist female readership. This 'tall dusky man' whom our heroine Amy meets on a plane on an air journey to London falls asleep with his handsome head on her stereotypically pretty shoulder. Ravenhill imbues this moment in the narrative with gloriously self-knowing, ironic Freudian symbolism. Amy has noticed the stranger's knife is in the pouch in front of them and she fantasises about bringing the knife down into his sleeping body with the melodramatic, mini-series rhetoric of 'This is for the Towers. This is for Civilisation. This is for all of us, you bastard.' Ravenhill's clinically witty edge glints again when James reassures Olivia through a stingingly barbed critique of every Method director everywhere by emphasising that this fantasy is an 'interior monologue' which she must play with her eyes. This vapid directorial note is laced with a further camp nod to Freud when James goes on to describe the character of Amy as not only wounded but being 'the wound'. The action continues with James articulating a mix of Californian psychobabble with the clichéd characters and dialogue of populist Hollywood or USA TV romantic melodramas.

Amy, who opens call centres around the world, is to have the most fantastic sexual relationship with the 'dusky man' who she and we discover is called Mohammed. We discover that Amy has a predictably emotionally loaded past in that Troy (not McClure, you may remember him?) her former lover was a victim of the aerial suicide-bombing of the Twin Towers. The sexually experienced Amy seduces the virginal Mohammed and in the worst traditions of tabloid romantic schlock she awakes in the cold light of dawn. In the predictable clichés of this genre she fears that she has been cheapened and used as a 'one-night stand', only to discover that her hero has not abandoned her but is mysteriously there with his knife and prayer mat. Mohammed remains with her as her lover in her ultra-fashionable loft conversion which with pop-Gothic symbolism had been formerly an abattoir. Other dusky-skinned men begin to arrive. Amy realises with mounting panic that Mohammed is part of a fundamentalist terror group, yet she can't resist him because, as James helpfully observes, 'The Heart is a bigger organ than the Brain, as we say in this business we call show.'

Mark Ravenhill's script scores very highly in terms of its consistently funny, satirically provocative evocation of a capitalist commercial media culture where the shakers and movers are as superficial as the mass consumable cultural products they end-lessly construct. The ice-cool subtext of the play's title com-municates that these fictional characters are themselves products and commodities. The play has a surreal sense of chaotic, postmodern assemblage and collision in terms of the hilarious roller-coaster ride of narrative events.

This trans-global and trans-cultural mix accommodates the outrageous entry of Osama bin Laden. He places a kiss upon our heroine's forehead ordaining her collusion with these 'men of evil'. Driven to want to share the suicidal terrorist death of her beloved Mohammed, Amy pleads to be incorporated into the terrorist cell of which he is the leading activist. Thus follows a wickedly funny nightmare sequence in which she fantasises about being strapped with explosives and entering Disneyworld Europe. With a clever fusion of the pop-Gothic and excruciatingly formulaic sentimentality, Amy's nightmare ends with

> Boom! From your back and your sex the force comes, the explosive comes, and in your last moment of your life that child's head, now ripped from its body, and the blood filling your eyes, that child's

head is blown towards you and her voice fills your head as you die: 'Maman.'

Ravenhill's play is a very accomplished and assured comedy that has some very serious targets in its sights. The inventive dramatic device of focusing the piece entirely in terms of the recounting of a potential film script doubly emphasises its fictional artificiality. This is not only of the preposterous film script but also, by implication, of the characters of James and Olivia. The political punch really lands with Ravenhill exposing the prevailing reductive stereotypes of Islamic terrorists within the context of a dominant popular cultural product, which is the Hollywood romance adventure. The audience is actively challenged to consider the means by which the technologically sophisticated media apparatus of our contemporary world acts as a kind of distorting Hall of Mirrors at the fairground.

Given the dangerous times in which we live and the terrorist atrocities of Manhattan, Madrid, London and Baghdad, there is a critical imperative to try to find and establish means of engaging and communicating with the broader Islamic world and communities. What *Product* also does is to expose the underlying ideological, political and cultural values that inform and define the mass global film and television product and its dissemination. *Shopping and Fucking* has transmigrated into 'Bombing and Fucking' in a world that continues to confirm Brian's enduring belief that 'Money is Civilisation – Civilisation is Money'. Equally significant in a play called *Product* is the fact that Iraq has some of the world's largest reserves of the twenty-first century's most desperately desired product – oil.

Citizenship (2004)

Citizenship was commissioned as one of ten new plays by contemporary dramatists to be written especially for both young performers and also young audiences. This young people's theatre scheme is called 'Connections' and is sponsored by Shell Oil in conjunction with both the National Theatre but also various professional theatre venues around the country. Schools, colleges and Youth Theatre are invited to workshop and perform one of the ten plays with a major workshop treatment of the plays at selected regional professional venues ranging from Plymouth Theatre Royal through to the Brewery Arts Centre in Kendal. Adjudications are made at each of the regional venues before culminating at the National Theatre where each of the ten plays is produced by those selected groups from the regional presentations. In addition, a smaller selection of the plays is then given a full professional production. This was the case with *Citizenship*, which I saw on its revival at the Cottesloe Theatre on the South Bank in the summer of 2006. It is due to be revived once again into the National Theatre's repertoire in either autumn 2007 or spring 2008.

From the mid-1990s onwards and most especially in this first decade of the twenty-first century 'citizenship', like 'community' which slightly pre-dates it, has become a buzzword in discussions located in the areas of youth culture, cultural and ethnic diversity. With proposed initiatives such as a new Public Bank Holiday called 'British Day', citizenship relocates itself more problematically in the wider forum about asylum seekers, economic migrants and concepts of national identity. Not surprisingly, these discourses exist in close relation to equal opportunities regarding issues of sexual orientation and gender within education and the workplace. In *Citizenship* Mark Ravenhill once again uses humour and a television-soap-opera-style dramatic format in which we meet a varied cast of characters consisting mostly of older teenagers and their teachers. The central character is Tom, a young friendly guy who is suffering the pains of growing up into adulthood. This rite of passage is complicated for him yet further by a recurring dream in which he is being kissed by a stranger. This mildly erotic fantasy is made more worrying for Tom in that he cannot be sure whether the stranger is female or male.

There has undoubtedly been considerable progress made in terms of positive and progressive legislation regarding gay men and lesbian women although lesbianism, unlike male homo-sexuality, was never a criminal offence. Most recently (2006) the government's introduction of civil partnerships giving same-sex couples equivalent legal rights with heterosexual (straight) married couples was a major achievement.

One of the play's central themes and concerns is the potential chasm between this important if overdue inscription of legal equalisation set against the actual attitudes, fears and prejudices of ordinary people regarding gay men and lesbian women. Of course, popular television and radio dramas, starting with *EastEnders* but more recently *The Archers* and *Emmerdale,* have all sought to play their part in demystifying prejudiced assumptions about homo-sexuality. Nevertheless, Tom feels anxious and unsure about what his dream means and more crucially what it means to be Tom.

Citizenship as a subject area has become a compulsory part of the National Curriculum and has replaced what in earlier decades was called Personal and Social Education (PSE). It is to his Citizenship teacher, Mr De Clerk, that Tom goes for advice. The scene is charged with a subtextual power of undefined feelings, needs and desire. It is also painfully funny. In the opening scene of the play, Tom has undergone an unsuccessful attempt to have his ear pierced with a cocktail of powerful painkillers as anaesthetic as his friend Amy does the task as a favour to him. His ear has bled over his piece of coursework for Mr De Clerk, who is under the considerable pressure and stress of having to show the class's work to visiting inspectors the following day. Tom, his ear still in a rough and unhygienic bandage, has been called in by his teacher to rewrite the piece of work and the two are alone after school has finished for the day. It becomes clear that it is not only because De Clerk is his Citizenship teacher that Tom hopes he may get some crucial advice and help. Tom suspects, almost certainly correctly although the play interestingly never confirms this, that his teacher is gay. Who else could be in a unique position to help Tom in his adolescent crisis of identity? As the teacher allows himself to admit his levels of stress and overwork to his teenage pupil, Tom offers and administers a shoulder and neck massage. Realising the potential proximity of other feelings being expressed through the social transgression of teacher–pupil contact, De Clerk brings the incident to a close. This is not before Tom has inadvertently managed to drip blood on to his teacher's designer shirt. Along with the humour that runs through the scene, there is an equally powerful resonance and pathos. This humour centres upon the paradox that despite De Clerk almost certainly being gay and that Citizenship as a subject promotes liberal-mindedness and the promotion of diversity and self-esteem, the issue most close to Tom's heart cannot be named or discussed:

Tom Sir . . . I keep on having this dream and in this dream I'm being kissed.
De Clerk Don't.
Tom Only I never know whether it's a man or woman who's doing the kissing.
De Clerk This isn't Biology, I'm Citizenship.
Tom I think I dream about being kissed by a man.
De Clerk I don't want to know about that. (p. 232)

Deciding that proactive action might resolve his dilemma, Tom makes a pass at Amy who is troubled and unsure herself, with a difficult home background. She accepts his advances as she also accepts Tom's honest admission that it's not she who appears in his dreams. There then follows a rather surreal moment when De Clerk appears in a stylised 'interior scene' in Tom's mind. In this alternative world of Tom's imagination, De Clerk is able to try to give Tom some advice and reassurance in a world of worrying choices and stresses, not least in an over-bureaucratised, pressurised school system.

Ravenhill may be acknowledging as a forty-something that the tensions between a traditional, prescriptive 'do what you're told' approach to personal choice might seem preferable for Tom to the apparent open-ended, person-centred choices of Citizenship.

Ravenhill is very sceptical of a contemporary liberal rhetoric which asserts that if a 'politically correct' vocabulary is used in public discourse, this somehow guarantees tolerance and open-mindedness. The confusion that this can induce for someone like Tom in *Citizenship* is disturbing at worst and unhelpful at best. Tom's journey of self-discovery does not end either easily or with a simplistic resolution. He endures a whirlwind ride of Amy having a baby after their initial sexual encounter. As complicatedly, Tom then finally meets a twenty-two-year-old gay man, Martin, via an Internet chatroom. The two enjoy a brief relationship although it still does not provide Tom with the answers and emotional security that he needs.

Ravenhill's play certainly presents a unique opportunity for those schools, colleges, or youth theatre groups with the commitment and courage to produce it or take a group to see it in performance. Whilst it's not exactly a campaigning or propagandist play, it does work most effectively for its young audience in terms of its intrinsic qualities of uncompromising honesty, robust integrity and unpretentious humour.

Pool (No Water) (2006)

Mark Ravenhill's unlikely collaboration with the Physical Theatre Company Frantic Assembly resulted in *Pool (No Water)*, which was a joint production between the Plymouth Theatre Royal, Liverpool Everyman and Lyric Hammersmith London. I saw this production whilst it was on tour at the Point, Eastleigh, in November 2006.

Ravenhill wrote a very interesting article for the *Guardian* ('In at the deep end', 20 September 2006) in which he described and discussed the challenge and creative processes of working in a way that was entirely new to him both in process and genre. This collaboration with Frantic Assembly was defined in terms of a performance piece which was not solely text-driven but necessitated the fusion and interplay of the language of movement and the body with the language of the spoken word. This of course becomes of even greater and ongoing relevance in the work of Tim Etchells and the avant-garde experimental theatre company Forced Entertainment, and also to David Greig's work with Suspect Culture. However, there is a significant difference between the Ravenhill–Frantic Assembly collaboration and the work of Etchells with Forced Entertainment. Forced Entertainment's creative approach in their devising, improvising methodology is to the making of work in which the spoken, written text emerges organically out of a wider process of trying out, sampling and mixing-editing. It is a process to which they have always been committed and have worked within for twenty years. Etchells's writing is not methodologically or ideologically 'privileged' in terms of the overall process of creating their work. Mark Ravenhill observed amongst other useful insights in his article that Scott Graham and Steven Hoggett (co-founders of the original Frantic Assembly in Swansea back in the early 1990s) 'operated as a unit . . . they often finish each other's sentences. Coming from the often lonely territory of the playwright's desk, I was deeply envious of this.' There are a number of issues that arise from this kind of collaboration and the frequent sibling rivalry that can break out between spoken/written language and physical, somatic language.

One which I felt quite keenly when I saw the show in November 2006 was that the narrative structure and delivery rested exclusively upon first-person address to the audience, which inevitably neutralises the dramatic textual possibilities of interplay and interchange. This also leads into the potentially dangerous territory of 'telling the story', rather than creating a piece of theatre which both characters and, crucially, audience can explore. If one is constantly being told as an audience what characters are thinking or what they are going to do next, or why they have done what they have done, it can invoke an effective redundancy in terms of shared interpretation. There were extended sequences within *Pool (No Water)* where the piece teetered and sometimes fell into this particular pool. This felt emptied not of water but of those elusive spaces in which diverse forms of reception and interpretation of meaning can take place. There is also another risk in this genre of work. As Ravenhill puts it himself in his *Guardian* article, 'I've never been a huge fan of physical theatre. Often the physical bit isn't as exciting as sport or dance, and the theatre bit isn't as substantial as a good play.' Certainly for me the best and most impressive parts of the show, which I nevertheless felt was more interesting and engaging than its London reviewers allowed, were when the two contrasting languages of movement and text spoke either simultaneously, or better still, in atonal counterpoint to each other. There were certainly sequences of movement that were quite breathtaking in their concept and execution. These sequences powerfully conveyed the emotional tumult experienced by the four characters in their tangled narratives of bruised egos, corrosive jealousies and destructive self-doubts. Imogen Heap's atmospheric soundtrack also contributed to an overall mood of darkness at the bottom of a pool where there was no water to catch even the faintest of illuminating sunlight on the surface.

Ravenhill had engaged in an initial creative workshop with Steve, Scott and three performers some eighteen months prior to the première of the final piece. He was unhappy at the end product of his own creative contribution as writer and had approached the two co-founders with an invitation for them to identify themes or material that were of creative stimulus to them. This proved to be a significant turning point. Their response lay principally in identifying the photographs of the counter-cultural American photographer Nan Goldin, who specialises in photographic portraits of the shop-soiled undertow of C-list celebrity culture of faded bohemia and drug-addicted excess.

A narrative began to emerge for Ravenhill and his collaborators of a parallel world of sub-Hollywood kitsch in which an infamous avant-garde artist holds a midnight party of multi-sexual, drug-fuelled, hedonistic celebration as a kind of reunion for three of her former co-artists. It is to be a poolside party with nearly fatal conse-quences as it is a pool with no water. The host falls backwards into it, suffering the most terrible life-threatening injuries. It is only in the context of her imminent death and a strange subtext shared by the three other characters of shared guilt for this personal tragedy that the audience realise that it is not friendship or admiration that has brought them to the mansion that evening. Rather, her lying on life support in the hospital provokes them to reveal through the means of direct-address monologues their savage jealousy and bitter hatred for this woman and her success. They are failed accomplices in a world of posturing postmodern experimental life-as-digitalised-alienated-art. In this world motives of financial gain and transient celebrity fame are barely disguised by working on 'worthy' politically correct projects such as murals for HIV/AIDS wards and hospices. As these characters await their former mentor's imminent death with a growing sense of transgressive, orgasmic fulfilment, they steadily realise that they can at last achieve the celebrity status they crave. Experimental, taboo-breaking art notoriety awaits them by filming her seemingly inevitable slide into death. This necrophilia-as-revenge involves their premeditated humiliation of her prone, unconscious body through the simulation of oral sex and other eroticised acts of degradation whilst filming it on their mobile phone and digital cameras. This will be 'art as life' which would make even Andy Warhol's multi-screen 'Marilyn' and 'Elvis' prints seem as staid and dated as the sentimental landscapes by the popular Victorian painter Landseer.

Their fantasies of fame and fortune are destroyed when against all the medical odds their victim in more than one sense recovers and returns to haunt and sentence them to the mediocrities of ordinary life.

Mark Ravenhill's initial reputation as a dramatist owed much, of course, to the notoriety of his entry into the public consciousness with *Shopping and Fucking*. It's important not to locate him solely and in perpetuity with a play that is now, after all, eleven years distant. Even then, it was always so much more than the problematic, eroticised thrill of the play's scene of violent anal rape. Ravenhill has shown himself to be more than willing to explore different theatrical forms and opportunities as his recent work has shown, including his first foray into pantomime. The remainder of this decade will be of great interest and significance as Mark Ravenhill enters his fourth decade if not in comfortable tartan-check slippers, then relinquishing the baseball cap with its *Enfant Terrible* brand name emblazoned upon it. It probably felt passé to him anyway.

Mark Ravenhill's dramatic voice is distinctive and unmistakable, particularly in the earlier work but also still evident in more recent plays such as *Citizenship* and *Product. The Cut* also signifies new generic and stylistic territory for him and possibly a deepening pessimism or problematic realism. He is a writer whose work is often infused with a provocative charm alongside a razor-sharp creative intelligence. There is an urgent, questioning moral sensibility about his writing that will not accept or tolerate cliché, soundbites or easy answers. This, along with a wicked sense of cutting-edge humour, looks to continue to evolve into a still more vibrant, dark-edged, satirical dramatic voice in the years to come. We should all hope so.

DOWNLOADS
- For a fusion of dark comedy, satire and social comment dealing with sexuality and sexual politics, try the plays of one of the major playwrights of the 1960s, Joe Orton.
- For a fusion of dark politicised themes with a deeply personal, pathological sensibility, try the plays of a major contemporary dramatist of the 1990s, Sarah Kane.
- For one of the major British playwrights of the post-war period and twentieth century, whom Ravenhill acknowledges as a profoundly respected influence, try the plays of Edward Bond – especially *The Sea* (a dark, biting comedy of social hypocrisy) and *The Worlds* (a powerful, darkly funny critique of corruption and hypocrisy in politics and business). Try also early classics by Bond such as *Saved* (in which a baby is stoned to death in a south London park).

5 TIM ETCHELLS AND FORCED ENTERTAINMENT

SHORT CUT

- Innovative, ground-breaking new experimental performance.
- Fusion of writer, writer's text and performance text emerging from long, extended collaboration, improvisation and devising process.
- See their excellent website on www.forcedentertainment. com

PERFORMANCES
(Bold titles are works discussed in the critical essay)
Jessica in the Room of Light 1984
(Let the Water Run Its Course) to the Sea that Made the Promise 1986
200% and Bloody Thirsty 1987–88
Some Confusions in the Law about Love 1989–90
Marina and Lee 1991
Emmanuelle Enchanted 1992
Club of No Regrets 1993
Hidden J 1994
Nights in This City 1995
Speak Bitterness 1995
Showtime 1996
Pleasure 1997
Dirty Work 1998
Disco Relax 1999
And on the Thousandth Night 2000
First Night 2001
Bloody Mess 2004
The World in Pictures 2006

Interview with Tim Etchells of Forced Entertainment

This is an edited transcript of an interview that took place at the offices of Forced Entertainment and the Showroom Cinema Sheffield in August 2006.

PB   I wonder, Tim, whether you could talk about some of the reference points and influences if you like that help to define the work of Forced Entertainment and also, by implication, your own writing?

TE   Sure, I suppose more than anything, my feelings about that is that as a group of people our first reference points are basically not the literary theatre – our first reference points are cinema, performance art, experimental theatre, music culture, trashy television, science fiction. Yes, there were some early influences upon our work, performance groups like Station House Opera, Impact, the Wooster Group, but pretty quickly from my not very well prepared list there's William Burroughs, there's the Fall, there's Mark E. Smith. If I was to try and identify current influences, well, there are some people who are working at the edges of dance, performance art, some people who are working at the very edge of theatre itself but I mean our range of reference points is quite wide and not in the direction of mainstream theatre. It's not really anything against mainstream theatre, it's just that we come from a different place. What feeds into our work is the way that we approach an hour and a half on the stage and that is not really with reference to the same things that one imagines the regular theatre writers and audiences are thinking about. To me that's healthy – it's not necessarily even an actual position; it's more perhaps a matter of taste. When we come to that space we bring a whole load of stuff that has nothing to do with that more mainstream theatre – that seems fine to me.

PB   As a writer, what kinds of challenges has working with a company like Forced Entertainment presented you with?

TE   Well, I think that's interesting. I see myself as a writer as very much part of the company's work and that can mean a lot of very different things for some projects. Historically within the company's work it's meant very different things and I think that's how I see it. As far as the company's concerned I'm not a writer who's sitting at home writing these things and then handing them over to a bunch of people and saying: so this, where it says that comma, don't forget it, I really need that comma, and where I say pause, again don't forget that, it's very important. Where it says so-and-so does this or that, make sure you don't forget. My writing as such is part of the messy group process which in a way has been going on for twenty years and being a writer over that period of time has meant that 'writer' has meant very different things.

I suppose the difference between me as a writer and writers who might work in different – more conventional – ways for the theatre is that I accept and actually embrace what it means to be a part of six, seven, eight, nine or ten other people who are working together on the project. I think fundamentally the big kind of important thing is that I work as a writer in the way that Richard [Lowdon] works as a designer in that we're all in a room trying to make something. We don't really know what we're trying to make and I'll pitch in some ideas, some text – it might be a paragraph, it might be a page – it might just be me running on to the stage and whispering into someone's ear 'Talk about blah – blah – blah' and very often these days that's what it is. Depending on the project, I try to write quite little in that sense and we work an awful lot with improvisation and a lot of it will involve me shouting 'Do this, say that' and we also work with a lot of transcripts of videotapes.

PB   How does the editorial process of developing performance work in that kind of environment?

TE   It's very much a group process. Everybody creates material, everybody discusses and critiques material, everybody watches back the videos and says 'That's really funny' or 'That's rubbish' or 'That's great' or 'That's not great' or 'That could be better if it were developed'. Then I have some slightly different role in that, in that nine point nine times out of ten I'm not on the stage. I'm watching and therefore I have a different perspective, an overview, if you like, which lets me have an opportunity to see it in a way that they can't see it because they're in it. Therefore, because of that I get to make some editorial decisions that they can't make although because we work a lot with a video camera everyone gets their two pennyworth to make a comment. Structural decisions are ultimately made by everybody: we all sit around and will decide those together, and we all run round and round in circles for months. That's very much how our process tends to work.

PB How long do you have in terms of rehearsal process compared to more conventional 'literary text'-based theatre where there's a very clear sense of how long you have to rehearse that pre-existing text into performance? If you're lucky I suppose the RSC – I suppose that's lucky – probably gets six or even eight weeks. How long are you able to fund yourselves through that making, devising, exploring and rehearsal process?

TE Five months.

(*They both laugh.*)

PB (*laughs*) This is without eating?

TE No, we . . . Most of the big pieces take five months or so to make, maybe longer, and oftentimes we'll do a couple of months' work on something and then we'll leave it alone. Simultaneously, we'll tour something old and then we'll come back to it and spend another month on it and then we'll leave it alone and then come back to it. Then we'll maybe do two months running up to the première and maybe in that early period we'll have done some work in progress. So as you can see, the process is very drawn out: normally over the period of a year, maybe longer. However, the actual rehearsal period in that time will be five or six months and basically in order to do that, we have an amount of money in the UK but in order to do those projects we have to bring in co-producers from Europe and elsewhere who put money into the production process. Otherwise we couldn't afford to do the work in that way, but to be honest with you, even when we *hadn't* got any money, we used to spend five or six months making the work and we were all on the dole or on various Thatcherite schemes designed to get the dole figures down. In the end, of course, we understood that to make this kind of work that we want to make, we all need to be in the room together for a long, long time. Therefore, when I say that we took five or six months I mean – if I talked to any of the artists working in theatre, performance or dance that I am interested in – that's what they do. Internationally that's the kind of timescale that people are talking about, if not longer. That's because basically what we do is born out of being in the studio together and trying things, it's not normally born out of someone sitting down at the computer and writing things. So the writing therefore is something in a way that gets done by everybody in the studio, trying things, maybe reading fragments of text, maybe improvising, but you know it's a hands-on, 'everybody-needs-to-be-there' kind of process and inevitably it takes a long time.

PB   I mean in a lot of the work, going right back to the very early shows, there are those very powerful moments where there is this sense of the reality of the performer in the space with the audience. It's a kind of two-way process between the performer and the audience with that marvellous sense of: 'Look, there's nothing up our sleeves – here we all are.' There are those moments when I think almost a kind of invisible boundary between – I don't know, let's call it 'the real' – and let's call it 'the performed' or 'of play' that seems to be such a strong characteristic of the company's work. Do you think that the making process that you've just described is what makes that sense of 'transgressing that boundary' in the work possible?

TE   Yes, I think so – that's right. I suppose we're very interested in the work in playing this boundary between real and not real, between pretended and just happening, between the deliberately staged and the accidental. This is 'the accidental' in a way that always wants to seem like it's just happening now, for the very first time, and I suppose we've gone about that in two ways. We've made pieces like *Quizoola* or *And on the Thousandth Night* or where there's a structure but within that, live, there's a genuine improvisation going on. Therefore, it really *is* like it's never happened before and the reality of that manifests itself in all kinds of ways that you can't necessarily explain or control. However, it's very clear that this is something that is really happening now in a certain way and it's not 'a winter's night five hundred years ago' or 'two thousand years in the future' but it's now, now, this thing is happening *now*.

By contrast then in other work, in the theatre work, in something like *Bloody Mess*, or in *Club of No Regrets*, oftentimes in those, what we've done is a lot of studio improvisation, a lot of fooling around in the rehearsal room. After that we've then gone back over the videotapes and rigorously scripted and controlled that material to make it look like it's just happening now, like it's some kind of 'crazed accident' or some kind of escalating 'tit-for-tat improvisation' or 'call and response' between two performers. However, actually what you've done is that you've sat down and literally notated everything you've transcribed: a lot of text, you've edited it, you've tweaked it around. This comes to the point where on a good night *Bloody Mess*, for example, feels like everything is falling into place. It doesn't look very deliberate – it looks like a mess – that this mess however is very tightly controlled and I think we like that because it kind of creates this sense of life now, real, even though of course everything we're doing is incredibly precise, strategic and deliberate.

PB Sometimes it feels like life or lives hurtling through space in a rather scary dangerous way?

TE I think that's also interesting because we work within a context, whereas performers who've been improving together for over twenty years, they take risks: they do things. They take themselves to places either deliberately or accidentally that are very profoundly connected to them – even if they are being silly or whatever. There's actually a quite deep-rooted connection between them, which again I think does contribute to this sense of blurring between the pretended and the so-called real. This kind of 'edge playing' between those two things is important to us and it's heightened in quite a few of the more recent performances [for example, *Bloody Mess*] where the performers use their own names and are often addressed by name and speak to the audience as if they were just standing there speaking to them. But of course, within that we're very carefully messing with that and fictionalising it – it's always a fiction – but it has this sense of a fiction that is quite intimately glued to or stuck to the people who are doing these things. There's 'acting' in what we do, there's 'fiction' in what we do and then drifting to the other end of the scale, there's this 'connection to performance'. It's the artists themselves who are on the stage doing these things, we approach it often in this 'workmanlike-task' kind of way and so I think, yes, we're very interested in the blurring of the real and the pretended.

PB   I was particularly taken by some of the recent work that I've been viewing and especially *Dirty Work*, which I think is an extraordinary piece and one of the things that really arrested me about it is a kind of formalism. But it's a formalism that allows for questions about acting in a space and the use of the makeshift curtains, the lamps at the front of the stage and a deliberately sort of halfway-to-declamatory style of performance and it seems to me that, through all those ingredients, you then enter into something that is very moving and poetic.

TE   There's two things. One of the things that we often do in our work is that we quote and we sample a lot of traditional or known theatre or performance apparatus. So therefore you get a lot of the pieces in which there'll be a little stage on the stage, there's some pathetic little curtains, there's some footlights made of some old industrial lights – you know, quite shabby attempts to delineate theatre itself, performance itself. It's then within this ruin of what theatre *could* be that we try to start and do something. The other way is, you know, when we were talking earlier about going around or above or through theatre, the other metaphor that we like is the quote from Baudrillard: 'The child's first relation to its toy is: how can I break it?' I think we have this similar sort of relationship to theatre. What happens if we pick this thing up, throw it away or sweep it up and put this thing in the bath? What will happen? And I think often the work invokes this idea of a rather shabby situation where theatre is finished, broken and you're picking it up and prodding it to see what can remain, what can be done with this . . .

PB . . . with this sense of very limited rather third-rate performers and materials . . .

TE . . . absolutely, yes . . .

PB . . . and also that these two performers are placed in 'quotation marks' and are performing in that very dated declamatory way.

TE Yes, that's right and I guess that the other thing to say is that, as I was saying before, our interests are very largely outside the theatre. However, it's very interesting to me that when we *do* look towards theatre, the things that we look to are often outmoded or discredited forms: pantomime, children's performance, vaudeville, cabaret, maybe stand-up. Then in something like *Bloody Mess* there are other modes of performance – the heavy metal gig, the cheerleader, the gorilla who seems to be a refugee from the pantomime, two clowns from some circus that's been shut down, so it's like the stuff that we grab hold of – it's not the literary theatre, it's actually of this finished-with, quite worn-out, quite discredited, lowbrow trash and that's the kind of stuff that we're excited about. That's what we want to pick up and see if we can play with it and wonder whether maybe we can make something happen.

PB Yes, that's right but there is also that sense in *Dirty Work* and then if we went back to early work like *Club of No Regrets* and more recently *Disco Relax* there is that strong feel of detritus, isn't there, of a kind of shitty world and this is all that we've got and what can we make of it?

TE That's two things on a kind of level of cultural politics that's like saying that there you are, you're sifting through this stuff that went before, you're trying to find something that might still speak – that you can do something with and create work through. You're 'quoting', you're breaking up things from the past and trying to do something with it, like it's not an original. There's no 'authentic voice', there's no masterwork arising out of anybody's soul, it's all quotation, it's all fragments and then on another level it's very like children's play. It's the dressing-up box, it's picking up stuff, it's taking something from a film that you saw yesterday on the flight and cobbling it together with something from a book that you've read or the story that somebody told you. Or, what you could do with this branch, if you like, hit your mate over the head with it? It's quite disrespectful of its own sources. So there are two ways of looking at that process but absolutely it's often just about us and a bunch of material that just happened to be there.

PB   I did feel that *Dirty Work* was a kind of elegy not only for the redundancy of those pre-existing historical forms of theatre to actually say anything to us in the contemporary world – it just felt to me like the most moving kind of elegy for Europe and the world?

TE   Yes, what interests me about it on the level of language is that I think there are really two major thrusts to the ways in which we've approached language over the last five or six years. One of them – you can trace it back further in the work – is the idea of or the fact of language as a means of summoning things into the room: the way that language makes images or events happen. Of course, Shakespeare has this thing about, for example, imagining the horses at the battle of Agincourt. The theatre has a problem because, of course, even when the stage is big, it's still small. I mean, you can't have a nuclear explosion on it, you can drive a car up to it but you can't drive a tank. In that sense it's empty in terms of what the cinema can offer and do, and I think what *Dirty Work* does is say, yes, theatre is rubbish, it can't really do anything. However, what we can do is sit here and describe this thing which has all the pompous and ridiculous ambition to bring the whole world in all its glory and all its comedy on to this stage.

So therefore it becomes something of a competition between Robin and Cathy [the two performers in *Dirty Work*]. Robin's first line is that Act One begins with five great nuclear explosions and of course in *Dirty Work* one of the things we're banging on about is the redundancy of theatre. You can't do it and then on the other hand, we're playing this rather beautiful game which is, if Robin and Cathy can keep this up and the piece sticks to its guns and doesn't do anything other than describe a show, then actually things *do* sort of happen in your head and you become a kind of complicit third author, which happens then very largely in your head. What happens then is that when you hear the line, 'The world stops and everything starts to float' – then mentally in your mind, you make the world stop and you make things start to float. It's a very hard thing about language that when a thing is spoken or read that thing in a certain way does become manifest and it takes you back to Burroughs and to Breton.

PB Language almost having an alchemical function? There is that moment in *Dirty Work* with the music, although it's not used in quite the same way, which is an echo, I felt, of that moment in *Hidden J* where Richard Lowdon . . .?

TE . . . Yes, that's right, he does this thing where he says this piece of music always makes me cry, I want to play it to you to show that I'm sincere. He says this to the audience and then he plays this record and he begins to cry. It's a typical moment from us: Richard, as an actor, is shooting himself in the foot in that he's declaring that this is what he's going to do and then he does it, and I think what we're most interested in is having basically turned all the lights on and ruining the thing. You then have to try and find a way to make it work. It's very much trying to create a problem around theatre and the theatrical, then somehow, from the ruins of it, managing to make that moment actually happen.

PB Can I just say that – leading question – to what extent might the aesthetics of the company's work be most closely and directly related to the company's purposes in the work?

TE Yeah, I mean, I think that the meaning of what you do *is* the aesthetic and *is* the form – in a way it's dangerous to think otherwise I think – what I'm trying to say is that what we're actually watching, what this actually looks and feels like, what the relations between the people in this thing are – that's what it means – what it's about is what's happening in this room now . . .

PB . . . and that's what's absolutely foregrounded in the company's work?

TE Yes, yes, that's right.

PB If we were to have a box with a jigsaw in it and were to give it to somebody and we said, if you can find some way of putting these pieces together and you might not even get a conventionally finished jigsaw – you'd get *something*. What kind of a jigsaw do you think that you as a writer and Forced Entertainment as a company have been working on and are you still working on it? (*Slight pause.*) And is there any blue sky in it?

TE Are you talking about the kind of tone or content of it?

PB Yeah, tone, content and purposes . . .

TE Well, I think that often what we're trying to do in the pieces – although it's not true of all of them – is that we're often trying to make an arrangement broadly speaking of what I think theatre and performance is: it's an arrangement of things and events in space and time. It's an arrangement of events, texts, music – stuff – and I think we're trying to arrange those things in a way that unfolds and takes you on a journey. In addition I think also that we're as interested in the gaps between things as we are in the connections between them.

There's the great quote from E. M. Forster: 'Only connect' and I was writing only just recently about the idea of 'Only disconnect' because I think we rather like this idea that separate things are allowed to sit separately in the performance space. That therefore you don't have to turn everything into a narrative and you don't have to explain what the relation between everything is. Also therefore that for an audience to be faced at the start of *Dirty Work*, Act One which begins with 'Five great nuclear explosions' and

'Spot the Mechanical Dog' is also presented. There's no logical way that we could think of to link these two things but as an audience you're left with a very nice space between those two things because you have to puzzle about the leap from the cataclysmic enormity of 'five nuclear explosions' to 'Spot the Mechanical Dog' who goes to fetch some slippers. I think that in all sorts of different ways – visually, rhythmically and with language, with everything – we're very drawn to make these constructions whereby disconnected things are brought together and leave the audience to do the work of joining them up – no, not joining them up –

PB   To return to the analogy of the jigsaw, is it thinking, 'Damn this, I don't care if the pieces fit together or not, I'll leave the piece in the box?'

TE   Or that an arrangement of those jigsaw pieces might not be hammering them into a rectangle, do you know what I mean? I would think the table is a part of the jigsaw – we *insist* that the table is a part of it.

PB   The table gets a 'walk-on part'?

They laugh.

TE   The table is the ground, the table is the theatre auditorium, and I suppose that the other thing that is interesting about that analogy is that you could approach this task with the jigsaw with a hammer, and hammering it all down and saying, 'Look, we've done my picture' but I think we're much more interested in saying, 'Well, yes, these pieces can be arranged in this way but they can also be arranged in a variety of other ways.' Oftentimes when we've stressed the space in between things, or where we make *Dirty Work* a kind of competition between Robin and Cathy, it's like saying, 'This could all have been different, it didn't have to be this way, it's not necessary that you make the picture like this,' so in a way we try and make people aware of those kinds of processes and their own agency.

PB   Yes, I see, and I suppose one of the reasons why the work has presented difficulties, or bemusement or challenges over the years for both some audiences and critics is that they want and need that rectangular jigsaw with every piece in place? Also, without of course doing any disservice to Ibsen, there is that notion of an Ibsenesque play of resolution where you have characters who are individuals with internal psychological dimensions, driven by a subtext to expose a social ill or corruption. It's something that I've been giving a lot of thought to. I'm beginning to think that that particular form of dramatic structure and strategy is far more redundant than its historical timescale.

TE Yeah, yes, I think so – I mean, on the one hand I would say that we understand that over an hour and a half or over two hours, you're just sculpturing time and space so things are set up: wants and answers want echoes, want refractions. In a certain way they want resolutions. I mean, we explicitly talk about that when we're making stuff; I mean, we'll say it's all very well him doing that there, where does that go to? What happened to that? In a way we'll get very annoyed with our own work when it fails in some way with these decisions about making a pattern. I think we're interested in quite lopsided patterns or patterns that break and seem to disintegrate, only to re-form, but you can't deny that you're in the job of making patterns, narrative or otherwise, and I'd be interested to see work that wasn't (*laughs*), I really would. But basically that's what you're doing when you're making work over one and a half or two hours, you're making patterns that unfold over that time – you have to be – but I suppose we're very interested in stressing the provisionality of that kind of pattern and stressing the audience's role in making connections and linking things. We are stressing the 'live nature' of what is emerging rather than stressing 'here is the finished jigsaw' where everything is hammered into place. The politics is very much in the process – understanding that it's a *decision* to put that there, it's not 'just there' – somebody *made* that decision.

PB Returning briefly to that idea of an Ibsenesque model, it's obviously part of a much wider and bigger historical project: liberal humanism and social progress – which early in the twenty-first century now seems increasingly problematic. Is there any optimism in the work?

TE   Entirely optimistic! Absolutely entirely optimistic!

They laugh.

PB   That reminds me of Edward Bond's statement in his preface to *Saved* that it's irrepressibly optimistic . . .

TE   Yes, the character [Len] fixes the chair, doesn't he?

PB   Can I twist your arm to say just a little bit more about that sense of optimism in Forced Entertainment's work?

TE   Well, I think that there are many possible reasons but two of them would be that the work stresses the kind of live, playful, subversive energy of the performance – that this is something that is happening – that this is happening before you, you're watching the performers make decisions – you're watching them throw things into the air, that you're watching them twist and turn with things – there's a great joy and pleasure in that. There are some shows we've made which are of course not funny but we're very, very interested in 'funny' and what does it require to provoke or create the possibility of laughter. This thing about the audience: there's a huge optimism in the work in the way that the work wants and needs to play with and disturb and celebrate and put on the table the presence of the audience at this event. Who are they, what are they, what are they doing, what will they take and what won't they take? What is the social organisation of doing something with the two hundred and fifty people who've sat down to watch this – what can you *do* with them? What can they do with each other?

There's a fantastic moment in *First Night* which is very provoking on the audience – quite relentlessly pushing – there's a great long monologue in that from Terry – the whole thing is titled in our minds as a kind of disastrous vaudeville – this big, grinning, cheesy show that is going wrong from the first moment that they walk on to the stage. Halfway through or so Terry does this long monologue about 'Don't think about the outside world, don't think about the bad times, don't think about people hidden away in oil tankers, don't think about the bombing that's happening right now in Beirut'? It's like ten or so minutes of Terry telling you all the things you shouldn't be thinking about when of course these are all the things that you're thinking about. I think some way into that speech, in Brighton at a performance of that show, someone – an audience member – shouted, 'Bollocks! You're boring!' Then another audience member stood up and shouted back across the auditorium, 'Shut the fuck up!' It was superb – now we understand that the three hundred and fifty people together in this room are here together by a very tenuous social contract – like this is now. This performance can be stopped or not – everybody in the room knows then that that is the case – the work is often about the preciousness and the inviolable 'nowness of now'. That, to me, is a huge optimism, and in a way its insistence that it is about theatre, that here we all are, to me that's both where its optimism and its politics lie. It's not about three hundred years ago, it's about now, this is happening now – yes, very optimistic.

PB I am going to ask you this question, I'm afraid you can't get away from it. Seriously, it's a question that I've asked the four other writers in the book and it's prompted by the final stage direction in David Greig's most recent play *The American Pilot*: 'The bombing continues. The gunfire continues. The End'. I've used that line as a way of reflecting upon where the world is and where performance, the theatre, the writer might be in relation to that world. I guess in a way that you may have just answered that in what you've just said?

TE I think theatre or culture in general in a way is a sort of fairly weak way of intervening if you would like to change the world, so to speak. So a very, very, very slow sort of twentieth-hand way of trying to nudge something into being. I think that, in a way, if changing the world is something that one wants to do, then probably there would be better ways to do that. But I think that what I do believe – it's small – is that the arts – whether it's theatre, literature, video, music – I think these things speak to and articulate things about individual or social experience and having these things awoken or spoken to I think that it does change people, but it's very small.

I mean we're in this hideous situation now with the conflict between the West and the Arab world led by America and backed heavily by Britain where you kind of feel that politically the opportunity to address that has gone (the way that one *might* have felt possible in the 1960s doesn't really seem remotely possible). Politics has become a dead game – you feel by gut instinct that the majority of the population in the UK would be very behind the call for an immediate ceasefire in Lebanon [the Israeli bombardment of Lebanon in August 2006, their target, Hezbollah, the militant Islamic organisation] but this falls on entirely deaf ears with Blair and the bizarre realisation that Bush is leading on every level. So you feel the impotence, really, of our political situation very deeply and it's quite hard to believe that any new show by Forced Entertainment is going to do fuck-all to change that. At a certain level and at a certain time there are ways in which works of art can bring issues into public debate through newspapers and other places, they awaken different ways of thinking in people – so I think that's clearly worth doing. What we're very painfully aware of now and what this stage direction nods to is the fact that those guys have got it all figured out – they're very, very good at riding the media and being totally fucking deaf in both ears when they want to – scary.

PB   Yes and I think therefore that – to use an old Situationist term – the work of the company might be seen to 'disrupt the spectacle' and surface reality, in and of itself a legitimate and creative thing to do.

TE   Yes, well, I think that that's one of the places where its politics operate with its insistence upon work and process, and upon seeing things done rather than the kind of instant effect – that's all very important. That's why I was saying before when we were talking about the relationship between the aesthetics and the content, that there *is* no difference between the aesthetics and the content – so at this particular moment it's depressing, to say the least, to reflect upon the impact of any art or anything at all upon those people who are pursuing whatever bizarre objectives they may have.

PB Thanks a lot, Tim, that's been brilliant.

TE Thanks, Peter.

Falling and Floating in Sheffield – Drunks, Dancers and Late-night Bus Rides: Themes and Strategies in the Work of Tim Etchells and Forced Entertainment

Forced Entertainment, the British experimental theatre collective, have played a unique role within radical, avant-garde new performance over the last twenty years. They have been described by the *Guardian* as 'One of the most influential new British theatre companies of the last twenty years'. *The Times* observed, 'Forced Entertainment has been pulling the rug from under theatregoers' feet for twenty years . . . they're not about to stop confounding conventions or exploding audience expectations.' Tim Etchells has remained their resident writer and was a co-founder of the original company in the mid-1980s.

While identifying Tim Etchells as their writer, this is a company whose ethos and working approach is collaborative and shared. He also appears from time to time as a performer and has a unique role as a kind of postmodern editor or dramaturge of their richly textured, open, improvisatory-based approach. Unlike the other cutting-edge dramatists discussed in this book, here is a writer working for a company whose approach embraces a diverse range of 'texts'. These are texts of the body in space, texts of images on a video screen, texts of live and recorded music and the found detritus of contemporary pop-trash culture. This dynamic montage and collision of texts gives his written text input and the dramaturgical synthesis of those multiple texts a special significance. Etchells's postmodern, poetic urban sensibility plays an intrinsic and a crucially defining quality in their work. He is a writer who does not write play texts separately or in isolation for a director and cast then to make artistic, interpretative decisions about in that usual sense of play production. This necessarily asks different questions, therefore, of the potential role and function of the writer outside that traditional Western context of writer-director-actor process and hierarchy.

Of course, one might say of David Edgar, David Greig, Mark

Ravenhill and Tanika Gupta that their play texts are also involved to some extent or other in a mutual and creatively collaborative process of interpretation and production. However, with Etchells and Forced Entertainment we have a counter-cultural phenomenon whereby not only the primacy but also the causal centrality of the writer is questioned and changed. As Tim Etchells observes in his essay 'Play On: Collaboration and Process' included in *Certain Fragments – Contemporary Performance and Forced Entertainment* (Routledge, 1999):

> If the process of direction in the theatre most usually has at its heart the interpretation of a text and the fixing of set meanings in it, the staging of one interpretation out of many possible ones – perhaps we have in mind something utterly different – of theatre or performance as a space in which different visions, different sensibilities, different intentions could collide [. . .] Collaboration then not as a kind of perfect understanding of the other bloke, but a miss-seeing, a miss-hearing, a deliberate lack of unity. And this fact of the collaborative process finding its echo in the work since on-stage what we see is not all one thing either – but rather a collision of fragments that don't quite belong, fragments that miss-see and miss-hear each other. A kind of pure play in that too. (pp. 55–6)

From political and ideological points of view their work is also interesting in terms of the influence upon it of the radical, revolutionary counter-cultural movement from the 1960s, the Situationists. The Situationists themselves owed their name to a radical French magazine from the end of the previous decade *Internationale Situationniste* (1958), but also, of course, from the wider, twentieth-century avant-garde of groups such as Dada and Surrealism. Situationism is a revolutionary political philosophy in which modern and contemporary industrial and post-industrial society is viewed as being inevitably and intrinsically oppressive and exploitative. It is a system in which the individual is no more than a commodity. The movement rejects all conventional politics (including those of the Stalinist and Trotskyite Left) and demands a comprehensive revolution in relationships, work and all aspects of contemporary living. Their declared aim was 'Disrupting the Spectacle' of the mass-mediated and controlled illusion of the apparent cohesion and inevitability of modern society. Simultaneously this also involved a radical critique of its social, cultural and political systems. There is a strong and central element of performance in their ideas and political activities. They played a major role in the strikes and student uprisings of May 1968 in Paris. This is a political and counter-cultural strategy of radically disruptive, interventionist performance. Through this they believed that the underlying political and economic factors determining and controlling people's lives, consciousness and perceptions will be exposed with subversive consequences.

Another major influence upon the performance style and collaborative creative process informing that is the work of the leading USA avant-garde theatre company the Wooster Group. Their multi-layering of what frequently seem like wholly irreconcilable source materials and references echoes and prefigures the performance methodology of Forced Entertainment. The use of these performative postmodern assemblages upon the conditional relationship between culture and consciousness was ground-breaking.

Etchells's writing explores and embodies notions of what I would define as a kind of post-Romantic English sensibility and melancholy. It is a kind of radical secular vision, revolutionary at the outposts of the imagination rather than at the street barricades; the beaten-up urban frontiers of the imagination where one might see William Blake staggering into the late-night store nearest to where you live, knocking back a bottle of imported Albanian vodka and then kicking off with his poetry and painting. As Tim Etchells observed in an earlier interview with me back in the 1990s, 'We are journeyers struggling to make something out of inadequate means, to enact and make sense out of inherited forms and structures . . . a sense of desperation to make meaning . . . we try to make spiritual work for atheists' (interview with the author, Sheffield, 1995).

Gatecrashing the radicalised imaginative world of Etchells and the company has frequently presented difficulties for critics, academics and audiences when attempting to discuss and describe their work. Problems arise of finding a meaningful critical vocabulary to discuss the complex meta-performance narratives and inter-textual collages of meaning in the making and performance of their work. This can take one down a blind alley but into the endless self-referential thinking of a postmodern cul-de-sac. It evokes a similar sense of frustration and strangeness to getting off the late-night bus at what you were sure was your stop, only to find yourself stranded in unfamiliar territory. I hope to make a contribution to relieving some of that confusion and disorientation. One acknowledges the conflicting demands for a critical objectivity whilst recognising that such conventional critical thinking will encounter the intrusive presence of one's own subjective experiential agendas in the work of Tim Etchells and Forced Entertainment. There is no way that you can entirely shake off that visionary poet-painter who followed you off the bus.

Forced Entertainment was set up in 1984 and comprised a core group of a relatively fixed number, usually in the region of six or seven including Tim Etchells as writer (as well as, sometimes, performer). The nucleus of the company has remained in place since the very early days: Tim Etchells, Robin Arthur, Cathy Naden, Richard Lowdon, Terry O'Connor and Claire Marshall. There has also been a growing network of collaborators over the years, with Hugo Glendinning as an ever present and indispensable visual design influence and also photographer-archivist of the company's work. One of his production stills of *Bloody Mess* provides the central image for the cover of this book. Also, John Avery has produced many of the haunting soundtracks that often accompany the work. His aural landscapes have infiltrated many of the performances like a half-forgotten Cure song or the Schubert lieder that won't go away.

The company is based in Sheffield in south Yorkshire and occupies rehearsal and administration space in converted post-industrial buildings in the city's cultural quarter. The company's decision to locate itself within a large, urban, northern post-industrial city is significant in relation to the ethos and concerns within their work. In terms of their artistic policy, one of their principal stated aims is:

> Developing ideas and theatrical strategies . . . concerned with urban experience, with ideas about identity in the media-saturated world, with the collision of cultures, languages and texts that make up and mark out our lives.

One of the prime British inspirations for the company's formation in 1984 and its subsequent early work was the Leeds-based Impact Theatre Company. Impact's experimental and innovative use of video and film as a performance text, and the deconstruction of narrative through non-linear sequencing, were significant influences upon early Forced Entertainment projects such as *Let the Water Run Its Course to the Sea that Made the Promise* (1986). Along with this went their creative and non-naturalistic use of source material for their work, raided from popular film and television culture. This subversive 'sampling' of contemporary media culture through its radically reordered juxtaposition creates an oppositional performance language as they counter what Robin Arthur described to the author in interview (1995) as a 'Hollywood mental colonisation process'. This sampled performance text also helps to locate the conceptual, ideological and performance dialectic within their work. This process, whereby the genres of dramatic form and performance are simultaneously the per-formance aesthetic and vice versa, is signified and communicated through the foregrounding of the work's own transparent constructedness and meta-theatricality. Therefore, within this pro-cess of ironic revelation, a complex iconography of performance, politics (though never in any doctrinaire or agitprop style) and radical aesthetics is created. This often signifies a latent sense of loss, desire and dislocation within the work. The performance text is placed in a wider meta-theatrical context that defines shifting concepts of meaning and coherence as a form of alienation. It is as if one sees performers playing actors playing characters that then drift into a kind of parallel world of alternative performers, actors and characters.

There is an ongoing sense of the company constantly seeking to explore the fragile boundaries between what we might call reality and performance. There is the added, crucial dimension and distinction that what is commonly thought of as socio-cultural reality and political rhetoric and debate can also be considered as a form of performance *itself*. The company's performers will often experiment and play along the boundaries of this no man's land, using devices such as a performer-in-character-as-performer establishing eye contact with individual members of the audience. This transgresses the usual socio-cultural conventions about eye contact and its intimate connotations. This making and breaking of eye contact also transgresses the socially and culturally con-structed relationship between actor and audience within main-stream theatre. In other performance formats such as cabaret, stand-up comedy and pantomime such knowing use of eye contact between performer and audience is, of course, accepted as one of the rules of those genres.

Forced Entertainment constantly reminds its audiences that they are not only passive spectators but active co-participants in the live process of making meaning through the transparent real-time creation of a world on the borders of reality and fiction. This is central to the paradoxes that occupy and inform their work. For example, in *Showtime* (1996) a performer (Cathy Naden) was dressed in the unconvincing costume of a dog who might have wandered out of a children's TV show or a second-rate panto-mime. The dog (or is it her?) is interviewed by another performer who questions Naden as someone recounting the steps leading up to a suicide attempt. This sequence asked profound questions about the reality of suicide and also about the increasing propensity through reality TV and Oprah Winfrey-style public confessions to trivialise and commodify deeply personal human narratives. The medium of the mass publicising of the private inevitably corrupts our sensitivity to and reading of the message. This placing of the performance event in quotation marks operates simultaneously with fictional locations that are paradoxically dreamlike whilst rooted in a contemporary urban aesthetic. They're often of the 'Bargain Basement', 'Five for a Pound', 'Topless-Pro-Celebrity Darts', multi-channelled, instantly selected satellite television culture.

Through this use of a performance process, which is broadly Brechtian in its revelation of its own constructed theatricality, the writing of Tim Etchells weaves its hypnotic way like a drunk who's convinced he or she is walking a straight line and that it's the rest of the world that's tilted out of joint. As in William Blake's yearning for an alternative vision of what he viewed as a spiritually empty and politically corrupt world, there is a strong sense in Tim Etchells's writing for Forced Entertainment of a subversive re-dreaming of the social, cultural and political world of late-twentieth-century and early-twenty-first-century Britain. Along with other, later artists in that post-Romantic tradition dating from Blake and disciples such as Samuel Palmer and, in the twentieth century, Paul Nash and John Piper, there is a sense of loss pervading Tim Etchells's writing and Forced Entertainment. This may be viewed as a loss of an earlier Utopia or 'golden world' that often carried with it a very particular sense of English location. There is also the association of a loss of innocence, of a consciousness corrupted by the values and pressures of a society, culture and political system that demeans or exploits the capacity to be human. Robin Arthur spoke of this sense of loss in the company's work and Etchells's writing. For Arthur it represented the consequence of living in a world that he likened to 'living in a cargo hold . . . in a second-hand culture'.

However, there is no room for polemic of the more traditional kind of oppositional political theatre, as Etchells has often asserted: 'We're not making sermons, tracts or cheerleading speeches to the disenfranchised.' The enemy is the mass-mediated global consumer capitalism that Mark Ravenhill exposes in such plays as *Shopping and Fucking* and *Product*. Tim Etchells and the company seek similarly in broad purpose though not in dramatic strategy to subvert and expose what is viewed as a mass colonisation of people's consciousness and lives. Blake's 'dark Satanic mills' may now have transformed into 'Heritage' loft conversions for aspiring young professionals but, like his visionary antecedent, Etchells imagines an alternative to a world where citizens become consumers and consumers become indistinguishable from the products they consume.

Because they grow out of an ongoing, open-ended devising and improvising process, Etchells's characters are therefore unlike those of any of the other dramatists in this book except perhaps Ravenhill's Robbie, Lulu and Mark with their diet of shoplifted microwaveable 'Ready Meals'. The characters in Forced Entertainment aren't intended or constructed to function as dramatic characters in the usual sense of that term. In the same way that the theatricality of their performance is constantly and often hilariously signalled and highlighted, so the 'characters' are constantly exposed as seemingly randomly constructed fragments from the Trash-U-Like warehouse subculture of porn films, news footage of bloody field hospitals in Rwanda, or Bosnian rape camps and confessional daytime chatshows. Consequently, both performers and their shifting, fictive shadows engage in a constantly frustrating, seemingly unsuccessful attempt to reaffirm and/or reinvent themselves.

Hidden J (1994)

In a piece from the mid-1990s, *Hidden J*, there were two evocative and powerful examples of this process at work. *Hidden J* presented a bleak vision of contemporary existence, mediated through a kaleidoscope of psychological and physical violence.

The first example is of Richard Lowdon playing the part of Frank, a best man at a wedding who struggles to deliver his customary post-wedding speech. The dysfunctional gestural signs of the performer-actor-character with his disjointed, self-destructing spoken text (by Etchells) communicated a complex code of the character and the performer-as-actor – exposed and at risk. There was also in this bleakly funny icon a potent sense of Lowdon trying to construct coherence out of inadequate resources: a powerful motif through Etchells's writing and across the company's work. This witnessing of Lowdon's/Frank's discomfort and dislocation within a familiar social context was exploded through a subsequent component in the performance. The worst best-man-as-actor sat and listened to a piece of music that clearly had deeply emotional connotations for him. As the music played, he wept in a way that undercut our previous laughter, arousing our empathy and concern. Once this vignette was established and set, Cathy Naden then approached Lowdon and discreetly enquired how much longer he would continue crying? At this point Lowdon/Frank automatically stopped crying, indicated that he would be about 'three minutes' and then returned to the performance of his grief. Approximately three minutes later, given a second and final reminder from Naden, he stooped as abruptly as he had previously. This puncturing of not only the conventional relationship of audience–character empathy, but also the convention of an alienation device created a motif of the 'space between' the 'integrity' and 'authenticity' of the performance event and its inescapable artificiality.

The second example from the same piece involved the performer Claire Marshall. For almost the entire show she sat downstage wearing a placard round her neck with the crudely written word 'LIAR' scrawled on it. Within the performance space, crude plywood flats were constructed on stage to define a kind of viewing space or viewing frame in which certain scenes are played out. One of the most harrowing sequences viewed through the 'window' of this 'room' was based on news bulletin footage of the panic, chaos and grief within a military field hospital in the Bosnian war. Along with Frank's chaotic ramblings and other characters' incoherent telephone conversations, images abound and collide of contemporary alienation, despair, violence and state-sanctioned terror. In placing Marshall in full foregrounding view of this performance action, she was offered as a silent witness to this nightmare collage of nihilism and destruction. She stared at the audience and in doing so seemed to question our own complicity with the performance events and our voyeuristic observation of them. In the dull, chilling tone and formal vocabulary of a Stalinist show trial, she proceeded to give a public confession of her alleged faults and crimes. Her subsequent punishment was to be forcibly made to drink and choke upon a bottle of spirits.

Marshall was the only performer-character with any semblance of coherence and meaning within the piece. There was a multiplicity of meanings potentially and actively present in that moment of performance. The roughly inscribed sign round her neck alleges that she is a liar and that, therefore, all that she says and embodies is a lie. There is a darker resonance also of the 'lie' of artifice, the 'lie' of the performance to the real, or the 'lie' of the so-called 'true' in the 'fiction' of performance. Her confession offered the only verifiable counterpoint of coherence in the disjointed nightmare world of *Hidden J*, a complex reality culled from Bosnia, wedding reception speeches and unnamed political prisoners confessing their alleged betrayal of oppressive regimes. There was a premeditated demonstrated tension between the existential, phenomenological fact of her presence in that performance event in disturbing contradiction to the inscribed, self-accusing denial of the legitimacy or possibility of her presence: LIAR. The combination and fusion of Etchells's written/spoken text with the collaged assemblage of its performance conspired to question the purpose and coherence of the theatre event itself and also our complicity in relation to its construction, interpretation and multiple meanings. These complex strategies of text and performance in disorientating but radical fusion asked serious questions of our relationship both to the production/performance but also, by direct implication, the actual violent fractured world that *Hidden J* evoked. Lowdon's worst best man and Marshall's silent-speaking victim-witness are powerful examples of those who make their surreal or reimagined journeys-without-destinations through Etchells's writing and Forced Entertainment's performance. In his words they are journeyers who struggle to 'enact and make sense out of inherited forms and structures'.

Nights in This City (1997)

In *Nights in This City* the motif and metaphor of the journey took on a decidedly three-dimensional aspect when the audience were taken on a coach journey around Sheffield. Two company members, Richard Lowdon and Cathy Naden, were on the coach as it travelled around what at that time was a familiar city landscape for me, the city of Sheffield where I lived throughout the 1990s. Lowdon again played a character that was struggling to make sense of himself and his relationship to the wider world and his environment. The existential discomfort leached into the actor and character. His character was a stereotypical tour guide on a holiday coach. The actor communicated an aura of hastily learned lines and an under-rehearsed part, whilst the fictional character himself seemed like someone who was not sure what part or lines (or how many) life had given him. Was he a leading man or a walk-on part? Lowdon plays the part of a tour guide who travelling through the city landscape of Sheffield constantly, repeatedly and rather desperately refers to that landscape in terms of other European cities such as Rome and Munich. This highlights and returns a prevailing theme and concern within the writing and the work. That is, the insubstantiality of the material geographical landscape and also the geo-metaphorical landscape of identity, memory and language. The piece asked: How does one truly and consistently locate one's place and sense of being in the world? This is critically heightened when consciousness is predicated upon a consumption and absorption of an inner-city, urban alienation. This postmodern angst stares back like one's reflection in a cracked, stained window. It is an interior experience of marginalisation. A performance-located tension was created between an experiential sense of 'being there' on the coach and viewing a familiar landscape. This was in conflict with another perspective created by Etchells's writing, of experiencing a simultaneous and disorientating sense of 'absence'. It was the familiar-as-alien. The more that Lowdon-as-tour-guide tried to offer coherence and meaning to his narrative and our journey, the further he slipped and fell into a defeated introspection. He ultimately relinquished both his task as tour guide and also his own problematic engagement with the world. His persona shifted from a likeable, if incompetent, tour guide to a melancholic urban poet, absorbed within his own memory journey:

> That's the place where you first met someone and that's the place where you fell out of love, and that's the place where you ran for a taxi and it wasn't raining, and there's a building you slept inside, once perhaps, or many times, and isn't this a street you used to live on, and weren't you always the person staring out the car window, watching the world like the movies, and weren't you always the one who'd travelled a long way, through the day and into the night?

The images of travelling and of a distanced and dislocated experience of life transacted *through* the car window 'watching the world like the movies', evoked a longing for engagement with a world one felt inescapably separate from. Lowdon-as-tour-guide exemplified that longing for language to give substantive, secure meaning of identity, location, purpose and memory.

Before the coach journey ended Lowdon left the coach on a desolate urban derelict site where it had temporarily stopped. Two company members appeared at the edge of this bleak landscape, reminiscent of two of the angels from Wim Wenders's iconic film of mortality and transience *Wings of Desire*. The coach journey was completed with another company-member-as-guide to replace

Lowdon and talk us through the final stages. As we eventually disembarked, we walked through a decaying inner-city building that was formerly a bus depot. At the far end of the space as one entered were the words 'Floating and Falling in Sheffield' in cheap motel-style neon lettering, suspended above the exit. In the former depot there was an avenue of industrial arc lights and a haunting soundtrack from John Avery. On the floor of the former depot the names of all the streets, avenues and roads in Sheffield were neatly and methodically written in chalk. Chalk easily smudges and disappears. If a chalk-written street name were scuffed and rubbed out, might the lives of the real people who lived there equally disappear? There was a very strong connection with the resonance of provincial war memorials with their neat and silent lettering naming the present, naming the past, inscribing the lost and departed. Within the space between the marked sign and its material context there remained a fragile possibility of reviewing and reclaiming a space that hadn't yet been sold as advertising space to sell us commodities *as* commodities.

Disco Relax (2000)

Disco Relax takes us to some recognisable and resampled material and themes from the first decade of Forced Entertainment's work, especially earlier landmark pieces such *Marina and Lee* (1991), *Emmanuelle Enchanted* (1992) and *Club of No Regrets* (1993). The piece took place in an unspecified location but one with distinct references of a run-down bar or drinking club. Cathy Naden and Claire Marshall played the two female characters. There were rough trestle tables delineating the downstage area with a sound-track of a sleazy Hammond organ that offered the subtle ambience of a seriously run-down strip club. Silver foil strip screens with crude coloured lighting completed the scene, along with an old TV set with a flickering screen. This screen jumped from images of the innocence of a young child performing simple conjuring tricks to another image of two anonymous bodies having sex in a third-rate porn movie, to a gun being loaded with bullets. On the central table Cathy Naden in a tawdry micro-skirt danced a lethargic photocopy of an exhausted lap dancer. Slumped at one end of the tables next to the TV was a drunk in a party mask with a sign round the neck (reminiscent of *Hidden J*) with 'Drunken Twat' scrawled upon it. Claire Marshall sat and mixed unending 'cocktails' of drinks taken from the dregs of unfinished glasses and half-empty bottles. A long-haired MC/DJ (later to reappear in *Bloody Mess*) sat slumped and occasionally picked up an electric guitar that he blasted a riff on.

The two women instigated and entered into the principal narrative within the meta-narrative of *Disco Relax*. This took the form of a daytime television, B-movie courtroom drama in which all the dramatic and textual clichés of that mass-produced genre were rehearsed and rerun. 'Write this down and write it fast!' ordered Naden to Marshall as she wound herself up for a melodramatic performance hilariously identifiable in its over-the-top flourishes and cheap rhetoric. 'What is justice? What is evidence? What is the name of the law!?' shrieked Naden's bar-room prosecuting counsel. 'Are we men or are we beasts of the field!?' This was contrasted by darker moments of underlying despair and exhaustion. The strain of having constantly to rehearse and perform this mascara-smudged, vodka-soaked purgatory overwhelmed both characters. 'I'm lost. I'm totally lost,' one said, adding, 'Is there a navigator in here?' The only comfort from Naden's companion (played by Marshall) was 'Take a look on the rosy side – you could be dead'.

These characters were dead in that their lives were emptied of all hope and purpose other than swilling back the next cheap alcoholic anaesthetic. *Disco Relax* is undoubtedly one of the more remorselessly bleak pieces from the company's back catalogue. It suffers to some extent from the more complex roller-coaster ride in texture and language that characterised the major work from the 1990s. In its unremitting darkness it communicated the impossibility of performance affecting any intervention or meaningful commentary upon the dangerous, violent and unstable times in which we live. *Dirty Work* (1998 and later revived) had reiterated this central and critical concern with its motifs and strategies of performers constantly apologising for the inadequacy of their work, whilst simultaneously exposing their deeper insecurities and competitive ambitions as performers-characters. This was resumed and explored to great effect in *First Night* and *Bloody Mess*.

First Night (2000)

In *First Night* the audience was confronted by a desperately poor variety troupe of performers who might alternatively have been the D-list cabaret act from hell. Their faces were smeared in an almost Day-Glo orange of amateur theatricals greasepaint with matching eyeshadow for the female performers of lurid mortuary green. Their expressions were fixed like masks torn between a superficial smile and a snarl of contempt. The visual setting for the show was the tacky scarlet curtains of provincial theatres. Also, at random moments in the performance crude spotlights of primary colour appeared on stage although usually missing any performer caught up in this nightmarish cabaret. These were characters playing for their lives, driven by fear, panic and exhaustion: a sinking in the pit of their stomach as they tottered on the edge of an existential and performative abyss. The show is full of artfully constructed visual, thematic and textual echoes from some of the landmark earlier work of the 1990s. No more clearly is this so than in the opening sequence of the show following a headlocked compère (Robin Arthur) being gripped by a grimacing, grinning partner (Richard Lowdon). They issued a wholly unconvincing 'welcome' to the audience, reassuring them that they would have a marvellous evening: 'We've got a lovely show lined up for you tonight, songs and dances, lots of jokes. It's got people – doing – stuff.' Arthur's character struggled to deliver these clichéd lines even as Lowdon's vice-like grip publicly humiliated him. These two characters appeared in this format throughout different points in the performance like some grotesquely surreal punctuating of the otherwise ceaseless performance of misery and alienation.

They were like some 'pantomime horse' trapped in a bad dream: Lowdon, the eerily sadistic 'head' and forelegs, and Arthur as the victimised, masochistic 'rear legs and tail'. When the other performers eventually re-entered, they did so employing the visual vocabulary of female hips swinging with dull, monotonous lasciviousness and their eyes and smiles pasted on to their taut faces. The performers all put on blindfolds.

This signalled a transition into an extended sequence in which the dated tricks and clichéd devices of the old Music Hall 'Memory Man' were evoked for all of their comic potential but with darker inevitability into the territory of fears and anxieties about the vulnerability of human existence. Terry O'Connor opened the sequence with 'Ladies and Gentlemen, I have a very great sense of loss in the house [theatre],' the text then immediately and skilfully moving from the comic banalities of 'A key? A dog?' to, as the charlatan 'Memory Woman' works her audience, 'Yes, I also feel loss of a more – personal – nature. A mother, father or uncle perhaps?' As O'Connor's character's panic suddenly intervenes, she 'improvises' with, 'Perhaps someone read about a death in the newspaper?' Claire Marshall's equally tawdry female co-performer takes over the theme with 'I'm getting a girl in a green bikini on a beach with a sticky face. Her message to you is she doesn't entirely blame you for what happened to her.' Other performers then joined in with: 'I'm getting a sore penis – there's a gentleman in the house with a sore penis – just to let you know that it's rather more serious than you thought.'

This fusion of crude double-entendre humour with the fear of terminal illness exemplified the skill with which Etchells and the company moved from one performance wavelength to another with an incredible sureness of touch. This has been facilitated by the closely intense proximity in which the company have worked with each other over many years. At the close of this sequence Cathy Naden's character entered like the drunk required to walk a straight line to prove that he or she is sober. In this case it was Naden in classic Forced Entertainment style who had to chart the walking of a performance-journey which premeditatedly threatened to tip over into the dangerous space between the real and the acted. Naden slowly intoned a text of mortality, disease and death that she (her character?) sensed in the audience. Her tuning in to the actual, life-located reality of fear, anxiety and loss regarding cancer, leukaemia, brain haemorrhage and a lover's 'broken heart' conveyed a dark pathos and poignancy. Was it that Naden's own fears and anxiety as a woman-within-herself as performer were revealed and channelled into her fictive persona? Might it have been that the 'mask-persona' itself responded at some deeper, intuitive creative level to the performer (Naden) who wears it? This would entail entering as a performer into a kind of heightened and deepened post-Stanislavskian emotion memory.

First Night is of course a well-known term in theatre for that anxious, adrenalin-fuelled moment when rehearsal and backstage process become visible in public and critical terms. It is used with some irony by Etchells as a title for this piece. Apart from anything else, it's clear that for those washed-up characters in *First Night* the vitality and freshness of a first-night performance is a long-distance dream or more likely a delusory nightmare. When their insipid, obsequious appeal to their audience transpired to be a masquerade revealing a bitter contempt for them the cast entered the final extended phase of *First Night* with a hilarious, 1970s-style cabaret dance routine clumsily choreographed to 1970s disco music. Each character entered with a large white card on which there was a capital letter clearly inscribed. After several embarrassing attempts (deliberately contrived) at bringing themselves and their letters into some kind of meaningful formation, they eventually pre-sented the word WELCOME to their audience. When they had reached this rare moment of coherence, Etchells's text took us into a long, penultimate meditation upon performance, performers and their audiences.

Robin Arthur's character assured his audience, 'When we come up on the stage and under the lights, we feel at home – we feel so at home ladies and gentlemen.' He followed this up with a desperate acknowledgement: 'I'd just like to say that there won't be any cats on roller skates here in this theatre this evening.' He also felt that he must remind the audience of a 'few rules': 'We're going to be in the light and you're going to be in the dark. We're going to be talking and you're going to be quiet as mice.' Terry O'Connor's iconic hostess tellingly reminded the audience that 'If you've got any problems, they're nothing to do with us' – flushing Aristotelian empathy and catharsis away with world-weary disdain. Cathy Naden's character tried to remedy O'Connor's disarming frankness with 'I'm reminded of an old saying that goes something like this: "All the world's a stage and we are some of the people on it." ' She followed this up with a knowing irony replete with Situationist ideas: 'It doesn't matter, ladies and gentlemen, if we're up here on the stage and you're not because the whole world is one.' There then ensued a post-modernist collage of caricatures from the lower depths of popular stage-based entertainment including a conjurer-illusionist with a saw on which he proceeds to cut himself.

Soon the performers reappeared with another set of large letters on cards, this time spelling out the word ILLUSION, once again resonant with Situationist self-revealing irony. This reiteration of the artifice and transience of performance was then consolidated through the superb execution of a marvellous Etchells monologue framed by 'Ladies and Gentlemen, whilst you're here with us this evening, we ask that you forget everything outside of here this evening.' This deft critique of theatre and performance as entertainment, or to be more precise, entertainment as sugar-coated anaesthetic, continued into a moving and dark litany of the many elements of what makes us human and fragile. 'Ladies and Gentleman, whilst you are here with us tonight, I'd like you to forget everything that makes you human – everything that makes you who you are.' Even as the audience were invited to forget, amongst other things, illness, loneliness, war, car bombs, O'Connor's crumpled, rouged face-as-mask suggested that she could not forget and that she knows neither could her audience. As this kitsch cabaret staggered towards its finale one was reminded of Etchells's vision of 'journeyers desperately trying to make sense out of inadequate resources'. Claire Marshall's aggressively confrontational drunk had to be violently and forcibly restrained as she shouted 'That man is a fucking charlatan!' and the piece, with carefully plotted chaos and depressed exhaustion, reached its final conclusion. *First Night* is a first-class example of Etchells's writing and Forced Entertainment's performance style constituting some of the best of their work over a twenty-year period of performances.

Bloody Mess (2004)

Bloody Mess was written by Etchells and devised with the company to celebrate its twentieth anniversary. Whilst there was no cake or candles, the piece burns with a vivid ferocity of late night, last orders and an end-of-time love song for human beings, and the 'Bloody Mess' they have made of their world and the planet.

Significantly, in its celebration and commemoration of twenty years of innovative theatre making *Bloody Mess* incorporates many of the motifs and iconic visual grammar of Forced Entertainment's work. Performers in gorilla suits, repeated, ritualised moments from B movies, moments of displaced Freudian longings, humourless roadies, iconic rock music blasted away at unendurable volume, two men with white clown mask-faces, skirmishes and fights, disco lights that disturbingly resemble the flashing emergency lights at the scene of some disaster, swirling clouds of dry ice. The list could continue.

The show opened with a seemingly calm and composed setting out of chairs at the downstage area of an otherwise empty performance space. The chairs were being positioned and repositioned by John and Bruno, playing two competing clowns. Their white faces were not able to conceal their violent competitiveness and destructive desire to be 'the funniest person on stage'. The 'backstage' ambitions and desires of the performers were foregrounded by the row of chairs that were eventually put in a straight line after a hilariously well-executed sequence of skirmishing, fighting and the crashing of chairs smashing the silence of the opening. The whole cast took a chair and with the aid of a microphone – another iconic device traceable back to *200% and Bloody Thirsty* (1987–88) – introduced themselves and revealed their principal aims, ambitions and hopes for their part in the performance that evening. This ranged from Richard Lowdon: 'I'm hoping very much that you will see me this evening as the romantic lead of the piece, strong and sensitive, caring, manly and very virile,' through to Bruno's disturbing 'Comedy is like a banana. I'm hoping that you might see me as representing that fruit's hidden white flesh of children's laughter.' This then went on to Claire Marshall's sexually charged and frustrated 'I hope that during this evening's performance, you're not going to be able to take your eyes off of me, your gaze will return to me again and again like a helpless moth drawn to a burning flame.' Most significantly, perhaps, in terms of both *Bloody Mess* and one of the perpetual concerns and themes within Etchells's writing and the company's previous work, Terry O'Connor told the audience, 'I hope you think when you look at me that I look like a *real person doing real things* – I hope that you'll think, "No one has written these lines for her, no one's told her how to act. *She is really living it*."' (My italics.)

O'Connor's sentiments helped to remind of the wider territory of the company's work and *Bloody Mess* itself. It has an epic quality and dimension in terms both of size of cast (ten) and also its intentions of demonstrating the bloody mess of a contemporary, bleak, postmodern landscape. *Bloody Mess* is like an apocalyptic, millennial end-time racked with futility and regret, with characters-performers competing for centre stage, even as all things disintegrate around them in some cataclysmic, post-nuclear final act. The dramatic tension and dialectic moved between fighting clowns and a sweets-throwing gorilla who, taking off its head, reminded the audience of her insatiable sexual desires and post-show availability. Manic drunken lap dancers and actresses with serious delusions of their talents continuously competed and argued. John, whose character proved to be something of a bar-room philosopher as well as a clown (perhaps the two are inseparable?), tried to tell the second of two stories 'both based on scientific fact'. Whereas the first story dealt with the potential for meaning, order and purpose in the universe, the second dealt with the inevitability of the final end of all things. Overcome perhaps by both the bleak, unswerving finality of his story as well as ultimately exhausted by the destructive tactics of the others, John's character, barely able to talk through his tears, could only repeat to his sympathetic interviewer (recollecting the suicide account recounted in *Showtime*), 'It's dust. There's nothing but dust.' Reminiscent of both the traditional Christian funereal invocation of 'Ashes to ashes, dust to dust' and also Trotsky's view of the 'dustbin of history', he was unable to continue.

Simultaneously, at precisely this moment of seriousness, the opportunity was then offered for comic counter-play with Robin Arthur as a nerdish roadie asking the competing comic (played by Bruno), 'Can you do the end of the world as, like, an impersonation?' Thrilled to score a potentially devastating and winning point against his comic adversary, the comic obliged with a convincing sound of multiple nuclear explosions conveyed via microphone whilst all visual chaos was unleashed around him. Lowdon's humourless, anally retentive roadie turned chatshow interviewer (another familiar motif and device from previous shows) tried to dissuade John's deflated clown from his conviction that *Bloody Mess* should not end as a 'bloody mess' by insisting upon a comic ending. With some telling and twenty years' hard-won subtext, Lowdon observed, 'The thing is it's not so important to be funny right now. This has always been the serious bit.' There is again a humorous counter-dialectic at work when Lowdon (the performer?) was questioned with mischievous insistence upon the veracity of his 'hippie' wig: 'Is that your own hair?'

'It's fully human hair.'

'Yes, but is it your own?'

The final and actual end of *Bloody Mess*, after several unsuccessful attempts to 'bring it to an end', reinstated Lowdon's sentiments that 'it's not so important to be funny right now' with a deeply moving and beautifully played piece of writing reflecting Etchells at his most potent and poetic. It was performed by the excellent Cathy Naden whose persona throughout the piece until this epilogue had been that of a self-obsessed, self-regarding drama queen. She then appeared in a simple, well-worn black dress with black smeared across her face, mingled with traces of cosmetic sequins. In this perfect visual paradox of crumpled exhaustion and barely lingering glamour, Naden delivered the final speech of the piece. As the stage lights slowly faded to blackout she spoke with the bitter-sweet finality of the last depressive left in the bar after everyone else has gone home. Her pace and focus were impeccable: 'This is the last thing that you'll see. You'll see me standing in this light and then you'll see me disappear into the darkness. It's the last thing you see. You think you know me but you don't. I'm a stranger to you . . . It's that quiet and then the lights will go and I will vanish, I'll disappear. I'm gone for ever and I'm never coming back. This is the final moment. This is the last light.'

Along with the critical acclaim that Tim Etchells and Forced Entertainment have received over the last twenty years or so of their ground-breaking work, they have also been vulnerable to the criticism that their work is too completely and simply an example of apolitical, self-referential, postmodern performance.

Tim Etchells and Forced Entertainment have never been in the business of manning the barricades. The agitprop political theatre of the kind that David Edgar and others were writing forty years ago has long since lost its currency as the dramatic genre through which to address the political and ideological climate of the late-twentieth and early-twenty-first century. Political debate has effectively disappeared from our national public life although there is still mercifully evidence of mass demonstrations from sizeable parts of the public in relation to the Iraq war, and also the anti-globalisation movement.

Forced Entertainment have produced some of the most ground-breaking, innovative, avant-garde performance work in Britain since the mid-1980s. In doing so they have fulfilled the function of creating 'a space like an airlock between you and the world outside'.

That increasingly precious and critical supply of the oxygen of radical freedom of thought, speech and counter-cultural pro-duction has never been needed more urgently than in our current age. Throughout their work they have succeeded in subversively resampling and reordering the mass-mediated propaganda of our time, in order to challenge and expose a system with all of its intrinsic inequalities, injustices and dehumanisation. Through their evolving process of the use of non-linear narrative and non-naturalistic performance strategies they have flagged up a sema-phore of the exploitative strategies of contemporary Western consumer capitalism.

In conclusion Tim Etchells and Forced Entertainment, in throwing away the wrapper from the product, don't simply expose a vacuous postmodern landscape of indeterminate relativity where surface triumphs over substance. In identifying and revealing the premeditated, mass-mediated construction of our contemporary world they also continue the struggle to name alternative potentialities in the spaces between the felt-tip pen, the placard and the inscribing of L-I-A-R or I-L-L-U-S-I-O-N.

Perhaps it's only half-time?

DOWNLOADS
- Try the work of the hugely influential experimental USA per-formance company the Wooster Group.
- Try the films of David Lynch, the writings of William Burroughs and the music of Mark E. Smith and the Fall for early and enduring influences upon Tim Etchells and the company.

6 TANIKA GUPTA

SHORT CUT
- Multicultural and youth issues.
- Women's and gender issues.
- Extensive TV and film credits and experience including *EastEnders, The Bill* and *Grange Hill*. Her short film for BBC2, *Banglatown Banquet,* was broadcast in March 2006.
- Pearson's Writer in Residence at the Royal National Theatre 2000–01.

PLAYS
(Bold titles are plays discussed in the critical essay)
Voices on the Wind 1995
A River Sutra 1997
The Waiting Room 2000
Sanctuary 2002
Inside Out 2002
Fragile Land 2003
Gladiator Games 2005–06
Sugar Mummies 2006

Interview with Tanika Gupta

This is an edited transcript of an interview that took place at the Royal Court Theatre in June 2006.

PB   I wonder whether we can begin with you sharing with me why you first started to write and whether there were any particular writers or practitioners who exerted an influence upon your early work?

TG   I think I always wrote, as a lot of writers do, I felt that I had always been writing from childhood. My family was very artistic, my mother was an Indian dancer and my father was a singer, and they used to perform Indian dance dramas. They both came from an educational establishment in west Bengal, which was set up by Rabindranath Tagore (the twentieth-century Indian poet, dramatist and philosopher). That was their background and so I was brought up in a family where stories were being told all the time and we always seemed to have had songs and dancing. I suppose it sounds quite 'bohemian', but in fact it just felt quite natural to us. My father used to tell me stories from the *Mahabharata* [the Hindu mythic account of creation and human history and destiny]. I guess I always wrote: I wrote letters to my grandparents in India and I think I wrote my first play when I was about six. I got all my friends at school to perform it and I remember that I was very, very bad at maths and everything else but very, very good at writing, so I used to write huge long stories and so, as you can see, I've always written. I was also really lucky in that my parents always encouraged me and they never expected me to be a doctor, lawyer or a teacher as so many other Asian people's parents did and still do now, to this day. (*Laughs.*) I was brought up on a diet of watching my parents perform in various plays – my father occasionally worked for the BBC Bengali World Service and he used to act in plays – he was an amateur actor – for example, he played Magwitch in a Bengali adaptation of Dickens's *Great Expectations* and we used to have sit through that. They also took me to see Brecht's *Galileo* in Calcutta in Bengali and I don't ever remember culture and literature being rammed down my throat, but that's just what we did and I did think as I got older that we were a little bit 'odd' because none of the other Asian kids did this. So, yes, it was kind of natural and then my father said to me that I should write a novel, which I did when I was about twenty-two. (*Laughs.*) It wasn't very good! I sent it off to lots of publishers and got rejected very politely by everyone and then, at this time I belonged to this very strange organisation when I was in my early twenties. I was working as a community and social worker, and I was still writing but not really thinking very much about it when I stumbled across this group called the Asian Women Writers Collective. They were these very fierce feminist Asian women who sat around reading their work to each other and criticising each other horrifically, but strangely enough they were very encouraging to me. Eventually, one of them took me to one side and said, 'Why don't you try writing plays as your dialogue is brilliant?' However, I remember thinking: I don't know anything about plays, whereas, of course, actually I did know quite a lot (through my upbringing).

Anyway, she shoved this piece of paper in front of me and it was something about the BBC Young Playwrights Festival and workshop and she told me I should go along to it. By this stage I was in my late twenties, and I was married and in the early throes of pregnancy, so I went along to the workshop and this was very funny, actually. You see, the workshop was at BBC Broadcasting House and I arrived and I said, 'I'm here for the writers workshop' and they sent me down this passage. I walked into this room and this guy said, 'Oh no, you're here for the black writers workshop, this is the writers workshop.' Surprisingly, perhaps, I didn't think anything of it at the time – it was only years later when I thought, how bizarre is that? Well, a black producer ran the black writers workshop and basically she made us record these monologues on these DAT recorders. I was heavily pregnant and I remember in between throwing up from early-morning sickness, I was recording this monologue and I really wasn't sure what I was doing. However, I just did this thing where I put on this Indian accent and pretended I was a seventy-five-year-old woman who was reminiscing about her life as she was burping and breaking wind and drinking champagne on the beach. The producer thought this was marvellous – apart from the fact that my Indian accent sounded Welsh! (*Laughs*.) From that experience I had my first play produced on BBC Radio 4 and that's where it actually started for me, in radio. Of course, when you actually look back and you realise, yes, I did go and see plays like *Top Girls* by Caryl Churchill, which was one of the plays that I really enjoyed but again it was like I always felt like a punter watching plays because that's what I did and that's how I was brought up. I loved Arthur Miller and I studied *The Crucible* as part of my A level English – this was one of my favourite plays. So therefore, I'd say in terms of plays, who'd really influenced me, it was very much Arthur Miller and Caryl Churchill, although I actually didn't read plays, I went to see them. What I read was Maya Angelou, Toni Morrison, you know when you're in your early twenties and you're discovering your racial identity? That was what was very important to me, writing about my Asian roots, which is not so important to me now.

PB Just taking a step back and thinking about the implications of your anecdote about the 'black writers group', how much of an issue, problem or indeed a burden has it been for you to be perceived or 'classified' as a black or British Asian writer? How much do you feel, 'I'll just get on with my writing' and/or how far do you see yourself as having some kind of commitment or responsibility to that group defined in terms of race, ethnicity and gender?

TG I think to begin with, because I was searching for and establishing my own identity, I didn't mind those labels in my early twenties. I think that it was very early on when I went to a workshop that Hanif Kureishi was running and at that time he had just done *My Beautiful Laundrette* and he was a huge hero, and also he was Pakistani so he was the bee's knees. I remember him saying, 'Don't let them pigeon-hole you, don't let them put you in a box' and I remember thinking, 'What's he talking about? What box is that?' Of course, at that stage I hadn't had anything produced. I think you do learn as you go along that 'oh, they see me as this': it's about what they ask you to write. About twenty times a year I'd get asked to write plays about arranged marriages and even now, although it doesn't happen so much any more. If *The Bill* had a new Asian copper, they'd ask me to write an episode for him, or if they had Meera Seeran in an episode of *Bad Girls*, they'd ask me to write her episode. They'll root around and think, 'Who's the Asian writer that we know?' and they'll ask me to write for them. I have to say that one of the reasons that I feel so comfortable in theatre is that that rarely happens to me there.

PB   I mean, from my perspective, it's such a knee-jerk reaction – it's a consequence of at best a well-meaning liberal politically correct viewpoint – but at worst it's a very patronising and reductive form of thinking?

TG   Yes, I'm very clear now, I'm much clearer about this – I'm not an Asian writer, I'm a writer. You wouldn't call Tom Stoppard a Czech writer or a white writer or an English writer, would you, so why should I be labelled? In the same way that writers who are women don't want to be called women writers because, again, you put them in a box. Actually, it happens less and less that, these days (*laughs*) – partly because they're so tired of me going on about it! – but in the early days it didn't matter to me and I was proud to be called an Asian writer. Of course, I'm still proud of being Asian, but the major factor remains that it shouldn't *determine* your writing because in a sense it denigrates you as a writer – I don't know, it 'corners you'.

PB   I can see the interface between an emerging network of black British Asian and Caribbean writers in the 1980s such as Winsome Pinnock, Maya Choudray – whom I knew briefly when I was working up in Sheffield in the early 1990s. I can imagine in that context that there's an understandable reason why you might want both to identify and be identified with a group that historically has been marginalised socially and culturally. However, I guess it's at that point at which that need for group identity ceases to be as important and hopefully because some initial territory has been secured. I do wonder now whether those kinds of terms are more aligned with certain (not exclusively) white liberal ways of thinking outside of the groups, rather than in the groups themselves?

TG   Yeah, yeah, the rules change, don't they? When I first started writing we were all called black and then we were all Asian or black Asian or Afro-Caribbean or African and now there's this thing, which is 'Muslim writers'. Now Muslim writers don't come under Asian and so where does that leave us who are (a) not Muslim and (b) not religious? Recently I was trying to get *Gladiator Games* made into a film for television and it was turned down by Channel 4 on the basis that they'd already done lots of Muslim stories and I thought, 'Where does it say anywhere in the play or in the treatment that this is a Muslim story? Does it say anything about him being Muslim and why is that not a concern – is he not still British?' Somehow or other, it was the attitude: 'Oh yes, we know Muslims have been treated badly in this country, we've done our programmes about that.' It's still a shock even now to hear that kind of talk. You think, oh my God we're still there, we're still at that stage of thinking.

PB   What was your first stage play, Tanika, the one that helped you to establish your reputation as a writer for the stage?

TG   It was *The Waiting Room* although it wasn't my first play – I think it was only my second play – so it was a big 'do-berry' for me – I was totally fazed by the attention and glamour of it all – of having a play produced at the Cottesloe Theatre. I think I drove up and down Waterloo Bridge about fifteen times to see my name flash up and off on the 'concrete box', which is terribly sad, but I did later discover that more famous writers than me had all done the same thing, except that some of them hadn't got a car and so went up and down on the bus! (*Laughs.*)

PB (*shares laughter*)   How did that opportunity come about? Was it part of a scheme or something?

TG   At the time they had an attachment at the [Royal National Theatre] Studio on The Cut near the Young Vic and we had eight weeks in which to write a play or whatever else we might want to attempt creatively. I was really fortunate in that the Literary Manager was so busy that he couldn't actually sit and work with you all the time, so they gave me a mentor and mine was the writer Liz Coughlin. She basically taught me how to write a play and although up until that time I'd written lots of plays for the radio and for the telly, I wasn't sure about what I was doing in writing for the stage and she taught me lots of basic things like 'Don't end your scene after two pages. It's not television; you have to go deeper into character and what's happening.' Very basic stuff, but really helpful. She sort of 'held my hand' and took me through the process and plus, when you were at the Studio, you got to see and meet people around the coffee machine: Alan Rickman or Alan Bennett. I didn't know who I was talking to, someone would say, 'Oh, that was Trevor Nunn!' (*Laughs.*) After eight weeks I'd written a play called *The Waiting Room* and we had a reading of it. They all loved it and so it went through a long process of workshops and readings, and within a year Trevor Nunn had read it and liked it and said, 'Yes, we'll put it on' – I can remember I got the call (from the Royal National Theatre) when I was ironing – I always seem to get those kinds of calls when I'm ironing.

PB   Were you able to earn any kind of income from your writing at that stage?

TG   Yeah, I was, I basically worked in a 'proper job' [as a social and community worker] until 1995, then I gave up my paid work when I started to get TV work. You can't afford to live on the income from the stage alone and I'd got two kids by that time, so I had to take on a lot of TV work – so I remember that at the same time that I was writing *The Waiting Room*, I was also writing for *EastEnders*, which was a bit of a headache.

PB   That's really interesting, Tanika, because I clearly didn't know that when I was first reading *The Waiting Room*, but I found it had strong televisual elements in it . . .

TG   Yeah, that's right . . .

PB   Although I'd known, of course, that you'd written extensively for *EastEnders*, I wasn't sure how close that work was to your writing your first major work for the stage.

TG   Yeah, absolutely, I was having to use some of my time at the Studio catching up on my deadlines for telly, but I also had the space to be able to write a stage play when I wasn't at home with the kids and washing machines, and where I had space to be creative. To a certain extent I think that some people got rather 'sniffy' about how, if you were a 'theatre writer', you shouldn't write for telly as it 'spoils you' in some way. At the same time I think that there's a lot to be learned from writing for television and 'light entertainment' like sustaining dramatic action and making people want to watch the next scene or episode to know what's going to happen next.

PB   Yes, finding a dramatic form that will appeal and communicate to a wider – possibly non-theatregoing – audience? *The Waiting Room* seems to me like a deeply personal play and I wondered whether it was, in any sense, autobiographical?

TG   Yeah, yeah, yeah, yes, it was, absolutely – my father had died, in fact, just before I had my first play produced. As I indicated earlier, we'd come from not so much an atheist but an agnostic background where the family was never religious and we were never hauled off to temple or anything like that, although my mum made some attempts sometimes. It was all rather half-hearted! He died very suddenly and at a very young age – fifty-three – of a brain haemorrhage. It was just totally shocking and I was pregnant with my first child and so it all happened at the same time. My father died, I was expecting my first child and I was having my first play produced all within six months and so it was an incredibly intense time. Also what happened immediately after his death was a lot of 'weird stuff' in the house: things that to this day we still can't quite explain – and we can't explain through faith or belief in God. For example, dreams, all of us having some shared dreams that we couldn't possibly have known. Then there was the whole thing about mourning and about how different cultures mourn. So immediately after the death your house is suddenly full of fifty or sixty people whom you've hardly ever met before – they're all sleeping on your floor, they're cooking for you, they're looking after your mum, they're arranging the funeral for you, they're all wailing. They're leaving glasses of water around the house, which you keep on chucking out and they keep on saying, 'No, no, that's for the soul to drink when it gets thirsty' and you're thinking, 'What soul, what are you talking about?' It was also the time of the first Iraq war and I remember that there was a hurricane and that on the day of his funeral – which was in January some time – it was just after the hurricane and it was extremely cold and I remember that the whole garden was full of yellow roses. It was January and . . . well, yellow roses were what my father had used to give to my mum whenever they'd had an argument and they never bloomed again in January. It was those kinds of strange things that marked that time and inevitably helped influence my writing of the play.

PB I felt that the very strong sense of the emotional location of the play was the sense of loss, which seemed both palpable and also very poignant. Some years on now from that painful time, are you able to identify a principal motive that you had in the writing of *The Waiting Room*? Was it perhaps to have a conversation with your father, with your culture, with your past?

TG I think that all of that is true and one question that's certainly there in the play is: 'What happens to us after we die?' I was so very much in the middle of it all that it took many years to get over a loss like that and even now, a sudden smell of something – oh my God, that's my father's aftershave – and it brings back so many memories. It's that kind of feeling and I was also really interested in the struggle that my parents went through and that whole immigrant story. I was aware of how many of my friends – my

Asian friends – have lost fathers at a very young age. So many of us lost our fathers when they were in their late forties or early fifties, you find yourself saying, what was it about that immigrant story and their struggles? They had to work so very hard. In the play – the deceased character is a woman and not a man – I had to remove myself from the immediacy of that loss of my father. It was that first wave of immigrants who first came to this country and, for example, making fish curry – the Bengalis are mad about fish – you can't walk past a fishmonger's without buying half a fish – like my mum says, they're just lying there on the ice winking at her. There's the pain of not being able to cook fish and the nearest you can get is fish fingers. Even today we sometimes have fish finger curry – it reminds us of that time, those early years, even though it's actually quite disgusting! (*Laughs.*)

PB The pre-play relationship and its history in the play between Ferez and Preea – I was so interested by that relationship in the play that I wanted it to occupy a more central ground – it was just such a powerful sub-plot – do you have any thoughts about that yourself?

TG Yes, yeah, one of the things that did inform me about the play was the old Satyajit Ray films. They were located in the same world that my parents came from, which is this incredibly idyllic educational establishment where people have classes sitting under the mango trees. It's all about bringing education to people rather than forcing it upon them and in that place there is no Muslim–Hindu divide in the same way that there is no Punjabi–Gujarati issue – people can all study together. It was therefore very important to me that, without signposting it too much, here is a Muslim man who has a relationship with a Hindu woman – and has an extramarital affair as well. It was something that got commented on a lot in *The Waiting Room*, although it's a relatively tiny little moment in the play. To an English audience it's not particularly big. To an Asian audience, however, they all shouted about it, commented about it. It wasn't that they were being negative, it was, 'Yes, we've not seen this on the stage before,' and that's why I wanted to keep it subtle; I didn't want to be heavy-handed with it. However, yes, I think there maybe was space to make it bigger.

PB I suppose that's all part of learning the craft of writing for the stage?

TG Yes, yes . . .

PB In terms of its autobiographical nature and setting, was this a play that you saw principally for an Asian audience and was that in itself a definite position that you wanted to take?

TG I've never ever thought about an audience when I'm writing a play. Of course I think about wanting to entertain them but I don't think about their racial or gender make-up, because I think if I thought I was writing a play for an exclusively Asian audience, all I'd be able to see would be rows and rows of my mother and that would stop me from ever writing anything! So I don't think in those terms. Having said that, at the first night of the play at the Cottesloe Theatre, I was absolutely shocked and appalled to see that the audience was all 'blue rinses' – they were all Americans. I remember turning to the director and saying, 'They're just not going to get this play, they're going to hate it' and she said to me, 'Well, this is the National Theatre, what did you expect?' I said, 'I thought there'd be at least one or two Asian audience members.' Actually, what it did teach me was that within ten minutes of the play starting, everyone was laughing and that at one point they all raised their handkerchiefs at the same point and cried, and I suddenly realised this as the universality of plays. There's the shared theme of death and loss: that's what they respond to – not that it's an Asian family.

They seemed to enjoy it – and quite a lot of these 'blue rinses' came up to me afterwards and said that they loved it. I thought later that I'd had some of my own prejudices about them challenged and that they were far more discerning than I might have given them credit for. Having said that, there were eventually a lot more Asian audiences who came to see the play, mainly because we had a Bollywood film star in the main role and there were some very funny moments. There was one night when there was a whole group of white-haired, white-saried old Asian women in the front row and underneath their saris, they all had the most high-tech, top-quality digital video recorders and they were videoing all the way through – of course that's illegal. One of the stage managers came down and tried to tell them off and confiscate their cameras, and of course they just stuffed their recorders up their saris! Now who's going to start unravelling an old lady's sari and they got away with it! The National Theatre just didn't know what to do – I thought, well, it's harmless, all they're going to do is sit and watch it at home on their wide-screen televisions. (*Laughs.*)

PB Did this pre-date the wider influence of 'Bollywood' in terms of British popular culture?

TG Yes, it did pre-date that kind of period – it was just after *East is East*. *The Waiting Room* was a quirky play in its own right but it did seem to have a big impact in that there were saris flapping on the Embankment in a way that I hadn't noticed before. I mean, I went to see a play at the National just last week and I'm still shocked that the audience is still predominantly of one age and racial background – I'm not saying that that audience isn't discerning . . .

PB . . . It's also, of course, about class and income . . .

TG Absolutely, we paid out £28 for our ticket – and I thought it's outrageous . . .

PB I think that there are some important issues about ticket pricing and the consequent problem of how people on lower incomes get to see plays. Did it lead to the possibility of further work coming from the National Theatre?

TG Yeah, yeah, I did a translation of Brecht's *The Good Person of Setzuan* for the National soon after that, which did a national tour and then came back to the Cottesloe and did very well. Following that I then got a 'Pearson's Residency' so that I was Writer in Residence at the National for a year and produced another play in the Loft Theatre, which was part of the 'Transformations' season

– yes, I did three plays in three consecutive years for the National and then – nothing since.

PB Looking back on that period, how important was it for you in your development as a writer?

TG Well, when I was the Writer in Residence that was great, it was about being part of the place and being known around the building. I never quite got over this feeling that I'd somehow broken into this terribly English 'bastion', that when I spoke, people were quite surprised when I could string a sentence together. They did get me mixed up with another Asian woman all the time – they couldn't quite remember who I was and I said, 'No, I'm not her, I'm the other one!' And they'd go [to try and explain their mistake], 'It's just that whenever I see you I think of her' and I thought, 'Yes, that's because we're the only two Asian people in the whole of the theatre.'

PB It's absolutely ludicrous, isn't it?

TG Well, it is, yes: the fact that I was mistaken for the other woman when she's about half my size and half my age. (*They laugh.*) Jack Bradley [Literary Manager at the National Theatre] was very, very supportive of my work and me, as was Sue Higgins. As Writer in Residence, it was about going to see plays in readings and rehearsals, and meeting other playwrights in a way that I'd not necessarily done before. At that stage I had no connection with the Royal Court – I wasn't 'in', as they say – and so my experience was very much exclusively with the National Theatre. Inevitably, it did feel like I had sort of 'made it' and people like Nick Wright and David Lan took me under their wing, so I learned a lot about the art of the stage and about what worked and what didn't work, but as you always do, you think you know better! It wasn't as if I especially liked most of what I saw at the National – I still thought much of it was really very stale and old-fashioned – and boring. I've got a friend who calls the National 'the beige macks' – but seriously, there were some fantastic people working there.

PB How did *Inside Out* come about?

TG *Inside Out* was the first time I got my foot in the door at the

Royal Court. It was a co-commission between the Royal Court and Clean Break Theatre Company. Clean Break is committed to working with female ex-offenders and they have this arrangement whereby every year they commission a woman writer to write a new play about the criminal justice system. You get a cast of three actresses; there are no men – men aren't allowed – that immediately turned me off. I have to say when I learned that I couldn't have any men in the play, I thought to begin with: I'm not sure that I can do this, because I didn't like that sense of being confined when a theatre company can tell you what you can or can't do. However, Graham Whybrow [Literary Manager at the Royal Court Theatre at that time] said that I should do it and that the Royal Court would support me and so I did it. As an essential part of the creative process I worked at HMI Winchester Women's Prison for about four months every week and I ran writing workshops there. That was intended to be the research period. One spent, in total, about six months working there and it was fascinating, a totally different world – it was eye-opening and life-changing. I think my former social work training did help me to relate to and work with the women in a way that, otherwise, I think would have been far more difficult. Within two weeks I had fifteen women coming regularly to my groups.

PB Were you running drama workshops with them as well?

TG Yes. Most of the women were 'foreign nationals' – mostly black women who had been used as 'drug mules'. But there were others – murderers and all the rest of it. They were from all over the world, so some of them didn't speak any English. That was quite a challenge but they blossomed and grew. At first I thought I'd be terrified of these women and I just wasn't sure about how I could relate to them, but actually, by the end of it the people I was terrified of were the prison officers. The prison officers had this wonderful ability to stare straight through you and treat you as if you were invisible. They didn't believe that any of those women should be getting any form of educational facility at all; it wasn't fair, why should they receive it? They should be punished, that's what they were there for. It was a real eye-opener for me to see what actually happens inside our prisons.

PB Presumably, without jumping too far ahead, echoes of that must have been formed when you were working on *Gladiator Games*? That powerful image that you've referred to of 'being looked through' and of becoming 'invisible', that's presumably how those prison officers saw all the women inmates?

TG There was one week when I went in with an actress because the women all wanted to read their work out at the end of the sessions and I not being a director or an actress, it would be good actually to bring someone in who could help them with their reading of their work. I got this woman who I think was on the board of Clean Break to come in and within three minutes of being in prison, she was being aggressively asked by the prison officers, 'What are you doing out of your cell? What are you doing?' I really was so stupid I couldn't work out why they were having a go at her. She kept on saying, 'I'm not here as a prisoner.' Of course, it struck me suddenly: she was black. She was a black actress, so the prison officers' assumption was that, as she was black, she must be an inmate, even though she'd clearly walked in with me who'd been visiting once a week for three months. Every single prison officer's reaction to her was to shout, 'Get back in your cell!'

PB That's just so disgraceful. How did she handle that?

TG She handled it incredibly well. She's done a lot of work in prison and she'd got used to it. She realised that the best way of coping was just to try to stay calm and not get worked up. Another instance was where we'd be in the middle of a workshop and one of the prison officers would just barge in and take one of the women prisoners off for some routine check. They'd do anything they could to undermine the project and our work to the point where you just felt like locking yourself in the room to get some peace and quiet.

PB It must have been a most traumatic play to write? There was the whole 'culture shock' of the conditions within the prison and the attitudes of the prison staff, as well as the tragedy of these lives. Was it a painful play to write?

TG   It was very painful in that every single woman said, 'For God's sake don't write a play set in prison – we've been in here for years and are going to be here a lot longer, we don't want to go and see a play set in prison!' Every play up until then that Clean Break had produced had always been set in prison and so I thought, OK, now I've got my task cut out for me. You have to, in a sense, kind of throw away all the research that you've done in prison and that in itself was hard – trying to do something different. Then of course you've only got three actresses and that was much harder than even I'd thought. The Royal Court decided not to do the play, which was a bit of a blow and I think that was partly because they disagreed with the ethos of Clean Break in not allowing writers to work with men – some kind of strange feminist backlash. I never quite got to the bottom of it. It wasn't that they didn't like the play, it was very much about the organisation and to this day they've never produced any more Clean Break plays – so we went to the Arcola [a Fringe venue in East London] instead and made a little tour, which was fantastic.

PB   I saw it at the Leicester Haymarket Studio, if you remember, which Kuli Thiari organised [the then Artistic Director of the Leicester Haymarket Theatre]. I like the play very much; it seems to me that in terms of your sense of confidence with dramatic structure for the stage it's quite a significant move on from *The Waiting Room* in that respect? Would that seem a fair observation?

TG   Oh yes, that's right. (*Laughs.*) I think I was learning and just getting better with that.

PB   I think that the structure of the play is actually quite sophisticated, especially given the constraint of only having the three characters to work with. I like the ways in which the characters are really allowed to live and breathe.

TG   No, you're right. I really enjoyed writing that play even though it was something of a departure for me. It did involve my working with and developing the sense of dramatic structure. A problem with Clean Break was that they didn't really have the means to give critical feedback during the writing process, which makes it rather more difficult for the writer in that you're very much on your own. It wasn't anyone's fault, they just didn't really have that facility, so it wasn't really until the director came on board that I finally felt comfortable with the work that I had done on the play.

PB   Let's go on to *Fragile Land*. Again, did this play follow on directly from *Inside Out* or was there a play in between?

TG   It was very interesting. It was one of those rare events for a writer when I had four plays produced in the one year. *Fragile Land* came out soon after *Inside Out* and that was a specific commission from Hampstead Theatre to write for their new space downstairs. The play had to be for fourteen- to twenty-five-year-olds and I was told not to make it more than an hour long and not to make the scenes too long either as 'young people have no concentration span'. (*Laughs.*) That was my brief and that was what I did.

PB   That's interesting because when I read the play – without knowing any of the details of that commission brief – it reminded me in terms of its themes, structures and characters of some of the Theatre in Education work that I'd seen back in the 1970s and 1980s.

TG   Yes, yes . . . I didn't do any formal research with young people – basically I hung around bus stops and listened to young people's conversations, and of course I have kids of that age range myself. I'd written for *Grange Hill* for about five years and I just slipped very easily into that world.

PB   I think that there are some authentic voices in the play. I taught in some tough comprehensive schools for the first ten years of my working life and I really felt I recognised some of these young people . . .

TG   Yeah, I'd just been to Drum Street on the morning that I was on my way to Hampstead to talk about the proposed play. I went to buy some Indian sweets and there were all of these young people and kids hanging around outside the sweetshop. I thought what a weird place to meet up. They looked quite a rough lot and they were all from many different kinds of cultures so I said to the Hampstead Theatre, I think I'll set the play outside a London Indian sweetshop. It did actually work quite well. I was also very lucky in that I got to work with Paul Miller as my director – this is an ongoing issue for any dramatist, trying to find a director who you'll feel is sensitive to and can interpret your work. He was someone I'd met during my time at the National Theatre Studio and whilst it was a struggle initially to get him, he came on board and he was fantastic.

PB   The fact that *Fragile Land* did follow on from *Inside Out* is also interesting to me because I felt that there was a kind of 'urban bleakness' about both pieces – even though there is some sense of the possibility of 'moving on' for at least one or two of the characters, there is also inevitably a very strong sense of bleakness.

TG   Well, of course, one doesn't write 'happy endings'. I think one of the things that I was interested in in *Fragile Land* was the dreams of teenagers – this came out of the same time that I went to South Africa with the National Theatre to run some writing workshops. The National Theatre wouldn't let us go anywhere without their prior arrangement because 'there are very dangerous and violent people out there'. Strangely, we felt like we were in prison and there was one day when I and two other directors 'broke out' and we asked some people at the Market Theatre [Johannesburg] to see if they could arrange for us to run some workshops outside the NT's domain. As a result we went into Soweto and we walked into a school. It was the most bizarre experience. It was like the most bleak, deserted environment with tumbleweed blowing everywhere and when we arrived it simply seemed clear that the school wasn't open. All the doors had been kicked through with broken windows. It didn't look as though the school had been vandalised, just that it had been very badly kept. So we asked this guy who was our contact and said obviously these kids are not here. He said, 'Oh, no, they're waiting for you, we're just not sure where.' We finally got to this classroom and there were about thirty Soweto teenagers waiting, all dressed in school uniform, and as soon as we walked into the room they burst into song, greeting us with their wonderful harmonic singing. We were so moved we nearly started crying. Then the director did some workshops with them and he asked them what the most important thing to them was and they all said, 'Our dreams.' After this, the director asked them to re-enact some of their dreams and one of them piled the most precarious pile of chairs almost up to the ceiling and one of them climbed to the top and acted falling in slow motion. As he did so he shouted, 'Mother help me!' Their lives are so bleak – they were amazing people. That was therefore very much a part of the making and writing of *Fragile Land*.

PB   Along with that underlying sense of bleakness, there is also, of course, a very hard-edged, young urban sense of humour – a kind of survival humour? Is there any specific sense in which 'hope' is located in the play for you?

TG   Well, I have to say I kind of fell in love with Omar [a central character in the play] even though I'd started off intending to place the two girls as the main characters. He was like so many young Asian kids that I knew – he was desperately trying to do the right thing but always ending up doing the wrong things. Basically, such young people are badly parented, often abandoned or left by their parents so that they [the young people] could get a 'good education' in England. Actually, of course, a good education isn't enough in itself; you need a sense of family and belonging. The hope was that therefore for Omar everything might eventually work out right because there is that energy there and a deeper sense to 'do the right thing'.

PB   He also has a quality of honesty and transparency; you allow us to see him in that very honest way and there is that sense of him starting on a journey, which might lead him somewhere better.

TG   That's right. It was so remarkable and affirming how successful and popular the plays was with its audiences. The play reflected their world; for example, there might have been fifty different cultures represented in the audiences – white punk-haired kids sitting next to young Asian kids who were perhaps sitting next to older Asian women. I was fascinated about that. I remember on the first night that there was this huge pile of skateboards in the foyer of the theatre outside the doors and I thought, where have all these come from and the Stage Manager said, 'That's what they all came on!'

(*They laugh.*)

PB   Gone are the days of bicycle racks.

TG   We were knocked out about how well the play was received and it led to me getting further work. You know, I wasn't interested in writing about that whole 'Asian gang warfare'. I thought, they're not all like that; when you actually do get to talk to them you realise what they're really like as young individuals.

PB   It's a deeply sad and depressing barometer of current British political, social and cultural life that those issues of race, ethnicity, asylum and youth culture that the play deals with seem even more resonant than – or at least as resonant as – they were at the time of the play being commissioned. Who approached you in terms of the writing of *Gladiator Games*?

TG   Well, I was actually approached by the young director who said that she had been commissioned by the Sheffield Crucible to get this play on in the studio and would I like to do it. She said that she had the family's permission and that we could meet up with them. I wasn't sure at first because I didn't really know who she was and also because Sheffield was talking about putting it on the same night as another play. However, I went along because I thought it was such a very important story. I'd read a lot of the reports and I went on to meet Imran Khan, the family's solicitor, and also the monitoring group who were running the campaign for the family and had also run the campaign for the Stephen Lawrence inquiry. I also got to meet Zaheed Mubarek's uncle and halfway through the meeting I realised she [the director] didn't have their permission but had been very clever in getting everyone to the table. The family did then agree to the play and I very much wanted to write it from the family's point of view. There was a lot of pressure on me to go and meet Robert Stewart [the young white neo-Fascist who murdered Zaheed Mubarek] who is currently serving a life sentence for the crime and I thought about it and then I thought no, partly because I didn't want to get inside his head. He is very disturbed and mentally ill. I didn't want to get involved in what I saw as – it might seem a strange term to use – the 'evil' inside of him.

Also, however, one of my main concerns was that I wanted to make Zaheed less of a victim and more of a real person, so I spent a lot of time interviewing the family. I wanted to try to get a sense of Zaheed as an ordinary young Asian man, but this proved more difficult because although his death happened five years before at the time of my writing the play, they were still so traumatised that they found it impossible to talk about him. His mother simply cried all the time. I felt like an intruder into their grief. It was just so raw for them, seeing that incredibly raw emotion of a family who had lost a really beloved son was very moving but also, of course, very painful.

PB   Was it always going to be verbatim drama or did you ever consider writing a play in the sense of *Inside Out* or *Fragile Land*?

TG   It was always going to be verbatim, although what I eventually wrote was much less so than had been originally envisaged. We had to be very careful for legal reasons because the inquiry was still going on and we got all sorts of problems from David Blunkett [then Home Secretary] saying that they were going to sue us. Therefore we had to be careful that we didn't defame anyone – which we didn't – we just had to state the facts of the case. There was a limit, therefore, about what I could do with the material and evidence we had. The people in the prison service were extremely cagey, extremely angry and extremely defensive. In the end, somebody put those two boys together in the same cell and they're trying to hide behind the cloak of the bureaucratic cock-up, but I feel that there is a far more menacing story underneath that is frankly very scary.

PB   One is left, inevitably, coming away from the play asking:

how much is the tragedy of his death a product of the supposed 'blip' in the system and how far is it a symptom of a system that is more proactively racist? I have to say, as one member of the audience, that I came away believing that both were true but also with a sense that the overwhelming context in which this tragedy has to be understood and responded to is in the evidence of a systematic and proactive racism within the prison system.

TG It's certainly the most overtly political play that I have done. At the end of every performance they would have a discussion about various themes and concerns in the play. They were fascinating because in fact you'd get ordinary members of the public standing up and getting very agitated about things raised for them by the play and these discussions could go on for a long time after the play actually finished. It was very Brechtian in that sense. We would hear stories of how, perhaps twenty years before, members of families had been arrested and either beaten up in prison or deliberately locked up in cells with racists as had happened, of course, with Zaheed. I managed to incorporate some of those post-performance statements and incidents into the play before it transferred from its original production in Sheffield to the second production and performances at the Theatre Royal in Stratford East.

PB Apart, of course, from the power of the piece itself, the other most memorable aspect of seeing the play at Stratford East was that on the night I went, I came out at the interval for a drink and realised, if I hadn't realised before, that (a) I was probably one of the oldest members of the audience – and I'm not 'ancient', honest! Secondly, I also realised that I was certainly one of the few white people there and that there was this incredible ocean of young black British and young British Asian people who defined the audience that evening. I sat in the theatre throughout the play and I heard collective intakes of breath and I thought, 'How often does it happen that what is happening on stage so moves an audience and so represents their own reality that they react in that way?'

TG   Yes, that's absolutely right and I was very worried at the beginning about the actor playing Robert Stewart, that he might be attacked because he uses such racist language, and what was fascinating was that he never got attacked and that even when he said those racist things or even when he beats Zaheed to death, the response from the audience was that they just went silent.

PB   Tanika, in bringing our conversation to a close, I'd like to ask you what I appreciate might seem both an impossible question, but also one which runs the risk of implying a simplistic or reductive answer. However, it's a question that has run through the conversations with the other four dramatists in this book and that is, what do you see as the prospects for contemporary British theatre and playwriting at present?

TG   I do despair quite a lot about the way in which individual building-based theatres are run and who is in charge, and I do think that it's become quite a misogynistic era. I do think that there are fewer and fewer plays that are being written and directed by women – what I mean is plays that have women at the centre. This is something that I feel most strongly about: there aren't enough women directors being given the breaks that they deserve and as writers we are very dependent on directors to champion our work. Naturally, what tends to happen is that male directors take male writers. I suspect that many women writers and directors don't want to be seen as 'desk-thumping feminists' – although I don't see anything wrong with that either – but it is my main concern for British theatre that there must be a diversity of voice. It would be great, of course, for any writer to be produced in the West End but if you're writing deeply political or thoughtful plays it isn't going to happen at the moment. I haven't seen that many great plays in recent British theatre – I long to see and hear another voice and, to be honest, my concern is that the theatre will die if we don't have those more diverse voices as both writers and directors.

Navigating a Journey Through a Fragile Land – Themes in the Plays of Tanika Gupta

Tanika Gupta is one of the most consistently articulate dramatic voices of those writers who are the second wave of dramatists from the Asian subcontinent and Caribbean. Her work is characterised by a passionate concern and occasionally nostalgic empathy for those multicultural and ethnic communities which were planted in the post-*Windrush* period and the awarding of independence to British imperial India in 1947.

Issues and matters of race, ethnicity, immigration and asylum have never been as prevalent and urgent as they are in this first decade of the new century. In particular, the debate surrounding religious and cultural identity has never felt as provocatively relevant as in the period following both 11 September 2001 and 7 July 2005. This debate of course provides a potentially celebratory field day for the political parties of the far Right in Britain, most notably and publicly the British National Party (BNP), formerly the National Front. Tanika Gupta's plays never deal directly with the politics of the far Right, as does David Edgar in *Destiny* and in a different sense in *Playing with Fire*. However, in *Gladiator Games* and *Fragile Land* she offers important and complementary perspectives on issues of race, ethnicity and racial prejudice and violence.

The debate surrounding the nature of Islam and the conflation of fundamentalist terrorist ideology has created difficulties for those seeking a vocabulary through which to defend religious and cultural plurality whilst retaining a more critical questioning stance on matters such as forced marriages, the role of women and the tolerance of other sexualities.

As she writes in the preface to her 2002 play *Inside Out*, her great-uncle Dinesh Gupta had himself been imprisoned at the age of nineteen by the British Empire authorities in 1929 for his involvement in the killing of the inspector-general of prisons. She says:

During a stint in Alipore Central Jail for six months, Dinesh wrote many letters to his family, in both English and Bengali, and it was reading these beautiful letters which inspired me to start writing plays many years ago. My great-uncle was in fact hanged in 1930 as a 'terrorist' and although I never met him, I felt as if I had a connection with him through his written words. He is now recognised as a freedom fighter in India and the main square in Calcutta's business area is named in honour of his and his fellow compatriots' honour. (p. 7)

As her professional writing credits clearly illustrate at the start of this chapter, Tanika Gupta is a writer of considerable achievement, as much in television and other media as the stage. Her immersion in writing for popular mainstream television series such as *EastEnders* enables her to locate a dramatic site and vocabulary in her plays to reach a potentially wider audience than the pre-dominant theatregoing, white, liberal, centre-right demographic group. This achieves at her best an impressive facility to employ narrative structure and dramatic language to create characters and situations that are immediately recognisable. This is especially so in the case of plays like the quasi-autobiographical *The Waiting Room* (2000) and also *Inside Out* (2002), which she wrote for the women's theatre company Clean Break. The latter deals with the lives of a family of three women and a fourth Brazilian woman, in the context of a play about domestic violence, mother–daughter relationships and the judicial system in relation to women. However, her latest play for the stage (at the time of writing), *Sugar Mummies* (August 2006), received a very negative critical reception from the London press. This focused upon the view that the play was in too close proximity to the characterisation and storylines of television soap opera.

Participating in an all-woman's writing group helped to give her the confidence to develop her dramatic voice. This kind of group characterised a wider movement within post-war and especially post-1970s contemporary theatre. They existed to facilitate and support dramatists, directors and performers who because of their gender, race, ethnicity or sexuality had been historically and culturally marginalised. The emergence of Gay Sweatshop and Monstrous Regiment were just two examples of gay, lesbian and feminist companies. Another similar initiative, which was eventually closed due to concerns from funding bodies about its administration, was the Asian Co-operative Theatre, which made producing new writing from within the broader British Asian communities its main concern. One production that that company did generate and for which it is still remembered was *The Bhangara Dancer* at the Royal Court in 1987.

A company which has enjoyed a much longer life than the Asian Co-operative Theatre is Tara Arts, which was founded by southeast Asians in 1976. Tara is committed to a multicultural ethos in its work and to provide both an actual and ideological stage on which contemporary British Asian voices could be heard. Tamasha Theatre Company was also set up in 1989 as and by a women's collective. Another, which directly included and involved Tanika Gupta, was that initiated by Sita Ramamurthy and Liz Coughlin to set up a new writing initiative for black writers at the Theatre Centre in London. Liz Coughlin, an Irish writer, became an important mentor for Gupta when the latter was Pearson Writer in Residence at the National Theatre. Writers, plays and their production never happen in a vacuum, of course. The creative opportunities that writers like Tanika Gupta, Maya Choudhry, Winsome Pinnock and Meera Syal have enjoyed could only have happened through a concerted effort on the part of particular women artists and activists to demand and help create a site and dramatic forum for their work.

The Waiting Room (2000)
In this, Tanika Gupta's first major play for the stage and produced furthermore at the National Theatre Cottesloe Studio, there is a powerful autobiographical emotional sub-current that permeates the piece. The setting of the play is a contemporary British Indian

family where the mother, Priya, a woman in her early fifties, has suddenly died. The play has a naturalistic setting, with stylised interludes, and explores the traumatic impact of bereavement upon the dead woman's family. It simultaneously opens up a number of subtextual and sub-plotted storylines relating both to the pre-play past and also to relationships between and within the family. With poignancy, pathos and unlikely humour, *The Waiting Room* also explores Priya's plight as she seeks to understand and navigate her post-mortal experience and predicament. She is helped in this by a 'spirit guide' who manifests as a famous, sexy male romantic lead from the 'Bollywood' film culture. This character is called Dilip and was played by an actual Bollywood 'heart-throb' actor Kulvinder Ghir. It is a good example of Gupta's sense of both the popular-cultural and specifically a dramatic device with a special resonance for a British Indian audience. This point is reinforced by Tanika Gupta when she recounts an anecdote about the performance at which a number of older Indian women smuggled their DVD cameras under their saris into the theatre in order to film their idol illicitly for later wide-screen home consumption.

It's worth noting that the director of *The Waiting Room* was Indhu Rubasingham, an emerging female director who was to work with Tanika Gupta on the later production of *Sugar Mummies* (2006). Also, the music for the production was commissioned from the British Indian composer and performer Nitin Sawhney. At the time of the production Sawhney was enjoying considerable recognition on the alternative contemporary music scene. His music is characterised by his powerful fusion of political statement and the use and sampling of traditional Indian music with contemporary cultural motifs and documentary audio footage (including the witnessing of the dropping of the first atomic bomb by the United States of America on Hiroshima). These factors help to locate and embed the play and its first production within an emerging creative network of contemporary British Asian artists. Albeit for a younger, though not exclusively British Asian, generation

Sawhney's music was an incentive for a non-standard theatregoing audience to see the show, as was the Bollywood dimension.

The inter-generational and cultural tensions between the traditional Hindu older family members (principally Pradip, Priya's widower) is explored early on in the play, even as Priya struggles to comprehend her death and subsequent out-of-body experience. A pre-funeral custom within that faith community is for the oldest son to place a burning coal on the lips of the dead person prior to their cremation. This difficult and unwelcome task falls to Akash, the twenty-seven-year-old son who consumes a considerable amount of whisky to try preparing himself for his ordeal. When he questions why he has to do this task and indeed, why it cannot fall to his father, he is reminded by his father of duty and custom. Matters are not helped by Firoz, the Muslim friend of Pradip and his departed wife, who from his non-Hindu perspective questions what he sees as a barbaric alien custom.

As an older British Pakistani Muslim, Firoz is an important character in the play and significant firstly in terms of the violent political-ethnic history between India and Pakistan post-partition in 1947 (deployed with ruthless political pragmatism by the departing British Raj). Secondly, Firoz's friendship with Pradip and his grieving family signals the possibility of friendship and under-standing between the two religions and cultures. The presence of a British Muslim character that is portrayed as three-dimensionally human and not as a negatively simplistic, reductive stereotype is doubly important in our contemporary society. Gupta understood this dimension only too clearly. The other tensions between the parents and their adult children run as a continuing theme through the play, cleverly positioning the critique of tradition and custom as not only 'generic' and expected but also in terms and contexts that prove to be deeply personal and painful.

For most people in our secularised, consumer-capitalist society the concept of any heaven outside its retail version of conspicuous consumption in the 'shop-until-you-drop' mall culture is irrelevant if not redundant. Therefore finding a way of signifying an immortal, supernatural world and its relationship to the affairs of the material world is a challenge within the play. Nevertheless *The Waiting Room* achieves a solution in a way that works within the play's narrative and thematic structure.

In conclusion, *The Waiting Room* is a play with an emotional and psychological range exploring the territory of bereavement in which family tensions, past disappointments and moments of warm humour convey an important snapshot of British Indian family life at the end of the twentieth century. *The Waiting Room* reveals a writer finding her feet in response to the demands, challenges and constraints of writing for the stage. Gupta's ear for the subtext of our humanity and its vulnerability is the defining strength and quality of this play. As in her later play *Fragile Land* (2002), *The Waiting Room* is ultimately about contemporary British multicultural society in which lives, hopes and aspirations are daily rehearsed by individuals and communities seeking assimilation and acceptance. Simultaneously, they also need to affirm the autonomy and independence of their own cultural, ethnic and religious identity. Such issues have not subsided in the first decade of the twenty-first century but remain more challenging and pertinent. This is exemplified through a reactionary tabloid press and media, which conflate the colour of skin with the most generalised racially prejudiced notion of Asian equalling Muslim and Islam equalling fundamentalism and terror.

Inside Out (2002)

In her next major stage play following on from *The Waiting Room* Tanika Gupta entered very different territory with *Inside Out* commissioned by the Clean Break theatre company in 2002. Clean Break is the only women's theatre company in Britain that works exclusively with women who are either in prison, former offenders or who have been sectioned under the Mental Health Act. Two women prisoners founded the company in 1979 and each year subsequently have sought to commission a play from a woman writer relating to women and the issues of crime and the penal system. The plays are also written to incorporate a women-only cast. This clearly presents a problem and challenge for the writer. The insistence upon a single-gendered authorship and cast echoes a stage in the development and emergence of a left-wing politicised feminism of the late 1960s and 1970s. That movement's determination to redress the imbalances and injustices in society was inevitably reflected by those women working in theatre and the arts. Nevertheless the insistence of Clean Break upon a cast of three women characters only very nearly dissuaded Gupta from taking on the commission. Mercifully she accepted the challenge, given that *Inside Out* is her very best play to date and the continuing relevance of its major themes of women caught up within the criminal justice system. This commission necessitated Gupta working with a group of women prisoners at Winchester Women's Prison and as she says in her preface to the published edition of the play (Oberon Books, 2002):

> Having never set foot inside a prison, this was to be a rather life-changing experience for me . . . I could not and still do not believe that locking people up is an effective solution. Almost all the women inmates I met at Winchester were from impoverished backgrounds whose lives had dealt them a very bad hand. I was shocked to see how many black women languished inside for relatively minor offences, serving long sentences for trying to cheat their way out of poverty and deprivation. (p. 7)

What makes it such a powerful play is that *Inside Out* isn't simply a campaigning play about the inequalities, injustices and arguably racist attitudes within the criminal justice and penal system. It is a play centring upon the relationship between two sisters. This relationship is forged in the crippling crucible of poverty and domestic violence. The sisters' single-parent mother is para-doxically its prime victim, but one who in internalising the role of victim effectively colludes with the prostitution and abuse by the abusive male partner of her daughters. It is in the carefully observed but non-sentimental empathy with the physical, emotional and psychological vulnerability of these women that Tanika Gupta's writing excels, discovering its true voice.

The two sisters, Di and Affy (aged seventeen and fifteen respectively at the start of the play), are allowed dramatic space and time in which to develop within it. In Act One the focus is entirely upon them and their relationship with their tragically needy and compromised mother Chloe, herself only thirty-two. Gupta allows these characters a developmental dramatic space in which metaphorically to stretch their arms wide and fly into a painfully convincing credibility. This dramaturgical sense of their evolution as dramatic characters is contrasted by the very dark and difficult journeys their emerging fictional lives are embarked upon. As sisters sharing the same mother, they have been fathered by different men. This is reflected in Di's mixed-race ethnicity. The identity of Affy's father also defines one of the central storylines within the play relating to her, her sister and mother.

At the start of the play, Gupta allows her audience to meet with the two sisters in a quiet location away from the unwelcome demands of school and home. The dialogue between the two characters conveys something of the harsh urban and emotional environment in which they live. It also reflects a deeply felt bond between the two teenage girls even as they exchange typically teenage dialogue about boys and sex. The two sisters also talk about a local folk-urban myth about a ghost-witch that inhabits the river banks and woods where we find them at the start of the play. Affy talks with naïve credulity of a tale told by their mother about how Chloe was once saved when she was thirteen from a dangerous sexual advance and assault from a strange man at the river bank. Chloe has told Affy about how the presence of a mysterious woman visible only to Chloe saved her from the man. The story ends with the grisly discovery that another schoolgirl is subsequently found strangled in the same location. The young Chloe has been able to give the police a description of the man who had preyed upon her and he is eventually arrested as the murderer. For Affy and her mother this story offers some promise and reassurance of a benignly spiritual, female protection in a world that is customarily dangerous and violent for women. Di's response, however, is to question the veracity of this protecting spirit that can protect one young girl whilst another dies a brutal premature death. Such earthed pragmatism that recognises the crucial need for self-empowerment against awaiting the miraculous intervention of others characterises Di's journey and ultimate survival as a young female character in this excellent play.

The story of the 'Water Witch' is given further resonance and meaning from a feminist reading of the play's concerns and themes in that the spirit's supernatural presence relates back to an earlier historical period when women accused of being witches were allegedly drowned along that stretch of the river. Therefore in the very first scene of the play, the vulnerability of these young, contemporary, female lives marginalised along with their mother by poverty and her desperate collusion with her current male partner's sexual exploitation and domestic violence, are given a wider historical context and perspective in the 'witch spirit' story. By implication, those poverty-stricken women that Tanika Gupta had met when working in the prison are also subliminally present in a world where poverty and discrimination still exist, and where society still seeks its scapegoats for social instability and economic uncertainty, even as earlier generations had stigmatised certain women as 'witches' and, much closer to our own time, Jews were signalled out as the 'cause' of Germany's social and economic ills in the inter-war years of the 1920s and 1930s. Even more proximate to ourselves is the malignant propaganda still spread by the far-Right BNP and the right-wing reactionary press that it is asylum seekers and illegal immigrants and 'Muslims' who are the 'cause' of whatever social and economic ills such as unemployment, crime and an under-pressure National Health Service are confronting contemporary Britain.

Chloe is in a deeply depressing sense more dependent upon her two children than they might reasonably be upon her as their mother. In Act One, Scene Two we return to the same location but this time to discover Affy traumatised by violence and sexual intimidation from their mother's current partner. It becomes clear that this is not a one-off or random incident, but that both girls have suffered in the present and their past from similar brutal behaviour. Di gives up her earlier aspirations to try to get some qualifications and improve her life by committing herself to get a job immediately after she leaves school and take herself and her younger sister into an alternative environment of safety, however materially vulnerable that might prove.

However, that determination and escape route are suddenly undermined when a storyline is introduced by Gupta in which Affy comes upon a hidden stash of correspondence between her mother and a former sexual partner, significantly it is discovered, Affy's biological father. She writes to this man whom she has never known and the partially unlikely scenario emerges and develops whereby she accepts his invitation to go and live with him in Brighton, his current home. Di is appalled at both her sister's instant willingness to receive the personal care and the material privileges that this man now represents to her. Affy's uncon-ditional acceptance of the life-changing alternative reflects her need and willingness in the opening scene of the play to believe in an unseen, benign presence that might 'magically' change specific people's lives and fortunes. Significantly, Di is equally angry and disbelieving that her sister, for whom she was prepared to give up her own ambitions, will now leave her. Di will have to survive alone in the continuing cycle of material and emotional need and domestic violence in the family home. The inevitable friction that results between the two sisters is nevertheless counterbalanced by the deeper sense of shared identity and care that they have for one another. This continues to survive against seemingly impossible odds through the play.

However, following Affy's departure to live with her father, the consequences for Di and Chloe are even more disastrous and ultimately tragic than could have been imagined. In a most powerful piece of writing Tanika Gupta brings Act Two of the play to a devastating climax. Di confronts her mother and her self-destructive dependence upon her brutal male partner in what proves to be their final scene together. Di is enraged that her mother has allowed this vicious, self-serving male back into her – and their – lives. Di and Chloe explode in mutual anger and disgust that will ultimately result in Di murdering her mother in self-defence:

> **Di** You let him back in again. He turns on the charm and you fall for it, hook, line and fucking sinker. He'll beat you, scare you, put you on the street, take your money and then he'll start on me. And do you know something? I don't want to fucking end up like you. You're disgusting.
>
> **Chloe** *looks at* **Di** *with fury.*
>
> **Chloe** At least I'm white, you bag of shit. (p. 71)

Even as Di continues, reinforced, in her intention to leave Chloe for good, the mother pulls a knife on her daughter. In the ensuing struggle that ends Act Two there is a fight between the two women with a single scream piercing the darkness of blackout.

Act Three, which is five years on, finds a new character called Mercedes, a thirty-something Brazilian woman, waiting at the gates of the prison to greet Di as she re-enters the world outside the prison, released before the completion of her sentence on licence, having been imprisoned for the manslaughter of her mother. The two women talk and celebrate Di's release; Mercedes and she had met whilst they were both in prison and had formed a strong friendship. Gupta cleverly sketches in a background world beyond the confines of a prison where Mercedes tells Di about the kind of poorly paid work available to women living on the margins of 'respectable society'. So 'respectable' that the rich woman for whom Mercedes house-cleans has a cocaine habit (which she can of course afford in financial terms). It is this world of illegal drug smuggling that Mercedes herself was involved in and subsequently imprisoned for. This dramatically neat and effective counterpoint of two individual women divided by social class, money, privilege and nationality challenges the audience to reconsider seriously its prejudices about stereotyped women and women criminals. Where does justice begin in such a world? Di relinquishes her friend's tempting offer to leave and start a new life with her, choosing instead to travel to Brighton to see her sister. This is despite the fact that Affy has not visited her or made any contact with Di throughout the five years of her imprisonment.

In Act Three, Scene Two, we find an Affy who is now married and with young children. It appears initially at least as though Mercedes's advice to her friend not to go back to a past, which could only ever be a weight round her neck, was correct. Affy's earlier, naïve dream of an idyllic future is contrasted by the very modest circumstances in which she and her husband, a cabbie, live. He has to hold down two jobs to make ends meet. Inevitably, given all that has happened, this scene between the two estranged sisters is pregnant with a powerful subtext of guilt, remorse, recrimination and loss – actual and metaphorical. However, the deeper ties between them hold firm. After telling Di initially that she would have to leave before Sean, her husband, arrives home ('he won't want you near the kids'), Affy invites Di to stay and meet her husband. This gesture at least offers the possibility of the two sisters maintaining some sort of contact. It also offers the possibility of building a longer-term adult relationship together as sisters and young women. Their early lives were irretrievably scarred but a better future is at least feasible. In the final short scene of the play, Mercedes and Di are together again, this time on the beach with a shared recognition that their lives will go separate ways but that this independence of the individual journey is a hard-won freedom and something to be celebrated. They do so as, at the conclusion of *Inside Out*, the two women walk off together to enjoy a celebratory 'last supper' of fish and chips.

Tanika Gupta found the experience of writing the play, and especially her experience of seeing and working inside the prison service, life-changing and traumatic. Her play captures the terrible circumstances of class, poverty, domestic violence and degradation that so many women still face in our contemporary society. Without ever being narrowly or reductively polemical, the play nevertheless has a ferocious heart and steely compassion and admiration for those women who are able to survive with any meaningful sense of themselves against impossible odds. For me, and notwithstanding the qualities in her other work, it remains her most powerful signature piece to date.

Fragile Land

The stage play that followed directly on from *Inside Out* was a play commissioned principally with a young, non-theatregoing audience in mind and one which would represent and incorporate the diverse youth cultures of both London and much of contemporary Britain. *Fragile Land* was commissioned from Tanika Gupta by the Hampstead Theatre and also served a dual function of being the first production to be performed in their newly redesigned theatre space. The play focuses upon a diverse range of young people living in contemporary London, defined in terms of their gender, race and ethnicity. The main setting for the play is outside a traditional Indian sweetshop in central London. The play follows the preoccupations and concerns of teenagers living in a harsh urban subculture: a microcosm of what for many young people in inner-city hardship and, for some, deprivation, is indeed a 'fragile land' of the play's title. In a way, these young people in this play inhabit a similar geographic and emotional/thematic landscape as the young Di and Affy in *Inside Out*. This is a world where school and schooling, so valued and prized by first- and second-generation immigrant communities to Britain, now seems very much at the edge of this younger generation's concerns and priorities. Theirs is more a world of illicit drugs and under-age drinking, of growing sexual awareness and attraction. There are also the problems and challenges of living within religious and ethnic communities whose cultural values are often in tension with secularised, commercialised British society and culture.

In what is very much an ensemble piece, the central character is Omar, a sixteen-year-old youth who lives above his uncle's sweetshop, the play's main setting. Tanika Gupta's extensive previous television credits included the iconic BBC school-based drama for young people *Grange Hill*. Set in an inner-London co-educational comprehensive, the programme was hugely popular over a number of series. It provided the first ever older children's TV series that articulated some of the ongoing issues, concerns and anxieties for young people in that eleven-to-sixteen age group. Not surprisingly, therefore, Gupta's characters in *Fragile Land* have just that right sense and quality of authentic realism. Given the current concerns in our society with youth culture and the associations of a violent knife and gun subculture, Tanika Gupta's play, whilst not presenting young people as 'saints', equally does not depict them as the 'hooded devils' of the popular lurid tabloid imagination. The play, with honesty, humour and genuine concern for the pressures upon young people today, examines those generational problems that are exacerbated by being, for example, a young Muslim or having only temporary, asylum-seeking status. Despite its own problems of crime and inner-city alienation, Britain is nevertheless an oasis for those who have fled political and ethnic persecution.

One such character is Hassan, a nineteen-year-old Afghan who is in a serious relationship with a female character called Tasleema, a seventeen-year-old Asian woman. She longs for the personal freedoms of contemporary youth culture, yet also wants to try to respect her own cultural traditions. Her father, Abba, is very concerned about what he sees as the dangerous and corrupting temptations of that contemporary non-religious world upon his daughter. Consequently he locks her in her room and ultimately decides to send her to Pakistan. Driven by this shared desperate need, Tasleema accepts Hassan's proposal of marriage. Unknown to her, he understands that a marriage to her would enable him to remain in Britain under British immigration and asylum laws. Tasleema comes to her senses with the help of her friends and has to break the devastating news to Hassan that she cannot marry him on grounds of political expediency despite the implications for him and his family. Hassan responds with a harrowing account of his mother's death at the hands of the Taliban regime in Afghanistan:

> **Hassan** Look me in the eye and tell me you would throw me back to the wolves. I have travelled long distances – you can be my shelter. I saw so many people killed. My mother was killed. She was dragged from our house because she was teaching girls secretly in our house.
>
> **Tasleema** I'm sorry . . .
>
> **Hassan** They executed her, shot her in the street and I wasn't even there! They imprisoned me, beat me and my father, and then threw us back on to the streets. We escaped over the border. I had to hide under sacks of salt over to Pakistan. I can't go back there.

This harrowing account of the human cost and suffering for thousands of asylum seekers contradicts the negative stereotypes prevalent in the media. Despite the terrible ordeal that he and his family have faced and the very uncertain, dangerous future that awaits Hassan, Tasleema has negotiated a difficult and painful journey in her own growing up and coming of age. With hard-won realism and insight, she recognises that a marriage built upon anything other than mutual and shared respect will never be strong enough to survive.

Fragile Land has the courage as a play to deal honestly but without sensation with the problems facing so many young people today. The cost of failing to support young people and their communities such as those in the play is disturbingly suggested in Omar's experience of being a young British Muslim in the inner city:

> **Omar** Don't you ever get fed up of this country, Hass? I mean, man, it's getting worse you know – with this war. They hate

Muslims. The other day some little shit called my auntie a 'Muslim Cunt'. They've even started picking on our women.

Hassan *looks sad.*

Hassan Sure, I get fed up. But what is the alternative for me? Go back to Kabul and sift through the rubble? Even with all of the aid they're supposedly pouring into my country, they cannot mend the damage their bombs did. The money is not enough to even begin to rebuild the houses and villages. (p. 33)

Tanika Gupta is careful not to engage in simplistic political viewpoints through any of her characters, which gives them the significant benefit of being able to function dramatically as human characters rather than as ciphers for ideas. For many thousands of British citizens, including those most vulnerable like Hassan seeking the safety of British citizenship, Britain is literally and symbolically a 'fragile land' and their only hope. Beneath the comfortable beneficiaries of consumer capitalism and Cool Britannia there is a very vulnerable social, economic and cultural underclass where race, ethnicity, gender and religion can consign people to limited educational opportunities, long-term unemployment and the attendant problems of deprivation such as crime and drug addiction. *Fragile Land* played to large and appreciative youth and multicultural and multi-generational audiences when it premièred at Hampstead. Gupta shows young people and their families seeking a safety raft of self-independence and the chance to dream of a better future: a future necessitating a more just and equal society based on sustained equal opportunities and inter-cultural, inter-faith and cross-class dialogue and debate.

Gladiator Games (2005)

If any event were to undermine savagely the hope of building a more just and tolerant society, then the murder of the young British Asian Zaheed Mubarek by a psychotic white racist fellow inmate at Feltham Young Offenders Institute was surely it. Not since Stephen Lawrence's tragic murder by a gang of known white racist thugs in the previous decade had there been such a shocking example of racist violence.

Zaheed Mubarek was born in 1980 in east London and was murdered in 2000 aged only twenty whilst serving a short sentence for the petty offence of stealing shaving razors and of interfering with a motor vehicle. Zaheed could have easily stepped out of the characters and multicultural subculture of *Fragile Land*, except that his real-life story was brutally and prematurely ended with no opportunities for him to try to rebuild his future.

For Tanika Gupta, the opportunity to return to some of the controversial and important issues about crime, its punishment and the criminal judicial and penal system that she had encountered with *Inside Out* was a powerful factor in accepting the commission. The play was a joint production by the Sheffield Crucible Theatre and Theatre Royal Stratford East, famous, of course, in the 1950s and 1960s as a base and home for Joan Littlewood and her Theatre Workshop company. Both the Crucible and Stratford East have earned deserved reputations over the last half-decade or so for being willing to produce challenging contemporary plays. Stratford East in particular has an illustrious history from the pioneering days of Joan Littlewood through the intervening decades under the artistic direction of Philip Headley to his recent retirement from that post at the time of the researching and writing of this book.

When Tanika Gupta was originally approached by the young freelance director Charlie Westenra to write the play she was inevitably taken back to the circumstances under which she had accepted the commission from Clean Break. She writes in her foreword to the published version of *Gladiator Games* (Oberon Books, 2005):

> Does prison work? What are we doing as a society when we are sending children and young people to prisons without giving them the means to change, to educate themselves, to rehabilitate? As I worked through the vast piles of evidence from witnesses for the

Zaheed Mubarek inquiry and looked at the way prison had failed to protect Zaheed or keep him 'safe behind bars', the systematic failures of the prison service at every level were astounding. The incredible story of Robert Stewart's long-standing mental illness, which was never addressed or recognised, his racist views and his long history of self-harm tell another story of a young man who has been failed by society.

The play *Gladiator Games* is in the form of a drama documentary or verbatim theatre piece in which much, if not most, of the dialogue and text is transcribed from various non-dramatic sources. These include interviews with Zaheed Mubarek's family and also transcripts of evidence given to the inquiry following his murder. Why the play's title? How could a young, harmless Asian man be placed in the same cell as a young white man with a history of violence and racist attitudes? It was alleged by some that the choice to place the two inmates together was a cynical, pre-meditated one. Why? One allegation made, but not substantiated at the time of the play's writing and production, was that certain prison officers at Feltham had deliberately chosen to place inmates together where that decision might provoke conflict and even violence between them. It was further alleged that certain prison officers placed financial bets upon the outcomes of these sickening modern-day equivalents of 'Gladiator Games'. In ancient Rome, the main venue for the pitting of gladiators against each other and also in fights for their lives against lions was the Colosseum. This explains how it is alleged that the prison officers' practice was referred to by those involved as 'Colosseum' or 'baiting'. One might see, too, how the play's title also reflects, as Zaheed's uncle Imtiaz Amin observed, the battle between the family and the Home Office to secure a proper inquiry into this tragic, savage and avoidable death.

On the morning of 21 March 2000, just hours before Zaheed's release, his cell-mate Stewart battered him to death with a table leg that he had previously taken and hidden from the crude table in the cell. Seven days later Mubarek died from the appalling injuries that he had received from the unprovoked attack. Following the charges brought against Stewart for murder, he was sentenced to life imprisonment in November 2000 and the Commission for Racial Equality (CRE) announced its own investigations into the events leading up to the death. Numerous attempts were made by the then Home Secretary, David Blunkett, to avoid any further governmental inquiry or discussion relating to Zaheed's murder. The family were successful in their appeal to the High Court, where Mr Justice Hooper agreed with the family, stating that the Home Secretary had failed in his duty to take into account his obligations under the Human Rights Act. There was then the reversal of that decision by a counter-appeal brought by David Blunkett and the Home Office in 2002. In 2003 the CRE's report included Chairman Trevor Phillips's statement that Zaheed would not have been killed had he been white. The family was ultimately and finally successful in securing the full inquiry they sought when, in October 2003, the Law Lords overturned the previous decision made in favour of Blunkett and the government by ordering a full inquiry. The inquiry's chairman, Mr Justice Keith, delivered his final report to the Home Secretary in April 2006.

Gladiator Games is a play that cannot fail to challenge and confront its audience about this terrible contemporary tragedy. On the evening that I saw the play in its revival at the Theatre Royal Stratford East in February 2006, I was moved and inspired by the very large proportion of young people who made up the majority of the audience that evening. Furthermore, the range of racial, cultural and ethnic diversity represented by that young audience was a remarkable barometer of the kind of contemporary urban, inner-city culture and society in which Zaheed had himself grown up and lived his short life. For one evening at the performance of one unforgettable drama documentary play, it was possible to look back not in anger but gratitude, those fifty years on from the Royal Court's production of Osborne's play; here was a play and an audience that was living evidence that Devine's vision of a socially relevant theatre was alive and kicking. Of course, one play on one evening in one venue does not a sea-change make. As I waited for my late-night tube train home, it was hard not to feel a powerful and evocative mixture of stunned sorrow at the play's themes, mixed with some tentative optimism. Surely those young people in the audience would return to their homes, schools and jobs, determined that a similar tragedy would not be allowed to happen again?

Owing to its unimpeachable moral power and significance as an awareness-raising, campaigning drama, it's problematic to consider the piece's finer details as a play. I found the amount and density of frequently direct-address commentary, facts and opinions difficult to digest at times. The scope for more dramatic interaction between characters was limited. One of the most powerful scenes dramatically was the interchanges between Stewart and Zaheed and also another young inmate, Jamie. These were predominantly fictionalised by the author and not the direct transposition of spoken or written testimony. The same critique could also be made, of course, of *The Colour of Justice*, the verbatim theatre piece of the McPherson inquiry into the death of Stephen Lawrence, and also *Guantanamo* whose title explains that piece's attempt to raise awareness about the detainees in that infamous prison.

I will always ultimately want to argue a case for authored plays rather than dramatic documentary reconstructions of events. Is it better that they are produced rather than that the voices demanding truth and justice should remain silent? There can be no question.

Sugar Mummies (2006)

Sugar Mummies opened at the Royal Court in August 2006; I was able to see it in repertory there. *Sugar Mummies* attempts to deal with a number of issues, perhaps too much in appropriate detail, and inevitably and interestingly revisits some of Tanika Gupta's previous plays. The central concern at the heart of the play is that of the politics of 'sex tourism'. This is made more controversial when the holiday setting of this play is the Caribbean island of Jamaica, a former British colony dating back to the slave trade. On islands such as Jamaica, African slaves lived the most terrible lives labouring in the sugar and banana plantations. Their suffering was the means by which businessmen and bankers back in Britain became wealthy beneficiaries of the slave trade, investing their wealth to fuel and fund the Industrial Revolution in the eighteenth and nineteenth centuries. The economic growth of cities such as Bristol and Liverpool are directly traceable back to the slave trade.

Gupta's play seeks to draw parallels between the slave trade and the exploitation of young, attractive black Jamaicans for sexual adventures by white women in the present. The characters of Kitty, a thirty-year-old white teacher, and Maggie, a white woman in her fifties, represent these women. There are two other women holidaying in Jamaica: Naomi, a mixed-race woman from Britain in her late twenties, and Yolanda, a black American woman in her early fifties. Angel, a forty-year-old Jamaican woman and masseuse and hair braider, and four Jamaican men: Reefie, a fifty-year-old Rastafarian and Yolanda's lover, and Sly, Andre and Antonio, represent the indigenous characters. Andre is Angel's son and a grill chef at the hotel where the tourists are staying. Reefie is a very experienced gigolo whilst Sly is, in a sense of that word, a young apprentice in that 'trade'. Antonio is also attracted by this lucrative trade of money in return for sexual favours. Andre has aspirations to better himself. He resists and is critical of the others in what he sees as a demeaning and exploitative trade for all concerned.

The character of Naomi is important and central to one of the play's key narrative and thematic through-lines. She is searching for her cultural and ethnic roots. Her sole reason for coming to Jamaica therefore is not to enjoy an 'eroticised' sexual encounter with a Jamaican as a stereotypical black 'sexual trophy' but actually to try to find out the identity of her unknown Jamaican father. In doing so, she hopes to deal with a sense of incompleteness and absence that characterises her life. Her white mother had had a brief sexual encounter with a Jamaican man who is her father.

The play's opening in London prior to a short tour to the Octagon, Bolton and the Birmingham Repertory Theatre received a depressingly critical mauling at the hands of the main London newspaper critics. Jane Edwardes, reviewing for *Time Out* (14 August 2006), conceded that 'Gupta's play is smartest when it's funny and the actors deliver their lines with a confidence that is not evident elsewhere'.

Naomi searches for her father who we ultimately discover is Reefie. Her falling in love with Andre possibly reduces the potential poignancy and pain in that storyline. It runs the risk of too easily 'resolving' the complex and tangled skeins of the past into the present. The difficult undercurrents of sexual desire and racial identity might have been further developed.

Kitty's explosive racist rage against Sly after he refused her proposal of marriage seems equally too sudden and insufficiently pre-established. Her final, appalling torrent of abuse: 'I'll bring the manager in and have you whipped. Have you thrown in jail, you fucking black bastard. NIGGER!' schematises her character. It also inhibits the deeper exploration of serious issues of race and the suspect economics of sex tourism.

I found the final scene very moving and challenging when with emotional and dialogic economy Gupta evokes the spectre of the human cost of sex tourism. Angel recounts that her man, a former male prostitute, has died prematurely: 'Las night. In him dirty room, on him own.' The haunting misery of AIDS and poverty permeates this final moment.

Tanika Gupta's plays take us on a journey through a 'fragile land' of racial, cultural and ethnic identities and communities. She always seeks the human scale and dimension in her work. Her work at its most powerful is crucial to the times that we live in and the challenge of creating a just and tolerant multicultural society. Her plays offer important insights and landmarks into the wider context of contemporary British theatre seeking to engage with those people and communities who have been historically marginalised or invisible.

The sons of Caliban and daughters of Bianca are given a voice.

DOWNLOADS
- For other writers from British multicultural backgrounds try the plays of Roy Williams, Hanif Kureishi, Ayub Khan-Din, Kwami Kwei-Armah and Winsome Pinnock.
- See also these writers of an earlier generation of black dramatists: Alfred Fagon, Mustapha Matura, Barry Reckord, Michael Ellis, Tunde Ikoli and Jacqueline Rudet.
- For other plays about generational tensions in family life (*The Waiting Room*), see Tanika Gupta's own adaptation of Harold Brighouse's *Hobson's Choice* and also *East is East* by Ayub Khan-Din.

CONCLUSION:
SHARPENING POINTS

Writing and researching this book has been a terrifically interesting and stimulating journey over a period of eighteen months from inception and commission to completion. Like any journey there were some expected destinations and stop-off points and others that came as a surprise.

Contemporary British theatre and playwriting is at a crossroads. There are admirable initiatives in place to try to facilitate innovative new writing. Theatre companies such as the Soho and Paines Plough lead the way in this, but there are many other green shoots of creativity looking to break through. The Royal Court has appointed a new director in Dominic Cooke during this book's incubation period. He will bring a fresh creative energy and intelligence to one of the most scrutinised jobs in British theatre. We are living in very different circumstances from those in which the English Stage Company and the Theatre Royal Stratford East emerged in the mid-1950s.

The late-flowering idealism of the 1960s in social, political and cultural life is not on such public view in the first decade of the millennium. The environmental pressure group Greenpeace manned speedboats to demonstrate at the recent G-8 Summit and proclaim their anti-globalisation message. Such inventive forms of protest show that the spirit of radical protest and activism hasn't entirely died by any means. What is more disconcerting and revealing is that another major show of citizen power, those one million people who marched through London to protest against the imminent invasion of Iraq in 2004, were summarily ignored.

Members of the English Stage Company were on similar demonstrations, of course, in the late 1950s and through the 1960s, most usually organised by CND, the Campaign for Nuclear Disarmament. They had no more success ultimately in preventing the arrival of American nuclear missiles on British soil twenty years later. Liberal, progressive, oppositional theatre has often emerged and thrived when there has been a wider current of sea-change in the social, cultural and political waters. Economic optimism and the sense of security it brings has also often facilitated a looking up and out to the wider horizons from where critical questions can be asked. Jimmy Porter caustically called for a British society in which we might at least imagine that we're alive:

> Oh heavens, how I long for a little ordinary human enthusiasm . . . Hallelujah! I'm alive! I've an idea. Why don't we have a little game? Let's pretend that we're human beings, and that we're actually alive . . . Let's pretend that we're human.

Osborne's angry reaction against the sterile conservatism of the post-1953 New Elizabethan Age enjoyed its window of opportunity in the context of an emergent economic prosperity expressed in Prime Minister Macmillan's 'Most of our people have never had it so good'. Shelagh Delaney's young, northern, working-class character Jo snatched her illicit 'taste of honey' in a British society that was belatedly moving away from its pre-war morality and social hierarchy. Arnold Wesker's heroine Beattie in *Roots* was also a catalyst of the tensions between reaction and radical change which characterised that period. This fusion of economic upturn and radically innovative playwriting stimulated the first sustained renaissance in British theatre since the building of the popular public theatres of the first Elizabethan era gave us Shakespeare, Marlowe and Jonson. What circumstances are needed now to stimulate a similarly sustained revival in British playwriting and theatre fifty years on from 1956 and all that (to quote from the title of Dan Reballato's stimulating account of that period)? Are they primarily economic? It's hard to imagine any theatre company, writer or director who would dismiss or turn down the opportunity of extra funding.

Yet one of the most richly stimulating pieces of theatre that I saw in the last decade was in the cellar of an abandoned house in St Petersburg. In the oppressive and uncomfortable conditions of a small, claustrophobic space, a group of rouble-less theatre graduates performed Chekhov's *The Three Sisters* with an intensity and depth so often missing from our contemporary British stage. Do we want a theatre that counts or is that far too passé and dated an idea in a contemporary mass-media climate of instant C-list celebrities, reality TV and *Pop Idol*? What is a theatre that counts? What kind of theatre or writer could claim to be at the sharp end of contemporary life without risking the charge of breathing in the rarefied air of the moral high ground?

Does theatre matter? Each of the five writers interviewed, analysed and discussed would say 'Yes'. They would be variously less certain of its continuing possibility and vigour. In his six provocative talks given to students and others whilst Judith E. Wilson Visiting Fellow at Cambridge University in 1979 and published as *A Good Night Out – Popular Theatre: Audience, Class and Form* (Nick Hern Books, 1981) the left-wing theatre activist John McGrath asserted:

> The work of Osborne, Pinter, Bond, Wesker, Arden and their heirs – Stoppard, Griffiths, Brenton, Hare and Keefe – may now seem to have developed beyond, say, *Saved*, or *The Dumb Waiter* or *The Kitchen*. But it is important to realize their aesthetic/social roots. The audience has changed very little in the theatre, the social requirements remain constant, the values remain firmly those of acceptability to a metropolitan middle-class audience, with an eye to similar acceptability on the international cultural market. (p. 15)

Twenty years previously, in 1959, the theatre critic and dramaturge Kenneth Tynan had expressed a similarly weary reserve in his end-of-year review entitled 'Look Behind the Anger' published in the *Observer* on 27 December and featured in the recently republished *Theatre Writings* (Nick Hern, 2007):

> I offer no prognosis, since the patient's condition is still desperately enfeebled, but I do think it undeniable that at some point in the past ten years the English theatre regained its will to live, emerged from its coma, and started to show signs of interest in the world around it. Assuming that it gets the proper nourishment, it may walk again ... My hope for the sixties is the same as my hope for the fifties; that before they are out I shall see the construction of the National Theatre ... The talent is demonstrably there. All it needs is financial succour, official status, and a permanent address. (p. 202)

From their differing modern historical and political perspectives, McGrath and Tynan identified what they saw as both the problems that faced British theatre and playwriting, and potential solutions to them. McGrath was sceptical about those accounts of the first two decades of the Royal Court post-1956, which depicted a radical change in the function and importance of British theatre and also of its audience. He viewed a contradiction between the liberally progressive and even revolutionary plays of writers like Wesker, Osborne, Bond, Brenton and Griffiths against the demands and restrictions of the economic-cultural conditions that theatre was inextricably located in. How radical is radical theatre if it only continues to play to a predominantly privileged, bourgeois audience? Tynan, whilst recognising the need for talent in terms of playwrights, directors and actors, was more pragmatic in his perceived need for British theatre to have 'official status and a permanent address'. This would certainly have excluded the cast and location of the 1993 student production in the St Petersburg basement. Nearly forty years on from Tynan's article and twenty years on from McGrath's published talks, a Royal National Theatre has been built with three auditoria (Tynan campaigned for two) whilst the late John McGrath's touring Scottish 7:84 company is to have its funding savagely cut at the time of going to press. It is questionable whether the 'official status' bestowed upon the building and ethos of the National Theatre is as uncomplicatedly benign as Tynan envisaged. The unofficial but equally influential 'authorisation' of the English Stage Company at the Royal Court over the last half-century, which McGrath criticised, has arguably created more problems in terms of external expectations of that theatre's work than it has solved. What Tynan observed forty years ago is still true. There *is* still the talent in British theatre. In the researching and writing of this book I've seen productions as diverse in scale and location as Sir Ian McKellen and Deborah Findlay in Mark Ravenhill's *The Cut* (splendidly directed by Michael Grandage) to the RSC's fine production of David Greig's *The American Pilot* directed by Ramin Gray, in an RSC/Soho season under the direction of Dominic Cooke, which undoubtedly illustrate this. Significantly, both plays were by writers who had made their initial breakthrough in the previous decade and both engage with serious questions of political and moral substance. Continuing with Tynan's metaphor of half a century ago of the health of British theatre as a critically ill patient, what do the five writers tell us about the health and condition of contemporary British theatre and playwriting? Is the insistent beep-beep one hears a box-office cash register at a new play sold out for its entire run or the warning signal on the heart monitor at the patient's bedside?

David Edgar

David Edgar's continuing presence in British theatre and playwriting is a powerful indicator of the ongoing relevance of serious-minded writing reflecting a well-informed, articulate understanding of post-war British and European politics. Plays ranging from *Destiny* through to *Playing with Fire* over a thirty-year period are a potent sign of the dramatic quality of his output as well as an impressive durability in the face of a vastly changing social, cultural and political landscape. The cool clarity of his analysis of complex social and political themes and precision of dramatic structure and characterisation define an unmistakable authorial voice. His work functions as a barometer of our times and deals with the major issues of political change across the post-Soviet-era 'new Europe'. Unlike any other modern British dramatist, he has drawn a dramatic map tracing the historical origins of racism in British society in relation to the end of the British Empire initially signalled by India's long-sought independence in 1947. In doing so he has reminded us that racism and racists can't be identified in convenient simplistic stereotypes. This is crucial in terms of our understanding of, debate with, and resistance to the neo-Fascist political ideology that underlies racism.

In *Playing with Fire*, Edgar also engages with some of the major political conflicts and manoeuvring of the post-1997 New Labour landslide election victory with Tony Blair becoming Prime Minister. The social liberalism of the Blair administration in terms of its legal equalisation of rights though civil ceremonies for gay and lesbian couples has coexisted problematically with an appeal to reactionary populist opinion in terms of asylum and the 'war against terror'. Equally significant was Blair's support of the Bush administration in the invasion of Iraq in 2003. Edgar's play accurately caught the schizophrenia endemic within the New Labour project and the potentially serious consequences for inter-cultural and inter-ethnic social cohesion and tolerance. Like other writers and political activists of his generation, Edgar has moved from an earlier revolutionary Marxist position to one best defined now as democratic Socialist. What has not changed is his conviction that political issues of race, democratic participation, cultural plurality and social inclusion matter enough for him still to write about them.

His inclusion as one of the five writers in this study reminds us as well of the span of serious-minded, socially committed writing of the last five decades. The recent generation of writers such as Ravenhill, Greig and Gupta are working within this timescale and tradition. This is a tradition that embraces an earlier generation of writers like Edgar to which social and cultural project their own achievements are a contributing part of its continuance. In June 2007 David Edgar was elected as President of the Writers Guild of Great Britain.

David Greig

Through plays ranging from early successes such as *Europe* and *The Architect* to later achievements with *Victoria*, *The Cosmonaut* and *The American Pilot*, David Greig represents a dramatic voice with a political sensibility for the 1990s and the first decade of the millennium. Whilst different in the detail of his political perspective and distinguished by the muscular poetics of his emerging and mature style, Greig may be seen to have some tangential points of contact with a writer such as David Edgar. There is a shared concern for structural elegance and symmetry but always, as with Edgar, to serve the plays' intentions and never purely decorative. There is also a similarly developed intellect and rational clarity informing their work. Greig's *Europe* speaks to Edgar's *Pentecost* in terms of those plays' concerns with the crisis facing post-Soviet, Cold War Europe. Significantly, whereas *Pentecost* maps in a geo-ideological territory in which the characters serve principally as channels for complex political dialectics, *Europe* focuses more particularly upon the individual and his or her personal experience. It is through Greig's proximity to his characters' subjectivity therefore that the wider geo-ideological landscape of the problematic new Europe is glimpsed.

In *The Architect* the clear resonance with Ibsen's *The Master Builder* and by implication the liberal-humanistic democratic project also places Greig and Edgar in familiar territory. This could be expressed as firstly, the view of theatre-as-resolution as a paradigm of history-as-democratic-progress. Secondly, there is the associated idea of playwriting being synonymous with social analysis and commentary. These two important ideas unite both dramatists. Greig's sensitivity towards the complex interior worlds of his characters and his experiments with a heightened poetic realism to navigate that territory give his work an authentic, subtle resonance. Through his use of a Brechtian episodic structuring and direct address by characters to their audience, Greig's *The American Pilot* also served as one of the few distinctively political plays of the decade to date that looked back and paid its respects to Brecht's pioneering methodology. It is also reminiscent in its parabolic structure of David Hare's early play *Fanshen* (1975), which was about a Chinese peasant community struggling to deal with the challenges of *fanshen*: the revolutionary restructuring of their community according to the principles of Mao's revolution. Whilst *Fanshen* did not idealise the Communist Revolution in China, it ultimately rested upon a provisional acceptance of that ideology.

This of course is a major and crucial distinction between plays and writers defined as political today with those of thirty or forty years ago: the absence of certainty. What characterises David Greig's work is an absence of ideological or political certainty counterbalanced by a finely tuned interest in people-as-people. The decisions taken by the villagers in *The American Pilot* against those taken by their fictional counterparts in *Fanshen* are different not only in the absence of political rhetoric and a wider narrative of revolutionary political change. They are also decisions reflecting a later generation's recognition that the paradox and dilemma of being human needs a new dramatic and political language to engage with and describe our world. David Greig is unquestionably one of the leading dramatists of his generation in seeking to create that new vocabulary.

Mark Ravenhill

Mark Ravenhill is a writer who has been inaccurately defined and trapped as part of the 'In-Yer-Face' phenomenon of the 1990s. His writing continues to interest and attract. The innovative stylistic challenges that he has responded to in plays like *The Cut* and the less convincing *Pool (No Water)* communicate a writer who still has much to say. He also has the confidence and openness to explore different ways of saying it. His ground-breaking and controversial

Shopping and Fucking is a high watermark of the new writing of the last decade, principally for its characters caught in the crossfire between postmodern assemblage and his critiquing of postmodern moral discourse inherent in the piece. The play also exemplifies the disenchantment with conventional politics by Ravenhill's generation. The play was written and first produced at the apex of the lingering death of John Major's impotent Tory administration and the ultimate disappointment and disillusionment with New Labour's Cool Britannia. Ravenhill expertly caught the *fin de siècle* weariness of political apathy set against an adrenalin-rush sub-culture high on Ecstasy and plural sexual freedom. It is one of that play's enduring strengths and qualities that far from idealising that subculture, it explores with frank candour the darker frontiers of hedonistic excess. In its invocation of a world in which 'Money is Civilisation – Civilisation is Money' it exposes the intrinsic moral paradoxes and hypocrisies of a consumer society and commodified lives.

Through plays like *Some Explicit Polaroids* and *Mother Clap's Molly House* Ravenhill continued to explore issues surrounding both gay sexuality and queer culture, whilst asking questions about the possibilities for change in social, moral and political attitudes. *The Cut* brought Ravenhill into for him the previously unlikely orbit of Strindberg, Ibsen and Pinter. It may yet herald a major new departure for him in the future. *Product* and *Citizenship* are more of a return to the cutting satire mixed with social and political critique in the early plays, although with more conven-tional characterisation and narrative structure. The stylistic diversity in his work to date makes one wonder what will come next. What one can be sure of is that he won't avoid a new challenge. His plays to date have shown a postmodern social commentator and critic, and an active celebrant of the gay scene and of the political and moral challenges facing a society becoming increasingly post-ideological even more than postmodern.

Tanika Gupta

Tanika Gupta's plays deal with some of the most important issues of twenty-first-century Britain. These are principally the issues and challenges of multiculturalism, inner-city youth culture, race and racism, and the role and rights of women. Gupta has had extensive experience and success in writing for television, which gives her writing for the stage a quality of accessibility in form and characterisation. It has also, however, led to some of her stage plays being criticised in some quarters for their close proximity to the conventions and formulas of television soap drama. This was particularly the case with one of her most recent plays at the time of writing, *Sugar Mummies*. At the risk of ticking boxes in a checklist of political correctness it is, however, true that one of the breakthroughs in British theatre of the last twenty years or so has been the emergence of dramatic voices from the black British and British Asian communities. Tanika Gupta, along with Roy Williams and Winsome Pinnock, has been one of the enduring voices to date from those communities within contemporary British society. Looking at the small percentage of plays produced on main-house stages from writers from those racial, ethnic and cultural groups, this is an area still requiring further facilitation and recognition. It's important, of course, that a writer like Tanika Gupta is no more pigeon-holed as an 'Asian writer' than Mark Ravenhill should be described as a 'gay writer'. Such narrowly simplistic categorisation is reductive and misleading. Nevertheless it is also important that a healthy, vigorous and relevant British theatre embraces writers and their plays that most reflect the racial, ethnic and sexual diversity that is contemporary Britain. This is increasingly so in a multicultural and political climate in which a young Iraqi Kurd woman living in Britain was murdered by her father and male relatives in an 'honour killing' concerning her choice of a partner from another ethnic Kurdish group.

Within the same week's news (week beginning Monday, 11 June 2007) Ruth Kelly, the Minister for Communities, had questioned whether the translation facilities available to immigrant communities were providing an unhelpful counter-cultural crutch. Her underlying argument is allegedly that well-meaning liberal policies of cultural assimilation were in effect discouraging and hampering multicultural cohesiveness. As Thomas Sutcliffe observed in the *Independent* on Tuesday, 12 June 2007, there is a more sceptical reading possible of Kelly's statement. This is that its implied sentiments were targeted specifically for her to create headlines for and credibility with what Sutcliffe calls 'White Van Man'. The *Sun*, a newspaper not best noted for its tolerance and inclusiveness, accordingly ran a front-page headline trailing Kelly's remarks with 'Learn Our Lingo'. As Sutcliffe went on:

> The *Sun*'s translation implied an unstated '. . . or else . . .' So . . .
> learn our lingo or else what? You fail to report that recent arrival
> from Karachi with the persistent tubercular cough? Or you ignore
> the vivid purplish blots on your feverish child's chest? (p. 32)

These two news stories from the same week, one a human tragedy of brutal ethnic prejudice and patriarchy, the other a government minister exploiting 'Little England's' xenophobic fears about asylum seekers and immigrants, signal why Tanika Gupta's plays remain so necessary and relevant. Plays such as *Fragile Land* and *Gladiator Games* in particular are urgent reminders from a dramatic voice charged with anger and compassion of the serious challenges facing our society.

On 29 June 2006, Judge Justice Keith's public inquiry into the death of Zaheed Mubarek established that the psychopathic killer Robert Stewart should have been identified as a risk and not placed in the same cell as Mubarek. The 700-page report, amidst a large number of other very serious criticisms, called for the Home Office to consider introducing the concept of 'institutional religious intolerance'. Whilst not able to substantiate the allegation of prison officers deliberately placing ill-matched prisoners in shared cells and gambling on the likely outcome of the ensuing violence ('Gladiator Games'), the report was absolutely clear that there were 'improper attitudes towards ethnic minority prisoners, particularly Muslims' and that this was a 'contributing factor to the tragedy'. Tanika Gupta writes with honesty and directness about these kinds of urgent issues in our society but without offering simplistic solutions. These plays, along with *Inside Out*, are in the wider tradition of politically concerned plays traceable back to David Edgar's generation and before. They remind us that even if the bigger narratives of left-wing politics have been necessarily subject to serious scrutiny and revision, the human need for justice, equality and tolerance, and drama's potential to engage in that process, remains as pertinent today as at the time of David Edgar's *Destiny*.

Tim Etchells and Forced Entertainment

Forced Entertainment were chosen and invited by Jarvis Cocker, former singer/songwriter with the 1990s Sheffield band Pulp, to perform *Bloody Mess* at the Queen Elizabeth Hall as part of a season of music and other arts events that he was commissioned to curate for the Meltdown Festival on the South Bank in June 2007. This was the first time that a theatre company had been invited to take part in this annual event. With earlier curators including 1980s icon Morrissey, Meltdown had previously been a platform for contemporary and modern music. Perhaps it's not surprising that someone like Cocker, who had written best-selling albums with songs like 'Common People' and who is from Sheffield himself, should issue his invitation to the company. It is certainly a high-profile indicator of the continuing presence, if not wider popularity, of Tim Etchells and Forced Entertainment after over twenty years on the avant-garde, experimental performance circuit.

Bloody Mess serves as a provocative amalgam of their back catalogue of work and some anticipated it as a 'farewell letter' from this writer and company who have engendered many imitators and inspired other practitioners in New British Performance. It's important and impossible to separate Etchells and his writing from the intensive devising and improvising approach that creates

Forced Entertainment's work. It's also true that the poetic urban melancholy and post-Romantic vision of Etchells's writing has played an important role in the unique distinctiveness of their performance language and style. The company faced closure in the early to mid-1990s after what would have been fatal threatened cuts to their funding were subsequently avoided. This was in large part due to a campaign of letters and e-mails to the Arts Council from Forced Entertainment's supporters. It is a testament to their own unyielding commitment to their work and the continuing audience for it that they received what was implicitly this accolade from Cocker in the summer of 2007.

Work on the margins of any art form and certainly work which challenges the assumptions of form, content and their aesthetic representation will always attract a similarly marginal audience. The questions that Etchells and Forced Entertainment ask through their work about the very nature of what theatre and performance are and what role, if any, they have still to play in the contemporary period are urgent and needed. Their exploration of the no man's land between the boundaries of the real and the fictional, and their evocation of an alternative ideological vision to mass-mediated conformity and empty consumerism remain potent and poignant ingredients in their work. Of all the writers discussed in this book, Etchells is the only one who does not function as the autonomous instigator and Prospero-like magician creating drama's fictions. He is more like an intriguing urban postmodern Ariel who, with other post-fall Ariels, imagines and makes an alternative England. Their reimagined England is an island like Blake's Albion where 'We are such stuff as dreams are made on'. Theatre will always need intrepid explorers of the uncharted territory beyond the known and mainstream. Without such new discoveries brought back, without protesting Calibans and burning tigers of the night, theatre, in Kenneth Tynan's metaphor, risks relapsing into terminal decline. Tim Etchells and Forced Entertainment continue to try to discover new and precious sources of such alternative creative oxygen.

Packing Away the Pencil Box

The future awaiting British society and theatre and the wider world is very uncertain and problematic. If the generation of socially and politically committed dramatists of forty or fifty years ago saw either liberal humanist democracy or revolutionary Socialism as a language for change, the questions facing writers today are more likely to be multinational globalisation, global warming and the powerful presence of either the Christian or Islamic fundamentalist God demanding holy war or jihad. We are living in times when effectively medieval ideologies and theologies of the West and the Middle East are disturbingly and dangerously allied to the twentieth-century technological innovations of nuclear weapons. With God – either Christian or Islamic – on your side, to quote the title from an early Bob Dylan song, you 'don't ask questions'.

Yet surely it's our capacity as human beings to ask questions and drama's unique facility and means for doing so collectively and communally that must be defended and reaffirmed? There are, mercifully, no easy answers to these challenges facing us because easy answers only satisfy narrow minds.

Perhaps it's irrepressibly optimistic to ask for playwrights, plays and a theatre that could rise up to and respond to the challenge of the first decade of the twenty-first century in the way that happened towards the end of the fifth decade of the twentieth century?

The writers in this book and other emerging dramatic voices outside its remit suggest that, in packing away the pencil box, we shouldn't put the pencil sharpener away – just yet.

A Short List of Recommended Further Reading and Indicative Websites

This list is not and cannot be either all-inclusive or exhaustive. However, what it does offer the reader is a very good selective introduction to themes and issues concerning the writers in this book and the wider field of modern and contemporary British theatre.

Howard Barker, *Arguments for a Theatre* (Manchester University Press, 1993)

Peter Billingham, *Theatres of Conscience – 1939–53: A Study of Four Touring British Community Theatres* (Routledge, 2002)

Edward Bond, *The Hidden Plot – Notes on Theatre and the State* (Methuen Drama, 2000)

John Bull, *New British Political Dramatists* (Macmillan, reprinted 1991)

John Bull, *Stage Right: Crisis and Recovery in British Contemporary Mainstream Theatre* (Macmillan, 1994)

Nicholas de Jongh, *Not in Front of the Audience: Homosexuality on Stage* (Routledge, 1992)

Tim Etchells, *Certain Fragments – Contemporary Performance and Forced Entertainment* (Routledge, 1999)

Christopher Innes, *Modern British Drama 1880–1990* (Cambridge University Press, 1992)

Stephen Lacey, *British Realist Theatre – the New Wave in Its Context 1956–1965* (Routledge, 1995)

John McGrath, *A Good Night Out, Popular Theatre: Audience, Class and Form* (Nick Hern Books, 1981, reprinted 1996)

Andy Medhurst and Sally R. Munt (eds), *Lesbian and Gay Studies – a Critical Introduction* (Cassell, 1997)

Michael Patterson (ed.), *The Oxford Dictionary of Plays*

Dan Rebellato, *1956 and All That: The Making of Modern British Drama* (Routledge, 1999)

Dominic Shellard, *British Theatre Since the War* (Yale University Press, 1999)

Dominic Shellard (ed), *Kenneth Tynan Theatre Writings* (Nick Hern Books, 2007)

Aleks Sierz, *In-Yer-Face Theatre – British Drama Today* (Faber, 2001)

Michelene Wandor, *Look Back in Gender: Sexuality and the Family in Post-war British Drama* (Methuen, 1987)

Websites

www.suspectculture.com/
www.theatrevoice.com/
www.forcedentertainment.com/
www.royalcourttheatre.com/